My First Years With Bing

by Kathryn Crosby

Collage Books Inc.

Copyright © 2004 My First Years With Bing by Kathryn Crosby

ISBN: 0-938728-12-1

Copyright © 1983 My Life With Bing by Kathryn Crosby

First published in the United States of America in 1983 by Collage Books Inc. Simultaneously published in Great Britain by Quartet Books Limited, London, and in Australia and New Zealand by Golden Books PTY. LTD., Sidney–Auckland.

All rights reserved. No part of this publication may be reproduced, stored in a retrieval system, or transmitted, in any form or by any means, electronic, mechanical, photocopying, recording, or otherwise, without the permission of the author.

Printed and bound in the United States of America.

A WORD OF EXPLANATION

I have spent much of the last two years touring with my second book, MY LAST YEARS WITH BING. Everywhere I perform, fans have been asking why in the world I began in midstream with the year 1966.

The answer, of course, is that I didn't. That volume is a sequel to the present text, which had a considerable pre-publication and contemporary sale, but has since lapsed into the obscurity from which I am hoping to rescue it with this new printing.

Another question concerns the pictures, which are in black and white in the first book, and color in the second. There the explanation is still simpler. Color hadn't come into its own when the earlier pictures were taken.

As to whether I have another book in me, I believe so, but all my time is presently occupied with painting, and with traveling to share those already written.

Dixie

PROLOGUE

I pick up a book in the attic, *The Incredible Crosby* by Barry Ulanov.

The inscription reads, "To my beloved husband—1948." The handwriting is dainty, regular, rather small, the antithesis of my juvenile scrawl.

As I seek out the references to Dixie Lee Crosby, I realize that this is a very good book. Bing's career is outlined with accuracy. There has been considerable research—interviews with schoolteachers at Gonzaga, neighbors from the old home town of Spokane, coworkers, film executives, fans. The only thing that is not discussed is what Bing the man was like, or to give proper albeit platitudinous emphasis—what he was *really* like.

There were two of us who knew Bing as a husband. One was Dixie Lee Crosby—née Wilma Wyatt. The other was Kathryn Grant Crosby—née Olive Kathryn Grandstaff.

The inscription in the book is significant because 1948 is a time when Bing and Dixie were supposed to be having difficulties. There was talk of a separation, perhaps even a divorce. Those were rumors stemming from the outside world—never from Bing. Let me tell you what Bing said about Dixie.

He said she was an angel and a wonderful mother. I appreciated that because I liked the idea of having a protective spouse. There were other things that I gleaned from the book that told me—and perhaps me alone—what Bing was like as a husband. There were questions asked toward the end of the book about the quality of Bing's voice. Was it fading? Was he losing important notes? Was he still able to sing with the same old effortless lilt? The year was 1948.

In 1948 Dixie discovered that she had cancer of the cervix. Treatment was still primitive, involving radium needles, packing, X-ray, surgery—all too late.

Bing's pain always went right to his voice. But he continued working, and together they tried to keep their sons from worrying, and the world from knowing.

By 1952 things were bad. Bing had to travel to Europe to shoot Perlberg/Seaton's *Little Boy Lost*. He didn't want to leave Dixie, but she insisted that she would be waiting when he returned.

Bing's return was slow. Flying terrified him, so he was crossing the country by train to arrive Saturday, October 25.

The first wedding anniversary

Dixie summoned Leo Lynn, Bing's boyhood friend, now his driver. She told him she was going to meet Bing without a nurse, though she had been under round-the-clock care for several weeks and in a coma part of the time. She prepared by receiving daily blood transfusions for two weeks. Only her youngest son Linny sat with her in the back of the car.

They came to the Union Pacific station at 5th and Alameda. Leo parked very close to the tracks. Linny waited in the car while Leo went to see whether Bing was coming. Then they reversed roles, with Linny going to look for Bing while Leo waited.

Finally Bing arrived. The emotional reunion was photographed; then he and Dixie were driven to the big house.

Bing gently opened the door and carried Dixie across the threshold of their home. They had lunch together in her room, and then Bing came downstairs and said, "Leo, Dixie wants to become a Catholic. Go get Monsignor Kincannon at Good Shepherd."

The priest came over, baptized Dixie, and gave her the last rites. She lapsed into her final coma at noon the next day.

What an amazing woman she was to live until Bing returned home—until she could do the one thing that would give him some comfort, and hopefully keep her boys close to each other and to God and their church in the adolescent years.

In Bing's jewelry box there is a large assortment of gifts from many people. The three that reveal the most to me are a watch, a gold book, and a bill clip.

The watch must have come from the early years and been treasured ever since. It has a plain leather band and lacks even a brand name. On the back is inscribed "Bing—All my love, Dixie".

The book is about an inch and a half by an inch in size. It consists of four gold pages with "Bing" stamped on the front. Engraved on one of the pages is a picture of Gary, Phillip, Dennis, and Lindsay. On the facing page is a beautiful picture of Dixie.

Imprinted on the bill clip is "Dixie and Your Boys." Inside a circle of gold slightly larger than a silver dollar is a tiny St. Christopher medal. Five dime-sized circles with the portraits of Dixie, Gary, Phillip, Dennis, and Lindsay form the spokes of a wheel. The date on the back is Christmas 1952. Dixie died November 1, 1952.

I met Bing in 1953 and we married in 1957. But there are big questions now as there were then. Why did he want to marry again? Why would he want to marry me? Wasn't I too young? Or might I have been just the right age? Dixie was 19 when they married. I was 19 when we met.

Were Dixie and I alike? There was no shred of physical resemblance. In the pictures I've seen, she was exquisitely beautiful with dainty features, the classic heart-shaped face that is so wonderful on film, large melting brown eyes, and the straight eyebrows that were fashionable in the 30's and 40's.

My face, on the other hand, was always round and chubby. As I grew more objective about it, I thought it looked rather like a pie plate with a nose stuck in the middle. That didn't change until I had had three babies, and what photographers euphemistically denominate maturity had begun to mold my face into some semblance of contours.

But the contrast between Dixie and me didn't stop there. Mrs. Senior, Bing's mother, was my source of information about Dixie's personality. Catherine Harrigan Crosby loved Dixie Lee very much. They were firm friends, and she was a beneficiary in Dixie's will.

"Dixie was shy," said Mother Crosby. "Painfully shy, particularly around strangers." As for me, I never met a stranger.

Bing did say that Dixie loved her mother but hated her stepmother. I too loved my mother and was blessed with not one, but two. Mother's younger sister, Aunt Frances Sullivan, helped rear all the Grandstaff children.

Mrs. Senior said Dixie hated movie work in spite of the fact that she was a rising star at 19, had already made major pictures for 20th Century Fox, and was destined to become the

With Dennis, Gary, and Phillip

queen of the studio before that ne'er-do-well crooner sang *I Surrender Dear*.

I loved acting in films, but experienced difficulty in conquering Hollywood. A year and a half at Paramount saw me playing only bit parts. It wasn't until I reached Columbia Pictures that the business started to make sense to me, and I began to feel that I might make the grade.

Dixie was content to retire from the industry and become a wife, mother, and homemaker. I asked Bing before we married if I could continue with my career and nursing studies. When he said, as a loving swain will, "Why yes, of course, anything you want," I thought he meant it.

He decided that having babies should be fulfilling enough. It wasn't for me, although it evidently had been for Dixie. For twenty years I tried to hold him to his rash promise.

Dixie's shyness was expressed in various ways. John Scott Trotter, Bing's friend in music, and mine in antiques and decorating, showed me a beautiful chaise longue by the window of the Pebble Beach house and told me, "This is where Dixie sat." It overlooked Monterey Bay, and seemed an ideal spot for contemplation of the lovely scenery or for silent introspection. But I never sat long enough for viewing or thinking—certainly not at Pebble Beach, where I was always trying to unclog the dishwasher or solve the mystery of the central heating.

Merle Oberon said that in spite of her shyness Dixie had a delicious sense of humor, and was celebrated for many a fine *retort propre*. I had no gift for repartee. From high school days on it generally took me about twenty-four hours to come up with, "When she said that, what I should have said was. . ."

Dixie was an excellent singer with a trained soprano voice. I sang in the choir, Baptist alto. And during our twenty years of marriage, my greatest musical accomplishment was to sing alto to Bing's tenor, or occasionally sing the lead in barber shop harmony while Bing sang bass, Trader Vic sang tenor, and Texan Lawrence Wood sang whatever was left.

Dixie starred in three marvelous performances put on by the Westwood Marching and Chowder Club. The first one, the Midji Minstrels, took place on Saturday April 16, 1938. For this performance Dixie, directed by Dave Butler, rehearsed in great secrecy with her co-star Johnny Burke.

The Program read: "Burke and Lee or Lee and Burke—Dixie and Johnny in appropriate chatter and patter and song."

My vaudeville appearances with Bing were limited to the Christmas shows; my only partners were Harry, Mary Frances, and Nathaniel Crosby. The program read. . ."and Family."

Bing and Dixie really loved horses. She shared his every experience at Del Mar, and all the pictures of them at the races seem full of delight.

My only relationship with a horse was transitory and tentative. I was Rodeo Queen of the Houston Fat Stock Show—which earned me the title of Miss Fat Stock among those who wanted to tease me.

I like to ride rocking-chair steady horses on wooded trails, but watching them run around in a circle seems futile. Furthermore I can't gamble. It's not that I don't like winning; it's just that I hate losing so badly that I'd rather not play. The few times that Bing did take me to the races, something horrible invariably happened. His horse was left at the gate, it rained buckets, or he lost our entire stake.

Our differences extended to little things. Dixie loved tiny pure-bred poodles. I had an assortment of dyspeptic mongrels and one sorrowful bloodhound.

I was as brunette as Dixie was fair. Shortly after we married Bing asked, "What would you look like as a blonde?"

Blazing at him from the depths of my insecurity, I snarled "Someone else." He never brought it up again.

What Dixie and I had in common was our love for Bing. But what about him? Having married Dixie and reared four sons, why would he plunge once more into the maelstrom of matri-

Wilma Wyatt Crosby
1911—1952

mony? And why would he choose to marry Olive Kathryn Grandstaff of West Columbia, Texas?

Even after twenty-five years I can't answer that, but I can tell you how it happened. Of course Bing, that master spinner of tales, could have narrated our story far better, but he was a shy, modest man, disinclined to speak or write of himself. Now that he, like Dixie, is one with Nineveh and Tyre, I, who suffer from no such inhibitions, am all that we have left.

Fortunately for all concerned both Bing and I were indefatigable espistolarians, who also kept voluminous diaries, daybooks, logs, and travel notes. As a consequence I am the custodian of some dozens of pages for every day of our married life. Thus I have not lacked for documentation, but have rather suffered from a plethora of paper, which carried the first version of this manuscript into the thousands of pages.

On sober reflection I realized that I had wasted words on many a subject that even Bing and I had found supremely uninteresting. In my ponderous tome our years together seemed hardly worth living, let alone writing about. I have therefore cut this final rewrite to the bare bones, and bequeathed a fantastic pile of original sources to future historians.

There was the further question of what to do about the gradual shift in style and point of view. The girl that Bing first met was a nineteen-year-old ninny, who behaved and expressed herself accordingly. Her subsequent association with his older and wiser friends throughout the world, and her own passion for accumulating academic kudos, while soaking her little lame brain in the literatures of four continents, altered both the matter and form of her narrative. Meanwhile Bing too was changing before her very eyes.

Should I attempt to unify the book by consistently adopting my present viewpoint and manner of expression, or should I let the reader participate in the development of its principals and of the relationship between them? I tried first the one, and then the other, but was unable to stick to my guns in either case. Finally I pusillanimously permitted my subject to decide for me. The resulting compromise is generally faithful to the wording in the diaries of the lost little girl, but also contains occasional waspish comments from an alas centuries older woman. And now, without further ado, I invite you to meet Bing as we both knew him.

That first fateful interview

1953

What kind of beau was Bing? What was it like to be wooed by him? What line did he use? What entreaties, what blandishments, what delights did he offer the fairer sex?

In his courting as well as his working life, Bing moved at a lackadaisical, nonchalant, insouciant pace. His was more an amble, a stroll, a meander through life. It never ceased to amaze me how he arrived at his destination so much faster than we hamsters who run incessantly on our treadmills.

When I came rushing through the front gate of Paramount Pictures, tennis racket in hand, petticoats over one shoulder, hurrying—always hurrying—to the drama building, there he was, leaning against the doorjamb of his dressing room, whistling a little tune, just waiting for me to walk into his life.

"Hi, Tex. What's your hurry?"

"No hurry, really." As I skidded to a halt the tennis racket brace came down on my ankle, leaving a scar that is still slightly visible in bright daylight. The petticoats jiggled off their hanger.

It was those mellifluous, floating, vowel tones that did it. It was like being pinned against an invisible wall by the vibration of his vocal chords. I'd have defied anyone to walk away from that voice.

Bing didn't make any abrupt moves to help me pick things up. He just watched in bemusement as I scrambled.

"I think you better come in and sit a spell. It's cooler in here."

"All right."

I limped into his dressing room, trying to hide my pain, and bumped into Barney Dean, his diminutive gag man. Bing and he must have been between set-ups over on Stage 10.

White Christmas was just moving into production. I knew that because I had tried out for the part of the granddaughter. Producer Bobby Dolan said I was too sexy, a new way of excusing one more disappointment. The producers usually said I was too young or too pretty. Tactful, but unrelenting.

I'd yearned to work with Mr. Crosby, and now I was sitting in his dressing room. Of course *I* knew about *him*, but how did he know I was from Texas?

Leo Lynn, examining the montage in Bing's dressing room

His clear, receptive gaze told me he thought I was attractive. That was no big deal. Attractive girls were all over the lot: Mary Murphy, Laura Elliot, Audrey Hepburn, Grace Kelly, Marla English, Sally Mansfield. Perhaps he had an allotment of girls from each of the 48, and this was his day to round out the Texas quota.

As my eyes adjusted to the shadowy coolness of his dressing room, an expanse of wall seized my attention. It was covered with pictures of Bing, Dixie, their children, horses, golfers, and baseball players—an enormous sepia montage with admixtures of cream.

"Oh, Mr. Crosby, tell me about that wall. Whose horses are those?"

"Just a few nags I have running. Some of them have done pretty well. That one's named Don Bingo. The one over there with the roses around his neck is Ligorati, another fast pony."

"And over here?" I pointed to a ranch scene.

"Those are the quarter horses up at the ranch in Elko."

"You know, Mr. Crosby, I prayed for years that God would give me a pony and a gold dress for Christmas."

"The dress seems the more likely of the two at Paramount. You know, I learned something the other day from a jockey named Johnny Longdon. He told me that horses have eyes that magnify things ten times. So when a Kleenex or a little bit of paper blows across the trail, it looks enormous to your horse."

He paused a moment to puff on his pipe. I couldn't endure social silences, so I jumped right in.

"Well, I was Rodeo Queen of the Houston Fat Stock Show."

"You were what?"

"Rodeo Queen of the Houston Fat Stock Show. Someone in high school started calling me Miss Fat Stock. How's that for a title?"

Well at least I'd made him laugh. I forged bravely on. "I rode a quarterhorse named Topsy in the contest. My poor mount was competing against palomino stallions with manes and tails to match their silver saddles. The number before our entry into the grand arena was a song which Roy Rogers sang; it had something to do with shooting and every time Roy's gun went off Topsy reared as if it were a signal to charge.

After the arena gate finally opened for us, my horse pranced out looking for his calf. When the spotlight hit him, he realized that we were in a grand parade and started dancing sideways, while I just tried to keep my hands off the saddlehorn. But do you know that horse could understand word commands? A judge said 'Turn and canter' and he did.

All this time the other girls, with their fancy saddles and showy costumes, were trying to keep their chargers from running away. Topsy knew what he was doing, so I could do my job, which was just waving at the audience and hiding my terror."

Realizing that I had been prattling on hysterically, I ground to an abrupt halt.

"I take it you won."

"Yes. Well at least the horse won, and I stayed aboard to grab all the credit."

Bing waited politely for the verbal torrent to continue, but noting that I had run out of breath he commented, "Horses are funny. They're really spooky in parades. I've been grand marshal in a couple of little things and you never know what they're going to do, but I like to ride. Do you, Tex?"

"Well, any self-respecting Texas girl likes to ride, Mr. Crosby."

Whatever my defects of character, veracity is not among them. Moreover I hadn't told a really big lie. I liked the idea of riding, but I was no Annie-Oakley-of-the-saddle. Indeed I was more a Marjorie-of-the-merry-go-round, so I thought it prudent to change the subject before Bing plumbed the depths of my ignorance.

"What are these pictures of ball players?"

"Those are the Pittsburgh Pirates." It was to be years before I discovered that Bing was part owner of the club. Among the golfers in the pictures I recognized Ben Hogan, Toney Penna, and Jimmy Demaret.

"You play golf a lot, don't you?"

Hard at work with Barney Dean, Leo Lynn, and Jimmy Cottrell

"Just days."

"How do you get out to the course when you're working like this?"

"You see that little strip of turf over by the goldfish pond?"

"Yes."

"That's for my pitch shots. If I stand at the back, the ball just clears the top of the fountain and lands in the patch on the other side. Then if we finish by three o'clock I can get in nine holes at Bel Air before dark. Are you a golfer?"

"Well, not exactly. Lefty Stackhouse, the pro at the Robstown Country Club, gave me lessons, but I'm not much good." Fortunately I was being modest since, as Bing later learned, I had a great deal to be modest about.

"I just played a few rounds in Europe. There are some nice courses over there. Different from ours."

He paused and I couldn't stand the vacuum, so I plunged back in. He wasn't the only one who had traveled!

"The studio sent me to Japan and Korea with Don Taylor, Joan Elan, and Audrey Dalton last April. I loved the trip. The world premiere of *The Girls of Pleasure Island* was in Seoul, and I was invited because Dorothy Bromiley had appendicitis."

"Did you enjoy the USO shows?"

"More than anything I've ever done. It seemed the only way a civilian girl could serve her country. Did you know that if we'd been captured, we'd have been shot as spies?"

"I had occasion to consider that possibility once when my driver and I discovered we were behind the German lines."

"Dear Lord, what did you do?"

"Turned the jeep around and advanced hastily to the rear!"

Here I was being entertained by Bing Crosby. I wanted to ask a thousand questions and hear what he had to say. That had been easy with other leading men at Paramount—Bill Holden, Charlton Heston, Ray Milland, Bob Hope. But with Bing I talked more than he did. He seemed content to listen, and let that deep rumbly voice of his flow only when necessary.

At length he eyed my racket: "But you play tennis?"

"Yes, and I'm late. It's been nice getting to know you."

"Well, since we're neighbors, when you're in the area why don't you stop by for a cup of tea?"

"I'd like that a lot. Bye."

I didn't want to leave, but knew that my time had come. I bounced off down the street with my ponytail swinging behind me, clutching the petticoats securely in my right hand, feeling as if I could fly.

Once I was safely away, I thought of all I'd meant to ask him. Then I fell to musing on what it must have been like to be Bing's leading lady. What impressions did Mary Carlisle, Judith Allen, Marion Davies, Carole Lombard, Miriam Hopkins, Kitty Carlisle, Joan Bennett, Mary Boland, Ethel Merman, Ida Lupino, Bessie Burke, Martha Raye, Shirley Ross, Beatrice Lillie, Francisca Gaal, Louise Campbell, Gloria Jean, Dorothy Lamour, Mary Martin, Marjorie Reynolds, Rise Stevens, Betty Hutton, Ingrid Bergman, Joan Caulfield, Joan Fontaine, Ann Blyth and Jane Wyman have of Bing?

What were his kisses like before the klieg lights? What did Marion Davies feel when he sang *Temptation* to her? How did Mary Carlisle react to *Learn to Croon, Down the Old Ox Road, The Moon Got in My Eyes* or *My Heart is Taking Lessons?*

Could I ever be his leading lady? Would he ever sing to me? Did he really mean it when he invited me for tea?

A couple of weeks later a lady named Gus Glenn phoned me. She had been our alumni advisor in Chi Omega sorority at the University of Texas. If that sounds like a grandiose title, it was supposed to be. Gus Glenn was a very important person in charge of making young ladies out of Chi Omega sorority girls.

Gus's southern drawl made her sound as if she'd been taking Scarlett O'Hara lessons all her life. At the age of seventy she still had flashing blue eyes, a wonderful smile, and enormous self-assurance.

She arrived with a friend, so I invited them both to lunch at the Paramount commissary, where the food was cheap and we could look at the pictures of all the movie stars lining the walls.

We finished lunch and walked out into the bright afternoon sunlight. At a loss for something to do I finally suggested, "Maybe we could go over and see the *White Christmas* set."

"Oh, that would be wonderful, Kathryn. We'd love to see Bing Crosby in person."

Right on cue Gus's words were followed by a loud rattling noise. Startled, I glanced around and saw two blue eyes bearing down on us from atop a bicycle sporting a big Minute Maid sign.

Oh dear Lord, I thought. It's bubble popping time. He'll never recognize me, and even if he does, he won't have time to stop and speak to us. I became deeply engrossed in conversation with the ladies, dimly aware of the fact that I was talking gibberish. The rattling stopped, but I didn't dare turn my head.

"Hello Tex. Who are your friends?"

Now you talk about being grateful! I would have blown up his bicycle tires, shined his Minute Maid sign, or run errands for him all day long just for those words.

With Gus Glenn, Bing slid easily into a quasi-Texas drawl, somewhere between Gus's accent and that of her friend, who was from New Orleans and had sorghum in her vowels and no consonants to speak of.

"Are y'all goin' over to Stage 12? I think that's where we'll be shootin'. Yes, there should be some pretty clever capers cut this afternoon. Rosie and Danny and Vera-Ellen will be there, and I'll be around too. Maybe I'll see you over on the set." With a reassuring smile Bing rode jauntily on.

When we reached Stage 12, there sat Rosie Clooney. I introduced her to Gus, and Rosie bailed me out, chatting comfortably and laughing with a characteristic throaty chuckle.

Then she said, "S'cuse me a minute, I've got to do a scene." She hopped into a section of the interior of a railroad car, and began a heart-to-heart talk with Danny Kaye and Vera-Ellen.

I watched from the semi-darkness that surrounds the bright lights. My friends were out of the way, but they could see perfectly. It was cool and comfortable on the set and I was feeling better, but not so good as I felt two seconds later when there was a subtle pressure at the back of my knees.

I turned around to find Bing holding a canvas chair with his name on it. After I plopped into it, he pulled up another chair and sat by me. Talking was impossible because the cameras started to roll at that moment. It never occurred to me to wonder why he hadn't given the chair to my seventy-year-old friend or her equally venerable companion.

I did understand that Bing didn't give chairs to everybody. We must have sat there in silence for five minutes, watching the scene. Then the director yelled "Cut," and an assistant ran up to announce, "Mr. Crosby, you're in the next shot."

With no sense of hurry Bing said, "I'll call you. Maybe we can have that cup of tea one afternoon."

"Lovely," I said, "and thank you."

He reached out toward me as if to shake my hand, then moved to clap me on the shoulder as my brother used to do. Finally he settled for touching my cheek, and quickly turned away.

"Well," said Gus, "if that isn't the sweetest man. You must be doing awfully well around here, honey, to have somebody like Bing Crosby treat you like that."

"I'm sure he's just as sweet to everybody," I lied. In my heart of hearts I was certain that he was nice only to me. Of course he couldn't be equally hospitable to Mona Freeman, Audrey Hepburn, and Jean Simmons. Surely I was the only lass in the world who had shared his canvas chair.

A couple of weeks later, having heard nothing from Bing, I decided to interview him for my weekly newspaper column *Texas Gal in Hollywood*.

Back on the *White Christmas* set I perched on a high stool with pencil and paper while he,

With the cast and director of *White Christmas*, Rosemary Clooney, Danny Kaye, Anne Whitfield, Vera Ellen, and Michael Curtiz looking very dignified in his officer's uniform, coolly chose his best camera angle, and filled my pages with utter blarney.

Ultimately I managed to conclude the interview on a more realistic and practical note by wangling an invitation for tea at Lucy's, where we sat in a dark booth, sipping the hot beverage and munching cinnamon toast. There we attracted no special attention because everyone in the restaurant was connected with show business.

This our first date lasted thirty minutes, during which the following topics were covered, to be duly noted in my diary.

"You say your father's a hunter? Do you hunt?"

"Well....uh...I....I've never really been hunting. But I helped Daddy sight in a rifle once."

"You're going to school, you say?"

"Yes, UCLA."

"That's good. You should continue your education."

"Oh, I plan to."

He said, "I hope my boys finish. School's awfully important, not for anything specific that you study, but just because you learn how to learn, and take your lumps, and have some unforgettable experiences, and say goodbye to childhood dreams."

Hardly a romantic conversation, but somehow it felt right. His words were warm and they included me. Why we even had mutual friends! In addition to Barney Dean, I knew golfer Jackie Burke, who was dating Joanne Stillwagon, a sorority sister of mine from the University of Texas. I had been terribly homesick at Paramount, but suddenly I felt better.

We walked back over to the lot, where they were just about ready for Bing in the next set-up.

"Bye Tex. See you soon."

"Bye. Thanks for the tea."

The week after Christmas, Nellie Manley called me to her studio next to Wally Westmore's makeup department, a place full of bustling preparation and gay camaraderie every morning.

That is where I first met Audrey Hepburn, who was having her makeup applied. Mine was put on by the same man, but somehow he didn't achieve quite the same results, so I consoled myself with doughnuts and coffee. At the time I supposed that the principal difference between Grace Kelly and myself was that she avoided the doughnuts while I, alas, didn't.

I never knew what the makeup artists were doing to my face because I invariably dropped off to sleep in their tilt-back barber chairs. Normally my blind faith in Nellie was more or less justified, but this time she decided to try something new. She washed my hair, and before drying it, combed it out and cut it off right at the jawline.

"They told me in the front office to get rid of some of that magnolia-blossom cuteness of yours."

"What kind of permanent will you give me?"

"None."

Nellie wrapped a hairnet around my head and sat me under the dryer until I came out looking a little like a lost lotus blossom on the Burma Trail.

"That's it," Nellie said briskly.

I risked only one horrified glance at the mirror. "Thank you," I muttered and left the department before tears started streaming down my face, thinking only of getting home before anyone saw me.

So of course Bing picked that moment to emerge from his dressing room.

"Well...where are you...say, is that you, Kathryn?:

It was the first time he hadn't called me Tex.

I raised my tear-streaked face and said, "Isn't this the worst thing you ever saw? Nellie just did it to me."

He brushed it off with a chuckle. "Well, you do look a bit like Joan of Arc on her way to the stake, particularly with those red eyes. Come on in and sit a minute."

I was delighted to hide since I felt that everybody at Paramount must be at the windows, staring at the strange new creature.

Montage from *White Christmas*

"I'll tell you what: Run up to see Wally Westmore's sister Pat. They have a beauty salon out on Sunset Boulevard called *The House of Westmore*. Surely she'll be able to make something *très* chic out of those few lank locks."

"Do you really think there is still hope?"

"Of course there is. No real harm's been done; just a little injury to your self-esteem."

The problem had been solved. Pat Westmore gave me an "Italian cut," and by the end of the day I was respectable again.

I know now why Bing was so sensitive to my situation. Hair had always been a problem for him. He didn't have enough of it, and all of our life together he was trapped in a special kind of purgatory: He couldn't be seen privately with his toupee, but he couldn't be photographed without it.

Since *White Christmas* was the big film on the Paramount lot, its star was there almost every day for the rest of the year. By a curious coincidence so was I.

1954

On January 6 Bing stopped me on my way out of the commissary after lunch. "I'm going to Palm Springs for a couple of weeks. I'll miss seeing you around here, so why don't we have dinner together when I return on the 24th?"

We kept walking. It was a chance encounter, nothing more, but the eyes of every studio worker, director, producer, and player were on us. Did they know that something of enormous importance was about to happen? I was going to have a dinner date with Bing Crosby!

"11345 Berwick is my new address," I told him. "I'm living in a guest house just off Sepulveda Boulevard, close to UCLA.

"It's close to me too. I was dreading the hour drive to Topanga Canyon. Besides, I don't think your uncle Walter likes me.

"Not possible. Why not?"

"I phoned there while you were in Texas over the holidays. Your uncle answered, and I asked for you. He said, 'She's not here. Who's calling?' When I responded 'Bing Crosby,' he snapped 'Yeah, well, I'm Harry Truman,' and hung up."

We had just reached the drama building. Why, he had walked me to work. My face was beet red, whether with pride or embarrassment I'd have been hard put to say.

January 24, 1954. The burnt-orange taffeta dress crinkled and rustled over the horsehair petticoats. My waist was nipped in to about 21 inches, but I could breathe if I planned each move carefully. I was wearing new black pumps and Mrs. Zibell, my landlady, had loaned me her black coat with the princess cut and the full skirt. I decided that I looked glamorous. There was just no other word for it.

Bing arrived in his Mercedes, and we met in Mrs. Zibell's front room. He was wearing grey flannel slacks with brown shoes; one sock was green and the other maroon. A large, smelly pipe was tucked casually into the breast pocket of his blue blazer. His hat was straw with a red band. It's never too early for spring. I thought he looked masterful.

We went to Chasen's and were greeted not only by Tommy Gallagher, the maître d'hôtel, but by Dave Chasen himself. Dave was an old vaudevillian, a juggler of note who'd decided

With Phil Silvers and Danny Kaye

that legerdemain with cuts of meat and stories about the old days with customers were more fun than trying to eke out a living on cross-country tours. He made the best deviled beef bones and chili in Beverly Hills and also did elegant things with less regional fare.

Bing and I sat in a red booth toward the back, where Dave put his special friends. On either side of us were Phil Silvers and Danny Kaye, who both came over to talk with Bing.

"What would you like to drink, Kathryn?"

He'd stumped me there. With the sole exception of Baptist eggnog at Christmas, I was a stranger to alcohol.

He sensed my uncertainty and said, "Maybe a little Dubonnet? That's a nice apéritif. Yes, a Dubonnet mist."

It looked like a grape snowcone and tasted wonderful, very sweet and flavorful. On about the third sip I realized that I hadn't eaten lunch. The crab came next, followed immediately by filet, salad, and one of Dave's specialities, a frozen eclair. The 21-inch waist was in dire straits, but I was in bliss nonetheless. For the first time no assistant director came to tap Bing on the shoulder and say "You're in the next set-up, Mr. Crosby," and I didn't have to run off to class.

Bing was very tan, which made the whites of his eyes much clearer and the blue more startling, even in the dim light of Chasen's. For the first time, he was able to concentrate on me. Nothing intense, mind you, just a bemused appraisal from time to time. There was no earth-shattering dialogue. We thoroughly covered the fact that Daddy had been the coach of a football team that had won the county championship with eleven starters and two substitutes.

Bing asked about the rest of my family: my brother, Emery, seven years older than I; my sister Frances Ruth, four years my senior. I wondered what he was thinking. Was he comparing this small-town girl to Dixie?

"What about you? Why didn't you stay home and get married?"

"I don't want to, ever. I want to be an actress. That's a full-time occupation." Obviously I meant it. I think it let him drop his guard and relax.

He told me about his family. How his dad, a wonderful storyteller, had been a trifle improvident, having once purchased a phonograph with money that was intended for the grocer.

'We have to have music, Kate,' Dad Crosby had explained to his frantic wife.

"Poor mother. She had to make things stretch to feed and clothe seven of us. She had some neat housekeeping tricks. We lived in one of those northern houses, two stories and a full basement. The laundry was downstairs next to the cellar, where the potatoes were stored. If we children didn't hang our clothes up, she threw them down the laundry chute. Since each of us had one suit for school and another for Sunday, there was a mad dash to retrieve the rumpled garb. Maybe that's how I developed my own peculiar style."

He looked at me slyly, but I hadn't read enough about him to know that Bing was noted for his singular lack of sartorial splendor, so my eyes just got wider. He must have thought, "This girl isn't from Texas, she's from Mars."

Unfamiliar with the popular music of the day, I didn't even know the names of Bing's recent records. Fortunately he didn't elect to discuss them, or his sons either this time. I learned much later that he had just realized that Gary was older than I. Children do date you. If it hadn't been for them, I wouldn't have seemed particularly young. I would have been just another contract player at Paramount, and he just another run-of-the-mill superstar.

The evening passed in a golden glow. I sipped coffee and felt fat but utterly content. The doorman brought Bing's car, and we slowly eased away from the curb, turned left on Santa Monica, right on Wilshire, right on Sepulveda, and left on Berwick.

The Zibell house was dark, even though it was only eleven o'clock. We worked our way around to the left of it.

"Watch out for the swings," I warned.

"The what?"

"Judy's and Naomi's swings." I touched

Bing as a boy, with his father, brothers and sisters

them first, and took his hand to pull him through. And there was the bougainvillea-covered cottage, with its porch light glowing.

"That's very sweet," he commented gallantly. "I think the size is right."

When we reached the door, I didn't know what to do. I couldn't invite him in. The house lacked a separate living room, and had no furnishings to speak of. So I just stood there and looked awkward.

Bing took my face in his hands, kissed my nose and each cheek, and jauntily disappeared into the shadows while I leaned against the door, covered with chill bumps.

He had kissed me!

About five seconds later I heard, "Dad blame son-of-a-buck." Of course he'd barked his shins on a swing.

Friday, February 11, I picked up the mail at the studio and opened three envelopes that should have been bordered in black.

UCLA was intransigent. The drama department would not accept me for their degree program because I had left a play in progress to do a USO tour of Korea for Paramount Pictures.

The editor of *The Citizen* in Brazoria county put it this way: "Dear Kathryn, we've had some recent cutbacks, and each member of our staff is going to have to double up on duties. Therefore we cannot continue to run your column, *Texas Gal In Hollywood,* but we do thank you for the work that you've done for us."

The legal department of Paramount Pictures was more succinct: "Dear Miss Grandstaff, we have elected not to exercise our option for your services."

I sat huddled on a bench in the mail room. Any one of those blows would have distressed me. The three of them left me numb. I had failed in the great world, and it was time to return to West Columbia.

I went to say my goodbyes to Bill Meiklejohn, head of the talent department, who had been responsible for hiring me and firing me, to Gene Zukor, whose father had founded the studio, to Pat Dugan, who was the producer of the movie *Forever Female* (the one for which I'd done my original test) and to Milt Lewis, the talent scout.

Only the latter commiserated with me: "They just don't seem to be doing anything that needs you, Kathryn.

"That's OK, Milt. Don't feel bad." I started for the front gate of the studio, hoping to make it home before I became very sick.

By some mischance I walked by Bing's dressing room. I didn't want to see him. My back already ached from walking tall. My quivering chin was held high, but the smile was frozen. If my eyes sparkled, it was with tears.

Suddenly his voice issued from the sanctuary. "Oh Kathryn, don't run away. It's tea time. Why don't we go to Lucy's—or perhaps Leo could fix us a cup here.

"Here please." I didn't want to see anyone else, but I felt a quick surge of relief. While Leo hummed and puttered in the background, Bing put all his charm into overdrive and told me some very funny stories. I've often seen him that way since when dealing with very old people, babies, and damsels in distress. At the end of our thirty minutes I'd forgotten that I had a care in the world.

As I took my grateful leave Bing inquired, "How about a little supper at the house tomorrow night? Lindsay is going to be there and I'd like you to meet him."

The next morning I rushed to the House of Westmore. Pat fixed my hair beautifully. It was close and straight at the back, but curled on the sides in a kind of modified flapper arrangement, making me feel perky and stylish.

I donned a skirt and sweater, with a pair of spiky heels for added inches and maturity (a mistake, as I was soon to learn), and waited for Bing to pick me up.

We wove our way through the commuter traffic and eased on down to Westwood Village. Bing turned left on Beverly Glen, then cut right by the Holmby Hills Park.

The big iron gate opened on a curving driveway which led through a jungle of unkempt foliage to an enormous flagstone courtyard. In the center was a lone star in a paler

Gary, Phillip, Dennis, and Lindsay

shade of flagstone, obviously fated to welcome a renegade Texan.

The architectural style savored of New Orleans. White grillwork covered the windows of the two-story brick building. The jacarandas were in bloom, dripping blue blossoms on either side of the wide front door. Red-flowered pepper trees grew against the wall.

Bing opened the unlocked door and ushered me into a vast hall. "Take off your sweater; the 'ladies' is right there," he said, dropping his hat on the right side of the entrance hall atop a rack loaded with golf clubs.

The ladies bath was a fairy tale of cut glass, painted mirrors, and silk-covered doors. I hung up my sweater and stared open-mouthed. A gold brush and comb stood beside crystal perfume bottles with gold stoppers. But alas all these objects had the name Rita engraved on them. I emerged, found Bing waiting, and demanded forthrightly "Why Rita?"

Bing laughed, paused a moment to get his story straight, then blandly averred that a male friend of his had needed a loan badly, and had put said *objets d'art* up for collateral before disappearing from the face of the earth. I wondered vaguely whether he would lie to me about other things.

Bing took me into the library, which had down-filled pillows on the sofas and a big Labrador lying on the rug. Just as I was getting acquainted with "Old Cindy," a yippy little poodle entered.

"That's Topsy," Bing said. She's getting on in years and a bit crotchety, but at heart she's a nice girl, aren't you Topsy?"

Topsy frisked around Bing's legs for a minute, and then hopped up onto the sofa in the bay window. She sat in an indentation which was obviously her place of rest, and stared out into the waning sunshine at the birds playing around the fountain.

"I'll be right down," Bing said, and left the library to walk upstairs. Abandoned to myself, I thought how lonely it would be in this huge house without company.

In a minute Bing brought down a package.

"On my trip through Spain with Lindsay I was given an assortment of bullfighter shirts. Will this fit you?"

It had a ruffled front with a stiff collar, and little glass studs and cuff links. I wondered what Mrs. Ptitsin could do with it. Perhaps a bolero jacket and a tight skirt simulating toreador pants, with a high cummerbund waist. Yes, that might just. . .well, I'd think about it later.

In the here and now, Bing was filling his pipe and tamping it down. He held a kitchen match in the fingers of his right hand, and struck it with the nail of his thumb.

A whistle and some noisy clomping on the stairs. Lindsay entered, paused at the little wet bar to fix himself a coke, and then joined us.

"Lin, this is Kathryn Grandstaff. She's at Paramount. Writes a column."

Instead of bothering to explain that I wasn't and didn't anymore, I compounded my crime with a third falsehood: "Right now I'm going to UCLA."

Lindsay Crosby had big brown eyes, a dimple in his chin, and a warm smile. This was his home, and he was very comfortable in it.

The sports of the day were discussed, but the repartee was a trifle fast for me, couched as it was in a Runyonesque vocabulary with numerous Crosbyisms that had evolved over the years.

Bing finally said, "Hey, phantom, where were you last night?"

"What do you mean? I was here all the time."

"Don't give me that."

"Is that why you call him phantom?"

"Oh yeah. . .you can never find Lin. He habitually 'yesses' you along, and then evaporates into thin air."

Bing gave me a look that was all perplexed innocence. Surely this wasn't the same man who had quietly disappeared from my life after pledging eternal fealty by kissing me on both cheeks and the nose. At any rate, now that I was in trouble he didn't commiserate with me; he gave me a drink and a present, and proceeded to feed me.

The couple from *The Country Girl*

Supper was in an oval room with a Sheraton table and crewel-covered chairs. Lindsay tilted his so far back that I thought he'd go over at any moment.

We ate fried chicken and English peas, with mashed potatoes and gravy.

"Say, this is real down-home Southern cooking."

"Sure is honey," laughed Rose, showing several gold teeth among her flashing white ones.

After a relaxed meal, we picked up our plates and took them into the butler's pantry, where I automatically started scraping food off the dishes.

"I can take it from there, child," Rose admonished. Knowing better than to interfere in her territory, I followed Bing's lead back toward the library, but this time he continued on instead of turning left.

We entered the drawing room. A Queen Anne table stood behind the overstuffed sofa, with captain's chairs drawn up around it.

"We can sit around the table or on the sofa."

"The sofa looks more comfortable."

So we all sat on it. Bing pushed a button, a television set rose out of an early American breakfront cabinet, and the fights came on.

After the main event Lin said, "Well, it's time to hit the books. Goodnight, dad."

"Goodnight, son. Stay off that phone now. I'll see you in the morning."

Once Lindsay was gone, Bing casually took my hand while we watched television for another half hour.

On the drive home he remarked offhandedly "I have a friend who is doing a series for television. I wonder if I might give him your name?"

"That would be wonderful." Tactfully I didn't add "because my option has been dropped and I will soon be broke." He had not mentioned my little problem, so neither would I.

Bing simply deposited me on the porch at the cottage and went whistling off into the dark.

I could hear swing hit seesaw as he expertly tossed it aside, picture of a man totally in command of his universe.

At 11:30 p.m., the phone rang. I awoke and staggered across the floor to my desk.

"This is Ken Murray," a booming voice announced. "I'm doing a television show called *Where Were You?* I told Bing that I need a couple of recurring characters, and he said you could probably handle an assignment, so I'd like to meet you tomorrow."

"Yes sir, what time?" I was wide awake now, and I remembered Ken Murray. He was a funny comedian with bushy eyebrows and a big cigar. So Bing had recommended me for a steady job. What quick work from such a lackadaisical swain!

The next day at one o'clock I met Ken at the Hal Wallis Studio, and the part was mine. I called Paramount, and was put through to Bing's dressing room.

"Thank you, thank you! I got the part! How sweet of you to recommend me."

"He's a good sort, and I think he'll do an entertaining series. How about some supper at Romanoff's?"

The Beverly Hills restaurant was presided over by Prince Michael Romanoff himself. The decor was early Roxbury rococo. Huge urns were filled with dollar eucalyptus branches to which I proved to be allergic. Alas how hard it is to be poised when your nose is moist, and your hankie is unironed!

Dinner was interminable, but somehow Bing didn't seem to notice my stifled sneezes and overt sniffles. For my part I barely controlled the urge to hurl myself into his arms.

Here was safety.

Here was an instant solution to life's problems.

Here was a man who made rejections by UCLA, the newspapers, and Paramount Pictures seem equally unimportant.

"Well, you appear to be pretty pleased with yourself."

"I am. Imagine! It happened so quickly. I have a job! I can miss school on shooting days.

The second interview

With Cletus Caldwell on my first trip to Palm Springs

That means I won't have to beg Daddy for plane fare home or funds to stay in college. Even though the drama department won't have me, I can still take courses in cooking and interior design."

I did not know that I was entitled to unemployment insurance, or that Bing Crosby Productions was doing *Where Were You?*

At the end of the evening, Bing walked me to the cottage, gave me the tiniest kiss on the lips, and left.

At Paramount Pictures photo sessions were arranged well in advance, and interdepartmental communication was non-existent. Publicity was blissfully unaware that I had been fired, so they had conscientiously set up a story.

When I foolishly explained the situation to the PR man, he insisted that it was a break even if my option had been dropped. "This will be fine exposure, and you'll get new material for your newspaper column. We'll focus on your reporting."

I couldn't tell him that I'd been dropped there too. How much failure can 5' 4" absorb?

We met at noon in front of the commissary. "There are about five movies in production. Who would you like to interview today?"

May all my decisions be just this difficult: "Bing Crosby again."

"OK, let's go."

When I arrived at the set where Bill Holden, Grace Kelly, and Bing were doing *The Country Girl*, the first person I saw was Barney Dean.

"What are you doing?" I asked.

"I mope a lot."

Barney was one of the friends who had helped Bing be affable for eons and never reveal a bit of himself, while referring to people who "told it like it was" as "soul barers."

Bing could tell Barney stories for hours, or better still listen to them. Theirs was the unending quest for the *mot juste*, or the sight gag that would break up Bob Hope. And now both were trapped in the depths of Odets' pessimism.

As we entered Bing's canvas dressing room his voice crooned, "Hi, Tex. Haven't seen you for a week or so."

"Has it been that long?" I purred.

"What's going on, Frank?"

"Well, Kathryn is doing a photo story and she would like. . . ."

"I want to interview you."

"Come on in."

Frank smiled in relief, and I realized suddenly that he hadn't known exactly what to expect.

Once again I borrowed a pad from Bing and perched on the same stool while we were photographed. Then, having satisfied Frank and the photographer, I sent them packing and promptly moved in, my pencil still poised journalistically.

"Tell me what the ranch is really like."

"It's quite a spread."

"What do you do there besides serenade the dogies?"

"We have a cattle-feeding operation which is experiencing a bit of trouble right now."

"Why?"

"The cattle spend each summer in the mountains where there's plenty of grass and water. When they move down to the lower pastures in the fall, we have to haul a lot of hay or sell off the excess calf crop. Generally we end up shipping them to a small place near Redding in northern California, where there is a feeder operation with good hay and plenty of water."

The precarious ranchers' tightrope-walk seemed cinchy the way Bing described it. "Well, what's the problem?" I enquired in some perplexity.

"We have to deal with three different unions. We haul the cattle to the railroad, ship them by rail to the stockyard in Redding, then truck them over Burney Mountain to Rising River. When they've been fattened, we have to move them to the slaughter house."

"That's very complicated. Couldn't you try a cattle drive like those on the Old Chisholm Trail?"

Bing's eyes narrowed slightly, but then he realized that it was just my idea of a joke. "I understand that during the past century squatters have built fences along the way."

At the Circus Ball with Bobbie Perlberg

"Ummmmm. Now that you're working on *The Country Girl*, Mr. Crosby, what do you do in your leisure time?"

Bing's eyes twinkled, "Well, I thought tonight I might go to The Brown Derby for supper. Want to join me?"

Mission accomplished, I breathed a sigh of relief. "That's a lovely idea, but now I must be going. Thanks for the interview."

"I'll pick you up at six o'clock, and we'll see a movie afterwards."

"Maybe a Western?"

Bing tossed my pad after me as I fled the set, feeling very smug and sure of myself. "Now that's what I call getting a story," Frank Riser commented.

Thenceforth Bing's evenings seemed to be occupied in rehearsing scenes with his co-star. I gave him until the sixth of April before writing a note: "Dearest Bing, there's going to be a closed house this Friday night at the cottage. Please come over after dinner for some cheesecake and Sanka, a walk around the block, and a talk before the fire. Party's over officially at about 9:30 so arrive by 7. Wear old clothes and bring your pipe. Kathryn."

Bing phoned on the 8th to say, "I'd love to taste your cheesecake, but I need a portion of protein too. I'll pick you up at 6:30 and we'll have supper at Romanoff's first."

At the end of the evening he kissed me, a proper kiss at last, and disappeared immediately into the shadows. "Talk about your phantoms," I fumed.

He phoned a half hour later: "I'm going to Palm Springs for a couple of weeks. I know you're busy in school, but what are your plans for Thursday, the 22nd of April: Think you might join me for the weekend?"

"Palm Springs? (I tried to sound as if I were balancing this against previous plans for Lake Arrowhead.) The sun might be nice." And ever so casually. . ."Is anyone else going?"

"Yeah, Bill Morrow and his girl, Cletus Caldwell."

Sigh of relief: "Lovely. I enjoyed Romanoff's tonight."

"I preferred your cheesecake. You have a pretty good stroke with the pastries. Can't eat too much though. Makes me fat."

"I can sympathize with your problem. Goodnight, Bing."

On the 10th of April he surprised me with a television set that had been in his dressing room. Louie Serpe, his mother's driver, brought it with this little note: "Dear Kathy, I keep forgetting to bring this to you. This way I know you'll get it and I can also say *Je t'adore*."

It never occurred to me to ask why I hadn't heard from him, and Bing never brought it up, but the fact is that he was dismantling his dressing room at Paramount, his home away from home for so many years. He might have had some feelings of discomfiture, but I never thought of consoling him, and as I learned later he didn't want me to.

At 2:30 on April 22 I boarded Western Airlines, Flight 317, at International Airport. One little hanging bag, one makeup kit. What a lucky break! Because I didn't own a suitcase, Bing mistakenly concluded that I preferred to travel light.

We drove to his house on the hill above Thunderbird Country Club. A gravel road threaded through tall palms. At the end of it we found Cletus Caldwell, a pretty, brown-haired, brown-eyed, wide-smiling girl who said, "Hi, I'm an Indian. What are you?"

"I'm a Texas mongrel, I guess."

"Do you wanna swim?"

"If it's all right with you, Bing."

"Sounds like a good idea."

I dog-paddled around the pool, slowly recovering from my air sickness. I tried to be careful because there was a party that night, and I hadn't yet learned how to take care of short hair.

The house was a one-story white stucco. Cletus and I had a bedroom at one end, opening out onto the pool. Next to us was the bath area, then the kitchen, and finally the living room, with records and a tape deck but no television because reception was still poor in the desert. A door on the side opened into a tiny

Mona Freeman

Rosemary Clooney

Betty Utie

Audrey Hepburn

office for Bing, which in turn communicated with his bedroom. Bill Morrow bunked next door.

For the Circus Ball, Bing wore a straw cowboy hat, a bolo tie, and a multi-colored silk cowboy shirt with chaps and boots. I thought him a vast improvement on Hopalong Cassidy.

I wore a peasant blouse with my purple Mexican skirt. After some hesitation I draped a mantilla over my short curly hair. The dogpaddling hadn't worked and I'd soaked most of it.

At dinner Bing chatted with Bobbie Perlberg who sat to his left. As I later learned, he had always been fond of her, and really cared what she thought. The next afternoon we set out to visit her. It was the only time we were alone that weekend.

Since Bing didn't talk much, I prattled on about the scenery. After I had alluded to the beauties of the terrain or inquired after the name of a certain bush, he would stare at the last-mentioned object as if he hadn't previously examined the problem, accord it serious consideration, and finally say, "Well, I don't know. That is something, isn't it?"

Bobbie was a petite, blonde lady with deep dimples, who had been one of the singing Noonan Sisters. She was now married to Bill Perlberg, a producer who did *The Country Girl* with Bing.

We sat in Bobbie's sumptuous home while I had a root beer and she looked me over. I now wonder what she saw. I suspect that it was a fat-faced girl who was much too young to have any sense, but who obviously liked her friend. That wasn't unique of course—everybody liked Bing. The question in Bobbie's mind must have been, "Does he like Kathryn, and if so, why for heaven's sake?"

Bobbie had a lot of people to appraise for Bing in those days. Actress Mona Freeman, dancer Betty Utie, French gamine Ghislaine, Oriental lovely Virginia Lee. Not to mention Mary Murphy, Joan Caulfield, Rosemary Clooney, Audrey Hepburn, and Grace Kelly.

I have no way of knowing, but I doubt that Bobbie approved of me. Had I been in her shoes, I certainly wouldn't have. The only thing that we had in common was our mutual esteem for Bing.

Bing trusted Bobbie. Her home was a safe place to take his friends. He knew that she didn't gossip and was as unswervingly loyal as Bill Perlberg and Jimmy Van Heusen. Years later, after her husband died, she married Jimmy.

Bobbie was saying, "We must go check with the Edrises. Their house is almost finished, and you'll love what they're doing."

Riding up the canyon, I couldn't get over the fact that the sliding shadows and the waning sun made Bing's eyes sparkle like forget-me-nots on ice. He was driving, Bobbie was in the middle, and I was on the outside, where I could look across and ostensibly be talking to Bobbie, while really watching him. Repeatedly he glanced across at me. I wondered if Bobbie realized that no one was paying much heed to her conversational efforts.

When we arrived at the house, Bing inspected the foundation, the quality of construction, and the enormous boulders around which the house was built.

"Well, there's only one thing to call this place," he opined: "It just has to be Edris-Over-The-Rocks." And indeed it was forevermore.

In retrospect, what was my weekend like?

It was a very proper house party, perhaps something unique to the time or man. It was also my first experience away from the world that I knew. But it was not an interlude with Bing, who spent the long solitary hours in his little office. Walking out to the pool with Cletus, I heard the continual murmur of a dictaphone. Occasionally I caught enough to make me realize that he was attending to business.

"Think I'd like to record the radio show next Friday. Get Buddy Cole with his boys and Rosie. Why not meet at her place about 4 in the afternoon... See about John Eckert's purchase of steers for Elko...Check on the new script with George Seaton...Sign the checks and send them air mail."

Signe Hasso

Ghislaine

Joan Caulfield

Mary Murphy

There was one inconsequential episode. Should I tell it? Well, the children are grown now.

After dinner at Don the Beachcomber's, we went back to the house, said goodnight, and I repaired to the ladies' wing. Cletus and Bill drifted toward the living room. I got into my shortie nightie with the bloomers, and popped into bed. About 20 minutes later there was a tap on the sliding door.

I went over, opened it a crack, and there was Bing in yellow cotton pajamas buttoned all the way up to the neck, and a blue-and-white seersucker robe. He whispered, "I just thought I'd come and say goodnight to you."

"How sweet. Goodnight."

He gave me a little kiss and started to squeeze in through the screen door. At that moment Cletus bounced into the room.

The princess in the shortie nightie turned into a Texas horned toad on the spot. Bing coolly murmured, "I just wanted to say goodnight to you girls," and sauntered off into the shadows, inspecting his hands for warts.

Cletus said something about "bad timing," as I blushed and mumbled "Goodnight."

About those p.j.'s buttoned all the way to the neck. People who didn't know thought Bing had difficulty expressing affection. Not at all. As I was to learn much later, the secret was in that top button on the pajamas. If it was fastened, it was going to be a quiet read in bed and lights out at 10 p.m. after chaste prayers. If it was unbuttoned, however, watch out.

Bing kept my silly thank-you-note: "Dearest Bing, My stay in Palm Springs has been just wonderful. You thought of everything to help me have a good time, and I did just that. The homes—Jimmy Van Heusen's and especially yours—are beautiful. Your pool, your golf cart, Cletus and Bill and Leo, I love. Your friends, the Perlbergs and Edrises met your newest flame with open-armed hospitality. The places we went—from the Circus Ball to the Racquet Club, and from Don the Beachcomber's to the Dunes—were all exciting. But best of all was you—kind, thoughtful, fun. Can you blame me for loving you? Kathryn. P.S. I left your thank-you in the cottage. May I give it to you Sunday?"

Bing's birthday was approaching. He had said he had no plans for May 2nd, so I felt free to ask him over for a birthday cake and tea. I deemed it imprudent to be with him alone. There was a strength about him that frightened me. Or perhaps there was a weakness in me. Without Cletus to interrupt, what might I not do if he started squeezing through my screen door?

I invited Aunt Mary and Uncle Guil Banks, who weren't really blood relatives. Aunt Mary was a self-righteous, born-again Baptist from Arkansas, married to an ever-so-proper Englishman. We met at Texas University, where Mary tutored me in government, fed me, scolded me, and made me feel right at home. Her daughter Marilyn was my age, and her son Guil Jr. was just entering his teens. After moving to California, the Banks had adopted me for Sunday church and fried chicken. Now I wanted them to meet Bing.

He arrived on the dot of 7 p.m. We had hot tea and cake, the latter decorated with a few horses and cattle representing Elko, and the words "Happy Birthday Bing". We chatted easily in the tiny room until all my guests left at about 9 p.m.

I had class the next day, and Bing and the Banks had to work. But it was an introduction and something of a happy accident because Thursday, May 18, I was invited to drive with Aunt Mary, Uncle Guil, and their son to Las Vegas. The minute we arrived, I had a brainstorm: "Why don't I call Bing? He has a ranch somewhere around here."

"Fine."

I reached him up at Elko.

"It's nice to hear from you, Kathryn. What are you doing?"

"I'm in Las Vegas with the Banks."

"Oh, How are Mary and Guil?"

"I thought maybe we might drop in on you if it's not too far."

"Well. . .it's up the road a piece, but you

Saddling up at Elko

certainly would be welcome. We have plenty of beds, and there's nobody up here right now. I'd like y'all to see the ranch."

I have never been able to read maps, a difficulty which I resolved early in life by avoiding them like the plague. Unfortunately there are occasional consequences. For example, I didn't know that Elko was not a suburb of Las Vegas. So on Friday, May 19, Uncle Guil, who didn't want to impede the course of true love, abandoned a prospective customer to drive Aunt Mary, young Guil, and me the full length of the sovereign state of Nevada.

We arrived in the late afternoon, having been further delayed by Aunt Mary's frantic quest for blue jeans. I had mine, and I had seen to it that the jeans were properly faded and the boots sufficiently scuffed. I might be a trifle weak in geography, but I had a firm grasp of essentials.

The Elko ranch had a totem in front of the main house, a white clapboard with a very steep pitch to the roof because of snow. It was a weather-beaten working ranch that looked half as old as time.

Guil Banks Jr. was a tall gangly boy, just starting high school in a strange place. After greeting the women, Bing turned to him and said, "Hey Guil, my boys work up here every summer. If you're interested and don't have a job lined up, maybe you'd like the life of a cowboy. Of course, I've invited some of the boys' friends to give it a try. Nobody's ever lasted the whole summer, but you can come if you don't mind hard work."

In the event Guil Banks Jr. worked there every summer for four years. I wasn't the only one to whom Bing offered gainful employment.

Next morning Guil, Bing, and I rode out with the cowboys to work cattle. The high mountain air was crisp and dry, but the summer sun was hot.

I was just managing to keep my seat on Spike, who was what Bing called a "good cuttin' horse." When a calf broke from the herd and Spike went right after him, I dropped the reins and embraced the saddle horn. To the relief of all and sundry, the horse got the calf and I kept my seat.

Bing and his cowboys tried not to laugh and failed. It was not the last time I would demonstrate conclusively that the title of Rodeo Queen of the Houston Fat Stock Show didn't imply any equestrian abilities. I felt fortunate to have escaped with my life.

Upon our return Bing took us for a long drive around the ranch, showing us the north pasture, where the cattle were driven in the summer to get that high mountain grass. He told us light, charming tales of western life, and afterward, when we were photographed, he put his arm around Aunt Mary instead of me. This time there was no repeat of the 'kiss goodnight' scene; indeed there was barely a peck on the cheek when we said good-bye.

As we drove across the desert, I watched the mountains gradually change form and color. Young Guil had found a job. Had I lost one? It wasn't the putative perils of Death Valley that furrowed my brow.

Bing finally phoned me on June 1. On the 4th he took me to a luau with his friends Francis Brown and Winona Love. He introduced me to two-finger poi, and told me that the pigs and the chef who roasted them to crackling perfection also came from Hawaii, as did the sweet potatoes and ti leaves.

Phil Harris sat to my left and kept me laughing too hard to eat, "Poi with the hoi polloi," he sniffed, demonstrating how it dribbled through his fingers.

"Someday I'm going to acquaint these poor benighted heathen with cutlery, the Apaches' greatest contribution to the march of civilization. What honest Injun could eat this miserable stuff?"

In point of fact we really didn't consume much until the watermelon arrived at the end of the evening. Phil, however, managed to make up for it with ample liquid refreshment.

His wife, Alice Faye, chatted comfortably with us. Bing seemed curious as to how these friends of his would accept me. He cast occasional concerned glances from across the room,

Bing and Mona Freeman double-date with Dennis

and I fervently hoped that my amateurish pig munching would pass muster.

The next night I fixed dinner for Bing in my landlord's kitchen. We had trout, parsley potatoes, French string beans, homemade cake, and hot tea. He arrived at 6 p.m., ate at 6:30, and went home at 9. His kind of evening. I prayed that it might become mine too.

I wonder now if my cooking disagreed with him. Or could this have been the time Alice Harris said, "You're crazy, Bing. Kathryn's just a child still in school!"

In any event he disappeared again.

Oh, he called a couple of times, sent a few postcards which amounted only to mini-geography lessons for a hopeless student. But the course of romance didn't run on. The water was smooth enough. There was no quarrel, no misunderstanding, no altercation. There was just a missing man.

What to do?

I continued shooting on my TV series, made a movie entitled *The Unchained*, completed summer school, refinished some furniture in the cottage, and signed a seven-year contract with Columbia Pictures Corporation, which finally gave me job security and the new alias Kathryn Grant.

At long last, on Saturday, October 16, Bing breezed back into town and my life with an invitation to attend a football game.

When we returned to the cottage, Bing said, "I want to talk to you."

"Come in."

This time he didn't have to squeeze through the screen door. Literally and figuratively I flung it wide open for him.

There should have been a cheerful blaze in the fireplace, but at least the sofa bed was made. He sat on its new grey corduroy spread, leaning against the bolsters. I sat opposite him in the straight-backed desk chair, ready to discuss the game, listen to stories, even boil an egg on my bottom-drawer hot plate.

"Come here."

I sat by him on the bed. He faced me, took my left hand in both of his and said, "You know, you're pretty special to me. I've been thinking about you a lot this summer while I fished Rising River, and golfed at Pebble Beach. I have a question to ask you when I know what the answer is."

"Well?" I asked. "Well?"

Where was the declaration? Where was the poetry? Where was the proposal? Was he now going to slip down on his knees and . . .

Not a bit of it. He just sat there and looked at me. When the vacuum became unbearable, I babbled, "Well Bing, we've known each other for a while now. I think it is very important to have roots. I've seen you at the ranch, and I like it there. I think maybe we should get to know each other a bit more, but I'm glad you missed me because I missed you too."

I was trying desperately to be cool because that's what he wanted. Or was it? Maybe he just liked himself to be cool.

Anyway I curled up next to him, and leaned on his shoulder. He scratched my head—not quite behind the ears like a Labrador, but something similar. I was getting comfortable, and for a moment he seemed to be. But after a brief pause he said, "I'll be calling you," and left.

One shoe had dropped. Or had it?

On October 30 Bing invited Marilyn Banks and me to Palm Springs, where he met us at the airport. We took pictures on his golf cart that record our new bathing suits and his old rig—the same Bermuda shorts, yellow socks, sensible brogan loafers, red belt, ancient paisley voile shirt, white Thunderbird golf cap, and pipe with a silver band encircling its extra-long stem.

Bing's powerfully muscled legs came complete with tan knees, a Palm Springs peculiarity. The tan stopped about an inch below the kneecap because of his everyday use of high socks. The resultant impression was that of a many-splendored layer cake.

Right after dinner Bing announced, "You girls must be tired, so I'll bid you goodnight."

The house above Thunderbird

We rolled up our hair, went to bed, gossiped like coeds in a college dormitory, and privately wondered what was going on.

Marilyn said, "Bing doesn't look too comfortable."

Well, maybe he isn't, I thought, and he's certainly not the kind of man I dreamed I'd marry. I think he is going to propose to me, but what will I answer? What does he make me feel, and what in the world does he want from me?

Little did I know that my sentiments that evening were a microcosm of my feelings toward Bing during the subsequent quarter century. There was uncertainty. There was a striving to figure out what he wanted, what he was trying to say. My antennae ached from trying so hard to receive non-existent signals.

I tossed and turned and mulled and anticipated the morning. It dawned with that sparkling clear air unique to Palm Springs and Islamic versions of Paradise.

I could smell bacon frying in the kitchen, so I pulled on some play clothes to see what Leo had prepared. Ah yes, a glass of Minute Maid and a cup of tea to keep me awake while I waited for Bing. In good time he arrived.

"Good morning, my dear." He gave me a perfunctory kiss on the forehead. And then, because I just sat very still, tilting back precariously, noblesse obliged him to transfer his attention to my lips. Suddenly I knew that this was going to be the day, and indeed it drifted by in a golden haze.

I'm sure that Marilyn must have awakened and we must eventually have done something or other, but all I remember is a quiet supper at home. Leo disappeared, I exchanged signals with Marilyn, and right on cue she yawned ostentatiously and declared that she'd just have to get some sleep.

By this time I was so involved with my own tensions that I was only dimly aware of how pensive Bing looked.

He put on a record and we went outside. It was María de Los Angeles in "Madame Butterfly." There was no moon, so we simply sat and stared at the sky. What can you say about the stars in Palm Springs on the eve when your love is going to propose marriage? Of course they're glowing diamonds in night's black velvet, and you are free to conjure up any additional clichés that might trip through a twenty-year-old skull.

I prayed that I would be able to hear Bing's declaration over the thudding of my heart, but still we just sat in the poolside chairs. What was Bing's heart doing? And what was wrong with his tongue?

He finally said, "You know, Kathryn, I have done a lot of thinking about you and me. We have started growing those roots that you talked about. I wonder what you want to do with the rest of your life."

It was a rhetorical question and didn't call for an answer. So for once I just sat and smiled. Hoping to look as if I were in control, I maintained a death grip on the arms of my chair to keep my fingers from trembling.

"I've had a very exciting life—full of adventures of one kind or another. I've had some luck with my singing, Lord only knows why. I've also enjoyed making movies. The fact is I have some health problems too, and if we did get married I could give you only ten years."

Bing was around 50, but age and infirmity are inconceivable to youth, so not knowing what to say I continued trying to look calm. Now I could feel the pulse beating in my temples.

"You know, it's hard to tell what people want from life. I mean, if we got married, what kind of life would you envision? Would it start with a long honeymoon, say a junket around the world?"

I hoped I had the answer he wanted to hear. "I wouldn't like a big trip then. You have to travel with your work and so do I." (Thus grandly equating my activities with his.) "I'd like to come home after my marriage and have my first memories there. The beginning of a new life is too precious to waste on Niagara Falls or the isles of Greece."

"Ummm, that's a novelty. I'd have thought you'd insist on Rome at least."

Clowning with Marilyn Banks

"I'll get to Rome. But if you're talking about a honeymoon after my marriage, I think coming home with the man I love would be the best part. In many ways I'm not prepared for marriage, but I know it's the coming together of two lives. If we could limit the initial cast to two people, I think I could cope."

"Do you mean you would marry me?"

There was such an innocent, plaintive, adorable quality to that rich voice that I quite overlooked the simple fact that the snake-in-the-grass still hadn't proposed.

"Yes," I said, nearly tripping on my tears.

Only then did I notice that the music had stopped. Next I heard a bump. With my remaining vision I made out Marilyn crawling toward the record-player in the brightly-lighted living room. She was in pajamas and looked very serious.

The operatic arias of Madame Butterfly were supplanted by Jackie Gleason's *Music for Lovers Only*. Bing and I listened to the new record and contemplated Marilyn stealing back across the tile floor.

"Do you think she's going in for basic training?" Bing asked.

"In one thing or another," I replied.

After a while Bing took my hand and we sat, feeling the stars shine on us alone, enveloped by the mystery of the night. Eventually he interrupted my trance by rising, pulling me to him, giving me a brisk kiss and saying, "Well, goodnight, Kathryn."

"Goodnight, Bing."

He walked me to my screen door. I slid it open and threw his back a kiss as he strolled off into the shadows.

Two seconds later the lights flew on. Marilyn, her eyes like saucers, demanded, "Did he? Did he?"

I gazed at her from another planet. My childhood over, I was all at once a committed woman, twenty years old, about to marry the most wonderful man in the world.

"Yes," I said distantly. "Yes, he did."

And I knew then that I would marry Bing Crosby and do everything he wanted me to do, if I could just find out what that was.

Whereupon Bing disappeared. I neither saw him nor heard from him for the next two months.

What happened? Why did Bing leave town and neither call nor write?

Dixie had died November 1, 1952. Had this anniversary brought back too many memories?

As I eagerly contemplated the beginning of our lives together, was he regretting what he had said? I had brought hope and ignorance to our discussion of marriage. Had he brought guilt and too much knowledge?

"I can give you only ten years."

Dixie had suffered for five. Did that have something to do with Bing's hesitation? I didn't understand anything, but I spent my nights in wild speculation.

Days I was acting at Columbia Pictures for coach Benno Schneider, and rehearsing for a USO tour to France and Germany, starring among others Forrest Tucker, Tony Romano, Jana Mason, Adelle August, and myself. We were to visit twenty-eight places in twenty-five days, with only one respite.

Our USO troupe landed in Paris on Christmas Eve, 1954. The next morning I found a refuge that would change my life, the cathedral of Sacré-Coeur. Some Parisians called it the wedding cake because of its round white domes. It sat on a hill above the city and sparkled in the brilliant sunlight. The church was full, and as I entered a hundred-voice choir joined the mighty tones of the organ.

In place of benches there were simply kneelers. I found a spot at the end of one and lost myself in the music.

I had been reared a Southern Baptist. And then, because my aunt and uncle were Methodists and I had lived with them while attending high school in Robstown, I had joined their church.

This Christmas morning I felt that I had at last found my own religion. I identified totally

Touring France with Adelle August

with the richness and beauty of the mass, and with the throng of people who had accepted me as one of them for the love of Christ.

After the service, with the church bells pealing in my ears, I found a rickety taxi and returned to our little hotel. I drank café au lait in the small dining room and pondered my destiny.

As I gazed out at the streets of Paris, the words of the doxology ran endlessly through my mind: *Glory be to the Father and to the Son and to the Holy Ghost, as it was in the beginning, is now and ever shall be, world without end. Amen.*

And I thought back to my Bible studies. "In the beginning, God. . ." Now I could find a church anywhere in the world and be accepted there. Furthermore, if I was going to become part of a family, there would have to be unanimity.

And suddenly I was face-to-face with my own subconscious and the motivating force behind my conversion. Bing was, of course, a Catholic. Perhaps we wouldn't have children. The subject had never been mentioned. He already had a grown family. But if we did have babies, there would have to be harmony. And now I was sure that they would be reared as Catholics. I must study this religion. Could it possibly offer me a whole lifetime of religious fervor such as I had experienced at Sacré-Coeur's Christmas Day Mass?

A letter arrived December 27.

It began "Dear Kathryn, I recall receiving a letter from you in which you said you didn't miss me when I was in Hollywood working, but when I was away in the Northwest the separation was acute. Now I understand what you meant, because that's my present experience. When you were in Kathy's cottage, or in your new Valli Sahara apartment, or at the studio, I felt in touch with you. You were at least within reach. But now—8,000 miles away—it's quite different. All of which is to say that I miss you very much indeed, and I'm eagerly awaiting your early return."

He went on about the Christmas celebration at his house, not mentioning that he had had a date. Then he discussed *The Country Girl* and wound up with, "Kathy, I think I'll go to Pebble Beach about the third, and get ready for the big tourney. Will you call me immediately after you arrive in New York? I want to hear all the tales of your trip."

Wouldn't it have been nicer, since he missed me so horribly, to stay in Los Angeles and hear my stories first-hand? I didn't know then that this pattern was to be repeated throughout our lives. When he had me where he thought he wanted me—at home, being domestic—the discussion of pablum, potty training, and rosebush pruning bored him to tears. When I was away acting, he caught fire, perhaps reacting to a sparkle in my eyes. He became agitated, distressed, demanding, jealous. In short—heaven.

Having been a magician's assistant and a dancer of the "Christmas Mambo" in 28 still-unidentified locales in France and Germany, I proceeded with our group to New York City, the *Ed Sullivan Show*, and some mad playgoing: seven performances in five days. Bing had given me the number to call for tickets. After all, tickets weren't mink or diamonds, we were engaged, and I loved plays, so I abused my privilege. When I phoned to thank him, he casually suggested that we be married in Carmel in early February. Little old New York wasn't big enough to contain my rapture. It was really going to happen. I would be Mrs. Bing Crosby at the beginning of 1955.

Gone Fishin'

1955

On January 9th a letter arrived from Bing: "I suppose you read Denny's publicity or heard about it. A pack of lies and a typical example of how the press can distort an incident to create a story. You know I never defend my boys when they are wrong, but this kid was not drunk, was immediately released, and the case was dropped. Nonetheless the papers ran stories about 'a wild auto chase, drunk driving, etc.' Actually the car was stopped one block away from The Townhouse where they had been, but the public will undoubtedly believe what they read, so there's nothing I can do about it but rage and suffer in silence.

"Well we had a nice Christmas and a merry two-week session. One night 16 boys were bedded at the old manse. Our grocery bill this month will be a beauty. Georgie, the housekeeper, tells me they average eight quarts of milk per day, a whole roast beef, and other items. But its worth it I guess. You know where they are some of the time. And there are lots of laughs with the endless ribbing going on.

"A great deal of muttering because of the Big 10 victory in the Rose Bowl...the 7th in 8 games. But I won a bet because I had 13 points. UCLA would have won I'm sure, but USC put up a gallant fight in the mud.

"Denny is now at Fort Ord and is seemingly happy about it. He knows where he's going to be for a couple of years, and is avowedly determined to make a good showing.

"Well dear, have a good time in New York. I'll call you in a day or so. Write me a note if you have time. All my love, Bing."

January 10, 1955: I returned to the coast and went into rehearsal for a Ford Theatre production of *Hanrahan* at Columbia Studios.

Because of jet lag, I staggered into bed at about 8 p.m. At 9 the phone rang. Marilyn started for it, but I had instinctively rolled over and picked it up in my sleep.

"Hello, Kathryn?"

"Bing!" I was awake immediately. Something was wrong with his voice.

"I won't be able to see you for a bit. I've had a kidney stone attack."

"Oh no! Don't say another word. I'll be there in four hours, or whatever time it takes to drive to Pebble Beach. Marilyn will come with

Singing to Grace

me, won't you Marilyn?" She was nodding, eyes alert. Whatever was up, she was game, even though she was now working in the wardrobe department at Paramount. She could call in sick, leave a message with the answering service there, and we would be on our way in 15 minutes.

"No, don't come. The doctor's here. I will probably be in Los Angeles in a day or so. You mustn't come."

"I have to, Bing. I have to see you. If you're sick, I have to be there."

"Kathryn, don't. It would be bad for both of us."

When he was direct like that, there wasn't much to say. I just sat there stupefied. How could he have a kidney stone attack and not let me do anything about it?

To break the silence, I finally said, "What's it like?"

"The pain's interesting. They say it's like having a severe case of triplets."

"Don't they give you medication? They couldn't just leave you hurting."

"They gave me some pills, but I don't approve of them. So I decided that they won't work...and...of course they don't." His voice sounded drowsy.

"Have you had something recently?"

"Yes, they gave me a shot half an hour ago."

"Well, why don't you try to sleep? Do you think you could if I hung up now?"

"Maybe so."

"Give it a go. If the injection doesn't work, call me back in 20 minutes. If I know you're getting some rest, so will I, and I'll be able to go to work in the morning." I felt clever, bribing him with considerations of my own welfare.

"Oh yes, you do that," he murmured, his tone growing sweeter and sweeter like a little boy going to sleep.

He hung up, and I lay there in the dark raging and feeling useless. In three minutes I was sound asleep. I'm not one of your longer ragers. At 8 the next morning the phone rang again and awakened me.

"Well, I'm better," Bing announced, and indeed his voice did sound stronger and clearer. "I just wanted you to know. Now you go on to work, and I'll call you tonight."

That evening at 6:30 he called again. "Uh Kathryn, I need to talk to you."

"Shall I come up there?"

"No, that's not what I mean. It's just that this old stone is not going to pass, and Doc Schlumberger feels that I need an operation."

That shot down our plan to be married February 7th in Carmel. Bing had decided to go to The Mission, only ten minutes from his Pebble Beach home, and slip in early in the morning. To him it was very important that our marriage be secret, or at least private. Why? I didn't know, but if that was what he wanted, that was the way it would be.

Jean-Louis had done a beautiful wedding suit—navy with a white piqué collar, full skirt, and black opera pumps with a wedding ring heel that reminded me very much of the stem of Bing's pipe. The trousseau was ready, but the kidney stones weren't.

Monday, January 17, Bing entered St. John's Hospital in Santa Monica, and I joined him that night. It was not much of a reunion. He looked very pale as he tried to make playful banter.

This was the first of many long drives across the mountain, from the valley to Santa Monica and back. Bing's inflammation was so great that the doctors decided to delay surgery, but they had to keep constant check on the position of the stones to be sure that the kidney function was not completely blocked.

I hated this waiting game. I wanted instantaneous results: immediate surgery, sudden healing, precipitate wedding. Forty-eight hours seemed as many years. Sadly I returned to work.

Surgery was finally performed late Tuesday night. Bing phoned me as soon as he came out of intensive care. "I just got the room in focus," he drowsed. "I could hardly dial your number, but I wanted you to know everything's all right."

I was elated. Fortunately I had not read the *Hollywood Reporter* that day. Radie Harris

Dining with Grace Kelly and Bill Holden

had written, "Kathryn Grant announced her engagement to Bing Crosby during her USO Tour."

My agent Mel Shauer called and said "There's a bit about you and Bing in the *Reporter*. Maybe you'd better stay away from the hospital for a few days."

"I don't see why. We haven't done anything wrong."

"It says you are going to be married."

"Oh dear."

It has always been hard for me to keep my big mouth shut. I had told only a few friends on the tour that Bing and I were engaged, but I sensed that I'd done it this time. Well, he was still under sedation. With luck maybe he wouldn't hear about it.

The next evening Bing called. He was so furious about my announcement that he had forgotten his operation. "I am sitting here in the hospital really fuming. You know how difficult things will be now."

"Bing, I swear I didn't tell anybody. Well, maybe one or two, but I swore them to secrecy."

"There is no one you can swear to secrecy. Don't you know that?"

"Well darling, I'm sorry, but it's not as if we'd planned to rob a bank."

"It might as well be. I guess I should be grateful to you though, because I'm so mad about this thing that I can't even feel the stitches in my side."

My lower lip quivered as I said, "I'll talk to you tomorrow," hung up, and flung myself on the bed.

What difference did it make if the world knew we were engaged? Would he keep our marriage secret too? And if there were children, would he pretend they didn't exist? This was a stupid tempest in a tiny teapot.

Bing had endured major surgery for kidney stones. He could have died of uremic poisoning before or during surgery. Now he was alive. He would be well soon. He loved me. He had proposed to me. I had accepted. Weren't we engaged? What was his problem? I hugged the pillow to stifle my sobs, and sure enough was soon asleep.

Next morning, as usual, I felt better and decided to proceed normally. What else was there to do?

Every day I made the long drive for a couple of minutes with Bing. He was unshaven and in pain, and I hated the tubes coming out of his sides. Eventually he ceased to harp on the wedding announcement, and as I just kept coming, he seemed to say with his eyes, "Glad to have you aboard."

With his mouth he'd say things like, "It's a long drive to Santa Monica from the Valli Sahara."

On the 20th of January I planned a short visit—no more than the recommended ten minutes. But miraculously the tubes had been taken out of Bing's side, and he'd been walking the halls. He was feeling himself—and feeling his oats. He almost ran up and down the hall several times before I helped him off with his robe and back into bed.

"Come here."

"Bing, you never know when a nurse will enter with medicine, or a doctor will make his rounds. . ."

"Come here," he repeated. "A fellow that's lying in bed all day thinking of you needs a kiss."

I needed a kiss too, so I sat on the edge of the bed and leaned over, and pretty soon there I was right on the bed beside him. The door opened and his nurse, with her round raccoon eyes and her gray ever-so-curly bob, marched in carrying a tray. Resourcefully she dropped it and beat a hasty retreat.

There was nothing to do this time. Bing couldn't stalk off into the shadows, so he just laughed. Before I left I picked up the tray, mopped up the spilled water, and threw the straws into the trash, trying to remove the blot from my escutcheon.

When I came to visit the next day, there was a screen in front of Bing's door, and the nurse knocked before entering with pursed lips and averted eyes. I felt less scandalous discussing

Emoting with co-stars Grace and Bill

our wedding-to-be, and perhaps Bing was embarrassed enough to humor me.

"You know what we might do, Kathryn? We might fly to Texas. I'd like to meet your folks, and certainly they should meet me.

"I've already written to tell them that we were to be married. You wanted me to do that, didn't you?" I asked hesitantly.

"Well I suppose your parents have a right to know what their daughter's planning to do with the rest of her life. You say your Dad's a Scottish-Rite Mason. Are you sure that he'll approve of your marrying a Catholic?"

"He has already lost one election because I was dating a Catholic singer. Now the least you can do is marry me, so he can come out and shoot a big buck at the Elko ranch."

Bing laughed as he recognized another *Field-and-Stream* man. I prayed fervently that in that regard, at least, they would prove to be kindred souls.

Convalescence was a time when Bing had to concentrate on me because he couldn't escape, when I could pour out all the fantasies that I had yearned to share with him. He was packing his bags for home when suddenly another kidney stone moved. Since the urethra is the only non-surgical path to the kidney area, he had to a have a cystoscopy. So instead of walking forth a free man Bing was back in bed again, suffering physically and mentally from the demeaning procedure.

The 9th of February was a glorious day. Bing had recovered sufficiently to leave the hospital. I had my last visit with him that evening, and he told me several funny stories about his nurse, who had always been a little nervous around him after she caught us *in flagrante delicto*.

I didn't see Bing again until St. Valentine's day, when I dined with him at his Holmby Hills house. I rang the bell, waited, and heard slow, steady footsteps coming down the hall. Bing opened the door himself and said, "Ouch, I'd forgotten that there's still a twinge there."

I eased in carefully. "Is Lindsay here? Will he be with us tonight?"

"No, he's out with his girl."

"Good, now I can kiss you." And I did, right in the middle of his own front hall. I knew that he really was alone in the house when he failed to back away.

We settled into the down cushions on the living-room sofa, Bing put his feet up on the coffee table, and we talked until the staff returned and prepared a quick meal. The ground round was good; the string beans were edible; and there's no way to hurt ice cream with chocolate sauce, even if you stick a pear under it and call it Belle Hélène. The fire was warm, and we were very comfortable.

"I'm excited about your award nomination."

"I'm pleased myself. Of course I have no chance for the Oscar in view of James Mason's fine performance in *A Star is Born*, and Brando's in *On The Waterfront*. Still it was nice to be included."

"Hogwash. Your performance was by far the best," I insisted loyally.

"Maybe Grace will get an Oscar."

I bristled, and then struggled to regain control. "She could. With your help she did a wonderful job."

"You know, Kathryn, I think that we should wait until after the Oscars to let our plans get around. Why don't we just keep it a secret till then?"

"Whatever you like."

He certainly wouldn't catch me making any more announcements. The important thing now was that we were going to be married, and Bing was getting well. I now think Bing's health should have come first, but I was young and greedy and lovesick.

"I'm all ready," I affirmed cheerfully. "I have a wedding suit that should look splendid in Carmel. Do you think we could get the Mitchell Boys Choir to sing for us?"

Bing cast his eyes heavenward. "Let's wait with that sort of thing until my innards have settled down a bit."

I assumed a penitent air, but secretly I was still formulating plans.

With John Eacret at the Elko Ranch

We watched a little television, but he looked so tired and drained that I took my leave. I longed to help him up to bed, but it was he who walked with me to the door. As I drove over the mountain, I pictured him turning and painfully climbing the steps to what he used to term his "monastic pallet."

When he could drive to my apartment, I tackled a leg of lamb and salad. After dinner I saw him surreptitiously reaching for his trousers leg. At first I thought perhaps his wool pants were itching. Then I realized that he held his pipe and was trying to get rid of the ashes. Since there were no ashtrays, he was putting them in his cuff.

I said, "You musn't," and ran for a saucer.

"Oh, it's good for the wool. Keeps the moths away."

To celebrate Bing's emergence from his "durance vile" at the hospital, we did something glamorous. I washed the dishes and he dried them. Then we kissed very carefully. Those stitches were still giving him fits. He talked about the test I was to do the next day for *Rebel Without a Cause*.

"I don't know what kind of gang girl you would make, Kathryn. It's not exactly your style but that doesn't necessarily matter to an actress."

Was he putting me on? A tone of lightly-veiled irony had entered into his voice.

"Mr. Arnow said I was to come in looking a little tough."

"A cinch. You're hard as nails. I've been envisioning a remake of *Tugboat Annie*, with you as the new Marjorie Main." He *was* putting me on.

"Only if you'll be Wallace Berry. I seem to recall that you played a drunk in *The Country Girl*."

"Sure, but I'd had a little preparation. Some called it typecasting. Well, give 'em your best, Babette."

"I'll try."

"I guess I'd better be easing back across town. Your apartment is hard to reach."

"Am I worth it?"

"Well. . ." he reflected dubiously.

"Watch it. Your stitches haven't healed yet. One good kidney punch and you'll be back in St. John's for life."

Bing biffed me on the cheek, gently bit my chin, ambled down the stairs, and disappeared into the night.

From eating at his house tête a tête, to starving at my house tête a tête, we graduated to dining out. The place was Perino's, the leading restaurant in Los Angeles at the time.

We were greeted formally by Mr. Perino, and ushered to the number-one booth in the flower-filled room. Friends welcomed Bing back into circulation, and eyed the young actress at his side with frank appraisal. After the stark reality of the hospital, I felt as if we were back in fantasyland, and as if Bing were floating away from me.

He was. The very next day he drove to Palm Springs, fading like a mirage into his desert habitat.

On March 11 he finally phoned from his house on the hill above Thunderbird Country Club. His voice sounded stronger as he told me that he was devoting his days to swimming and lounging in the sun. Even more therapeutic for our relationship was my casual mention of a try-out for *Picnic* in the Sombrero Theatre in Arizona.

Bing phoned on Saturday to inquire, "Any news from Arizona?"

"No."

He called back Sunday morning. Still no news.

On Monday he again phoned very early. My continuing lack of news had spurred him to return to Los Angeles.

Later that day I learned that I had lost the part. Bing consoled me at dinner.

"They've no brains at all. You'd have been wonderful in the role." But the danger was past, he was growing stronger, and the gypsy in his soul next took him to his Elko ranch.

"Dear *Vin Rosé*, I arrived here 6:35 *le soir*.

At the Academy Awards

Nice trip—clear, sunny, and crisply cold. Hope *tout va bien pour vous et les journalistes ne vous donnent pas d'ennuis*. Love, Bing."

That, after my apotheosis at Perino's. Having presided over my debut there, he might have expected the press to react, and indeed we had made all the gossip columns. Now he neither threw bouquets at me nor brought back my rose and my glove.

On March 16th he did, however, send me a letter on a dictabelt from his Spring Creek Ranch: "I am dashing off some dictation at the office, and though I know it is a very impersonal way to carry on correspondence, it will enable me to get a message off to you today that would otherwise be delayed.

"After that involved and doubtless unacceptable explanation, I will proceed forthwith: We drove up in one day from Beverly Hills, reached Elko about 6 in the evening, had dinner, and came out to the ranch.

"The roads were in wonderful condition all the way. There was little traffic and the weather was clear and sunny, so my ranch superintendent, Johnny Eacret, let me take my turn at the wheel.

"I should be heading for Palm Springs in a few days. I'll phone you and let you know my schedule. In the meantime don't become embroiled with any columnists. And try to avoid all those loose characters around the Valli Sahara. Love, Bing."

A phone call March 25, 1955: "I'm in Palm Springs."

"Did you have a good trip?"

"I sure did. It's a lot warmer here than it was at the ranch."

"How are your stitches?"

"Not bad. The horseback riding didn't give me too much trouble, but the cold weather up there really got to me."

"Naturally if you're going to contrast it with Palm Springs."

"I guess you're right. Why don't you come down here for a swim?"

"Just let me grab my suit."

Lindsay and his girl arrived as I was fixing tea after our swim. I met them by the pool with a small tray, two mugs, Bing's white Hammacher-Schlemmer teapot with its copper cozy, and a plate of oatmeal cookies.

Bing didn't interrupt his conversation with Lindsay as I approached. Somehow he seemed more comfortable with me around now. I felt instinctively that he was no longer viewing me as a contemporary of Lindsay's dates. He added his dollop of milk to bind the tannin English fashion, dropped in a Sucaryl, and asked, "How about the Academy Awards? Do you think you could scare up a long dress for the big do?"

"Oh, I think I can find something," I murmured casually to conceal my sense of triumph. A girl who was engaged might assume that her fiancé would squire her to the Academy Awards, but there was no ring, and there had been no public announcement. With Bing it seemed best never to assume anything. So many people had wanted so many things from him that he had become a slippery devil. Burlesquing his own leave-takings, I gave him a peck on the lips, threw a towel over the car seat, and vanished into the purple shadows of the desert.

Awards night was an event! Ballyhoo! Hoopla! Bleachers full of fans! Limousines! Whole constellations of stars! Photographers and columnists waiting in the foyer. Garboons in the lobby! Quite a change for me since my first grand event, when fans had leaned toward me screaming, "Who is it, who's that?" and had received the flat, final answer, "She's nobody!"

Bing and I were backed up against the wall like a happy pair of convicts. He looked debonair, and not at all self-conscious in his white tie and tails. I now think that he was amusing himself by pretending to be Fred Astaire.

I wasn't pretending. Here I was an exposed engagée, a flagrant fiancée, a merry married-to-be. I revealed nothing and neither did Bing, but the press saw the light in my eyes and we made the front page in papers all over the country.

I sat with clenched teeth while Marlon Brando accepted his award. To my mind he was good in *On the Waterfront*, but Bing was better

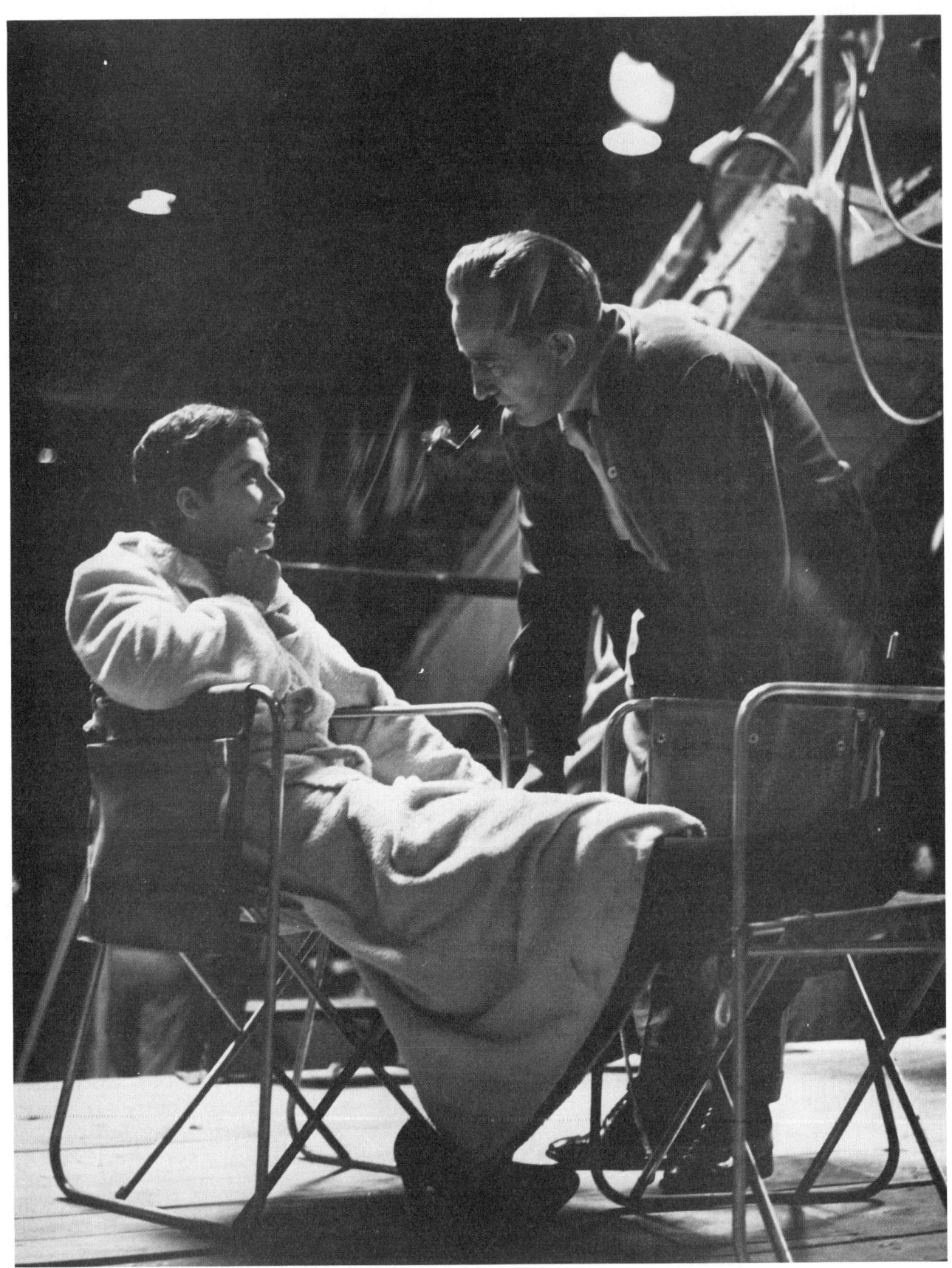

On the set of *Anything Goes* with Zizi Jeanmaire

in *The Country Girl*. I felt a real sense of loss, but Bing remained unruffled.

We danced at the party at Romanoff's. Again we were photographed, and Bing still seemed very much at ease. He had perfect rhythm, but following him was tricky because he didn't have any set one-two mapped out. He might go in one direction for four steps, and then in any other direction for five. Or he might stop and take a riff on the drum—either mentally or with his hands. In the interest of survival I reminded him of the choreographed routines from his movies, and soon the other couples were pausing to watch and applaud.

Bing was effervescent until we arrived home, and then the sparkle changed to tender sadness as we talked softly in the living room.

"Things will be different now Kathryn."

"Why?"

"The word is out."

"Well, how long did you want to keep it a secret?"

"I didn't want people to bother you, who are so very young and have no understanding of what public life is all about. Just remember that you are precious to me, and take good care of yourself in Phoenix City. There'll be hard work, and never enough time for rest. When there is a break, I want you to take a nap in your dressing room or get back to the hotel."

Now he was playing what was to become a familiar tune. It ran "Whenever you're away from me, Baby, I want you all alone and blue" in the key of B-flat. I would come to know it as an old and dear refrain, a constant in the relationship of Harry Lillis Crosby and Olive Kathryn Grandstaff. I hadn't yet played the flip side enough to become familiar with it, but I was to learn that it was "And I'll do exactly as I please and tell you nuthin' at all," in the key of C-Major.

It seemed that Bing had a schizophrenic streak. He said he hated reporters, photographers, and newspapers, but he never failed to forward clippings about himself. His first letter to me in Phoenix City was stuffed with accounts of the Academy Awards. Written Friday morning, April 8, on the set of *Anything Goes*, it referred frequently to the delicate state of his health and concluded as follows: "These are long days for an invalid and I'm exhausted, but I feel I'll get back into it soon. We have a great director in Bobby Lewis, who prepares each cut perfectly. Now I must jump back onto the set and participate in more deathless dialogue. Je Vous embrasse de tout mon coeur, Bing."

April 17. "Received your last epistle Saturday. It sounded like a short piece by William Faulkner, a moody, broody contemplation of a decadent southern scene. That Phoenix City must be a depressing town. My but you have been in the news lately! What with immersion in the Chattahoochee, and accompanying the sheriff's car on riot calls. (Gathering background for my sordid role as a crooked card dealer.) Anything for diversion I guess. But really, Kathryn, don't overdo it and get yourself hurt. Write soon. I miss you like hell, Bing."

The fall into the Chattahoochee was planned like a mafia murder to advertise *Phoenix City Story*. I was told to leave the cabin as if looking for sunken slot machines, steal to the end of the boat, and throw myself off. But not before signaling the cameraman, who caught me in mid-flight. Bing, the old pro, actually believed it was accidental.

But I was to suffer for my deception. There is always a down side to doing a stunt that works. From then on the publicity men at Columbia did nothing but push me into cataracts. I had two recurring themes in my life: Marrying Bing and falling into water. To this day I tend to avoid swimming and baritones.

"I miss you like hell, Bing." Now any time that prudish cavalier waxed profane with me, it meant he really was over the edge. So his swearing delighted me and vice versa. Throughout our marriage, any time I was fed up to the teeth I could fix him with a sullen glower, and without raising my voice one iota say "Go to hell." It was enough to make him fall giggling to the sofa.

After finishing the movie, I went home to Texas. A letter from Bing spoke only of his sons:

Montage from *Anything Goes*

Phillip was in town for a couple of weeks, taking a leave before reporting to Fort Sam Houston in San Antonio. Dennis had come home toward the middle of the month for his two-week furlough before going to Germany. Gary had gone to New York to appear on *The Ed Sullivan Show*, and then do a couple of weeks of vaudeville with Louis Armstrong in and around the Chicago area. Linny was neglecting his studies.

Then my ears pricked up as the letter ended, "If I don't hear from you, I'll call in a few days. I tried once or twice but never could catch anybody home at West Columbia 73. All my love, Bing."

Hey, pay dirt! For him to say "All my love" in a typewritten letter that went through his secretary. . .Well, if this wasn't a bona fide engagement, at least it was becoming a solid romance.

Then it really happened. Bing phoned with a complete itinerary for our wedding on May 13th in Carmel.

I flew straight back to Los Angeles, arriving at noon, and spent the afternoon and evening sorting clothes. Tomorrow was the big day. We would fly by private plane to Carmel. Bing would call to tell me the take-off time.

I waited all day on the 13th. Then I waited all the next day. Bing finally phoned the night of the 14th! "There is a bit more work to be done on the film, and I have some business dealings to clear up."

He sounded lost and frightened, so I swallowed the lump in my throat and asked, "Do you want to come over for supper?" He did.

Afterwards Bing said, "Now you've got a few things to do. Are you going back to college?"

"Yes, I'll attend the second semester of summer school at the University of Texas. They've accepted the work that I've done here, and I'll take exams for my last 30 units. Lillian Barkley is tutoring me now, so I hope to be ready."

"What time will you be through?"

"Around the 5th of September."

Fine. Why don't we plan to be married in Hayden Lake around. . .oh. . .let's say the 10th of September. That's a nice round figure, don't you think? 9-10-55." It was indeed, and its diameter would increase with each successive disappointment.

"What about your folks? They'll want to come out, won't they?"

"I'm sure they would, but if it is a problem to transport or lodge them, it isn't essential."

I watched his eyebrows knit slightly when I invoked logistics, and relax in relief at "it isn't essential." He really wanted a simple ceremony. If for example he left me at home, he could march down the aisle alone.

On June 3rd Bing invited me to dinner. I was not only tired but angry. It was his first call in two weeks. "I just can't make it," I told him.

"Fine, I get the picture. I trust that when the situation is reversed you'll be equally understanding."

On the 10th he called and said "I'd like to come over." Without giving me a chance to protest, he did just that.

In the 45 minutes it took him to reach me, I bathed, dressed carefully, stashed Marilyn with Maggie Eastwood, and broke a previous engagement.

"Well. . .looks like you're going to have a little supper. Were you expecting someone?"

"Just Marilyn."

"Is she going to be here with Maggie?"

"No, they both prefer Maggie's cooking to mine. Come in and sit down.'

It took me an hour to soothe his ruffled feathers. He watched the telly while we sampled my first meat loaf. If he'd been sure it was meant for another, it would have stuck in his throat, but he puffed contentedly on his pipe as I finished the dishes. Finally he drawled, "I'm planning to attend the U.S. Open in San Francisco next week. Ben Hogan is playing. Would you like to go?"

"I'm doing a TV show, but I'll manage to finish in time. Why don't I fly up and meet you?"

Inspecting the wine cellar at the Blue Fox

"Let me know what time your plane arrives, and I'll pick you up at the airport."

"That'll be fine."

"I'd better be heading back over the hill."

"I hate to see you go."

He looked at me with deep scrutiny. "One day," he promised. "One day soon." Then he gave me a tender kiss and simply evaporated.

I wondered if his silver stallion was waiting at the foot of the steps. I seemed to hear the faint echo of "Hi-ho, Silver, away," as the masked stranger disappeared into the night, possibly forever.

During the noon break in *Father Knows Best* I bought my ticket for San Francisco. We stopped shooting at 3:30 and I zoomed to the Burbank airport. I was on the plane at 3:59.

As I scrubbed my face in the ladies room, I grimly determined to enjoy myself. Though wholly ignorant of golf etiquette, I would feign a passionate interest in the sport. By the time I arrived in San Francisco, I was also feigning poise, maturity, and a relaxed queenly grace. All in all it was practically raining feigning.

Bing took me to the Palace, one of the oldest hotels in the city. I could imagine carriages driving into the garden court. For a time I was so lost in fantasy that I misplaced Bing, whose room was some floors above mine, but we finally met in the lobby and dined in the Venetian Room of the Fairmont Hotel. There Peggy Lee gave the impression that she was singing just for Bing. (As it chanced, she was. They had dined together the previous evening.)

The next night I had Bing to myself in a corner of the Blue Fox Restaurant, and he directed all of that thousand-watt charm at me alone. Moreover, he presented me with a little pin, a ballerina with pearls and diamonds on her skirt. It was not, however, an engagement ring. I read his note in the soft illumination of the candlelight "Dear Kathryn—so you won't forget San Francisco and me. Love, Bing."

Then I did something that I was to repeat countless times in the next 20 years. I magnified what he had written by several thousand diameters and came up with what I hoped he had meant. Thus in the Grandstaff translation the note really said, "I'm madly in love with you and want to drag you off to my cave posthaste. Your devoted slave, a pawn of passion."

My memories of Ben Hogan's near-flawless play and Jack Fleck's last hole victory are hazy indeed, but I retain total sensory recall of Bing's brave kiss at the bottom of the ramp which led to my plane.

As I stumbled up the steps, his sweetest tones wafted skyward: "I'll call you from the Ranch. I go to Elko next week, then Northern California."

Bing was going to Church Falls to raise funds for a sorely-needed hospital in that sparsely-populated area, but he always mixed pleasure with work: "Dear Kathryn, the fishing with Beulah Martin (who later sold us Rising River Ranch) is just great, and the weather fine but windy. The fairground is out on a prairie. If the gale continues, the performers will have to be tied down. But we must manage somehow. The spectators are coming from a hundred miles away. I miss you and wonder how you are faring. Will call in a few days. . ."

The show at Church Falls was a triumph. Sufficient funds were raised to build the hospital. "We ran three hours and fifteen minutes, and there was great enthusiasm on all sides," wrote Bing, flushed with success.

Eight years later he still reddened at the thought of his contribution to the world of medicine: "Kathryn, I've just received word about my hospital."

"What happened?"

"It has become an abortion ring. Planes are flying in from all over the country. With the collaboration of the pharmacist and a doctor of some kind, girls are being relieved of unwanted pregnancies."

"But just think, darling. All those little girls can tell their grandchildren 'I had my abortion when it was still naughty at Father O'Malley's Friendly Country Hospital.'"

As usual, I'm getting ahead of myself. Our paths went in different directions in the summer of 1955, but I steadfastly pursued the goal

The house at Hayden Lake

of becoming a mature, brilliant, thoroughly-educated matron by September 10th, the date of our scheduled nuptials at Hayden Lake.

Bing's new house in Idaho was nearly finished. The area where he had been so happy as a boy would be the place where our lives together could begin.

Meanwhile I was still subject to occasional lapses of sanity. On July 12th I wrote Bing at Elko: "Why don't you tell me how to reach the Mitchell Boys Choir? Then a friend of mine could make all the arrangements. You needn't be involved at all."

Did I really plan to import a boys choir for our wedding service in Hayden Lake, Idaho? They'd have had to fly to Seattle, then to Spokane, and finally, since no private plane could possibly have carried them all, I must have expected them to come through on a school bus, or perhaps to cross Hayden Lake on a barge.

Bing traveled constantly, whether working, golfing, or fishing. I remained at Texas U, attending summer school, taking 30 units of final exams, being instructed in the Catholic faith, and dreaming of the time when all loose ends would be neatly bound up. I would become an R.C. B.F.A. and MRS. all in one splendid summer.

As a tentative step toward joining Bing's family, I shared his concern over Phillip, who had driven off a bridge, landed in mud a preposterous distance below, and miraculously survived.

As an equally tentative step towards becoming a genuine actress, I toured for *Phoenix City Story*.

As a final farewell to childhood, I wept at the Philadelphia airport when Mama, who had been with me all summer, said "Goodbye baby, you'll be fine. Go with God."

And hopefully He accompanied me to Spokane, where Bing met me.

The latter tossed my luggage into the back of the car, opened the door for me, and said, "You've arrived, Miss Grant."

Then he slid across the seat from his side, checked the surroundings to ascertain that we were not being observed by eye of man, mouse, or low-flying owl, and gave me a quick peck on the lips.

"I'm not going to let you go home," he drawled. "You've traipsed around long enough." He continued in the same vein, but my ears were ringing so that I couldn't follow his words. Was it something about my chatting with Father Corkery about final instructions for the wedding service?

Whatever it was, Bing's hypnotic tones were occasioning a tickling sensation in my interior, which threatened to emerge from my ears as champagne bubbles, while my toes were frost-bitten in the dead of summer.

Hayden Lake, Idaho is situated near Coeur d'Alene, just across the Washington state border, not 50 miles from Spokane. Our route led through tall timber where huge pines cast deepening shadows across our path. There was no traffic for the last several miles, so Bing took my hand.

At last! Here was our home! It was of only one story, so the silvery spruce seemed to grow right out of the roof. Huge wooden tubs were filled with scarlet geraniums. I wouldn't have traded it for paradise.

At the door Bill Morrow and Mary Henderson awaited us. Behind them were Mrs. Lemmon and Mrs. Morris: "I just came over today," said Mary, as she helped me unpack in the guest room. "I'd been a house guest of Mrs. Soterberg until last night, when Bing took me aside and asked if I'd move to his place. I told him my mother'd warned about that kind of Yankee, but he paid no attention.

"I don't mind Bill crossing the lake every night," he told me, "though with his mechanical ability he will most likely drown himself. But a lady from Texas is going to visit me, and she needs a chaperone."

"So I just moved in this afternoon. Did I leave enough space? I hope you can manage."

I surveyed the room, which had a statue of St. Francis in the corner, exotic birds all over the curtains and bed covers, and Hayden Lake sparkling at me through the windows. "So do I."

On the road with Bob and Dorothy

When we rejoined the men in the living room, Bing showed us draperies of manta with a musical clef and the notes of *White Christmas* woven into the pattern, and photographic montages of his movies *The Country Girl, White Christmas, Anything Goes*, and *Road to Bali* in simple frames.

I sank luxuriously into the down-filled sofa by the stone fireplace. All this was pleasant but not overly pretentious. Surely a woman of my new-found maturity and erudition could cope with it.

"Come on," Bill shouted from outside. "The steaks are almost done." We were to join Bill and Mary for a barbecue, which also featured corn, home-grown tomatoes, and Mrs. Lemmon's lemon pie.

I made only the feeblest efforts to help. "No, you rest," soothed Bing. "Leave this to us stalwart cook types." Gratefully I dropped into the nearest chair. All that coping could start tomorrow.

Two of Bing's sons were visiting, but both were out for the night. After supper Mary and Bill took a walk, while Bing and I sat on the terrace looking out at the water, which was now navy blue. The stars were coming out, and there was a hint of a silver moon.

"Well, I guess we'd better make plans. I'd like the ceremony to be at St. Aloysius, the church at Gonzaga University. Father Frank Corkery has been a lifelong friend. He wants to meet you, of course, before he marries us. I know you'll like him."

"I'm sure I shall," I murmured, delighted at this unexpected precipitancy but wondering what in hell I could possibly wear. My entire traveling wardrobe consisted of one pair of pedal pushers, one skirt and blouse, and one silk taffeta dress which I'd purchased to wear for my baptism, and which made me look twelve.

The next morning I was awake at five. A beautiful day was dawning and I was at last near Bing. I lay in my bed and listened to Mary's regular breathing, wondering dazedly what the years ahead might hold.

Was that the distant hum of a motorboat on the lake? I slipped out of bed and dressed for church. Medium heels, the blue taffeta, the faintest hint of lipstick. Bing didn't approve of heavy make-up. I passed by his door, realizing that it would soon lead to my room too.

There was no breakfast before mass in those days. Only the pure of heart and empty of stomach received communion. I had supposed that we'd take the car up the road to the little settlement, but Bing revved up the motorboat and angled it toward Coeur d'Alene just across the lake. There I sat with windblown hair in a very wet silk dress, suffering from incipient *mal de mer* and offering up a silent prayer for those in peril on the sea.

It was answered with a miracle. Suddenly all about us there were boatloads of nuns, with their habits flapping wildly in the stiff breeze. Someone might lose a wimple, but there are no atheists in lifeboats and I would not die alone.

The church held no more than twenty people and thus barely accomodated the nuns, forcing the laity to stand throughout the service. I remember that the priest was a Jesuit on retreat, but I don't recall much of the mass, except for the delight of being with Bing and envisioning many a hairy ride across the lake on glorious Sundays to come.

I was all too conspicuous, standing there in the aisle, and I noticed several heads turning toward me, Bing's among them. Suddenly I felt dreadfully young, wet, and windblown.

After the service we greeted the priest, and then raced back to the launch for a relatively uneventful return trip with the wind at our backs, and a breakfast of waffles.

Next we attacked Bing's project for the day, a picture frame that had been sent from Los Angeles, already filled with a montage of *High Society*. Bing had decided that the stain was too dark, so we laid the frame on the club table in the front room, and started sanding the bejesus out of it. The improvement in the appearance of the wood may have been marginal, but the splendid destruction wrought upon the table top was beyond dispute.

When some guests arrived, I seized the op-

Masking heartache with hysterical giggles as Mary Henderson and I bade farewell to Hayden Lake and matrimony

portunity to race to the bedroom and phone Aunt Mary. "Where's my trousseau?" I gasped.

"I'll bring it when I come."

"When are you coming?"

"I don't know. I'm waiting for word from Bing."

"Hasn't he invited you?"

"No."

Now for the question of the day: Why in the world didn't I ask Bing, "When is Aunt Mary coming?" I could see that there was no room for her, but if she'd just bring me some clothes, I could be married and she could go home.

Did I have a foreboding? Perhaps, but at the time I thought it was fatigue. I'd expended all my energy in finishing college and converting to Catholicism, and now it did seem to be Bing's move.

But he in turn was playing some other game. His *modus operandi* was to whisk me off to paradise, away from civilization, work, and friends, and maroon me there. It was up to me to decide what was going on. If I had taken the bit in my mouth and said, "Darling, Aunt Mary's coming up today to bring my clothes, so let's be married tomorrow," perhaps we would have been.

Wednesday, September 7. Bing and I breakfasted, but our hearts weren't in it. He was alternately hiding behind the sports page and staring at the telephone. Finally it rang, and he leaped upon it only to bark angrily "Yes. . .no. . .keep trying," and hang up. He was obviously at such loose ends that my social instincts prompted me to fill in the obvious gap.

"I think I'll make some divinity."

"What's that?"

"A creamy white candy."

"Fine," Bing grunted and disappeared. I made the divinity. Sure enough, it was ghastly. Fortunately I was the only one who tasted it.

At about noon Bing materialized at my elbow: "Kathryn, there is a complication in my life. That's what the phone call was about. I can't really discuss it with you, but maybe it would be better for us to wait." He looked absolutely miserable.

There didn't seem to be any point in saying, "Wouldn't you like to share your problems with me, dear? After all we're engaged. Your life is my life. Tell me about it." In point of fact, he had just informed me to the contrary. His life was not my life, and I was obviously superfluous.

"Perhaps I'd better go on home.."

"I've already called Ralph Scott. He'll have the plane here in the morning." Couldn't he at least have let me take the initiative in leaving him? I bade farewell to beautiful Hayden Lake.

September 10. A letter pierced my gloom. "Problems, doubts, impediments. . .but I love you more than anything else in this world. Bing."

September 27. Bing called with the old lilt in his voice. Could he be happy only when he was away from me? Would he pursue me only when I had freed him unconditionally? He told me light golfing stories of Pebble Beach where he was staying, and promised to call me again very soon.

October 12th is not my idea of soon, but evidently it was his. I had been in Santa Rosa filming *Storm Center*. Maybe he was a trifle nervous about my falling into the clutches of the Redwood Forest, the wine country, the Russian River, and Bette Davis's histrionics.

"Kathryn, do you think you could come up to Pebble tonight?"

"I'm working, Bing."

"Tomorrow is Thursday. Could you come then?"

"I'm afraid not."

"How about Friday? I really have to see you."

"Well, no matter what happens on the set, I'll be off work Friday evening. Why don't we plan on Saturday?"

"All right. My problem has been resolved, and now I can tell you about it."

For a proverbially cool customer, he did sound eager. I took the early plane for Monterey, but only Leo met me.

Back at the Pebble Beach house there was tea. Mrs. Lemmon had prepared a plate full of

The triumphant return from our walk at Pebble Beach

the crisp fried cookies that she called "palm leaves." Bing nibbled on one while I devoured the rest.

If Bing had brought me up here to pour out his heart to me, I was willing to catch it right in my lap, but he persisted in light banter, a cheerful, evasive, non-communicative monologue. So I ate cookies. When the plate had been thoroughly emptied and his conversation too had run out, in desperation I suggested a walk on the beach.

The sky looked threatening. The still-calm sea was an oily gray.

"Hold on while I get you a sweater. You'll freeze in that blouse."

Bing bundled me up in one of his heavy pullovers and a Jackie-Coogan-style golf cap, which fit me so badly that he ended up wearing it. We walked across the 13th fairway to reach the beach, but by the time we'd arrived there Bing's hitherto cheerful face had begun to mirror the mood of elements.

"Oh dear God no," I thought. "Don't let it be Hayden Lake all over again."

For once I had the good sense to permit the silence to become oppressive. We had walked over a mile before Bing broke it. "I have to tell you the reason we couldn't marry last September. I wanted to confide in you then, but I didn't dare."

Horrible thoughts raced through my mind. Had his stable of slow race horses at last bankrupted him? Was he a closet queen? Had he contracted some dread social disease? Was he—heaven forbid—impotent?

I listened in vast relief as he recounted a romance with a young actress while I was away at school. In his innocence Bing really felt he was the only one in the world who could have told me a story familiar in its most intimate details to every bit player, bartender, and taxi driver in the greater Los Angeles area. I had already been asked about this particular dalliance by five different columnists. I had feigned ignorance with all of them. Not one to quit when I am winning, I affected it again with Bing.

"Really?" I said wide-eyed.

"You were gone for a very long time, you know, and it started out as just a party after our movie wrap-up—and then I suppose I had too much to drink and one thing led to another. Weeks later, when I told her of my previous commitment to you, she utterly lost her composure. She had always been so calm and serene, but now she wept and screamed at me. I can't understand why a woman would carry on like that. It was just terrible. Then she disappeared!"

I listened in silent glee while he reenacted their parting scene, her threats of suicide, public exposure, perhaps a suit for breach of promise.

"I had to have her found, to be sure she wouldn't carry out her threats. I couldn't let her harm herself or cause a scandal that might hurt you or your family."

Bing thought for a while and then added, "I must be rotten to the core to have treated you like this."

We were striding down the beach at a brisk clip while I struggled to stifle my laughter. Here Bing was apologizing for having chosen Olive Kathryn Grandstaff from West Columbia, Texas over this regal blonde, the most adored lady in Tinseltown. Whoopee!

The old clichés were all true. No man would ever understand his woman. While Bing had to be my first love, I was interested only in being his last. He was too preoccupied with the preservation of my virginal innocence to notice that I didn't require an equally spotless record from him. With a superhuman effort I controlled my facial muscles, stopped by a sheltered dune, turned to him and softly whispered, "I forgive you."

Expressions of surprise and relief chased each other across Bing's face. He took my hand and started walking back toward his house. In a moment he was whistling. Shortly thereafter he began to sing.

Inside I was singing too. He had chosen me over her! Well, I could now forgive him anything; even his all-too-evident lack of taste in women.

The newlyweds, Bill and Mary Morrow

That night we went to dinner with Francis Brown and Winona Love. After his first few drinks Francis, who had lived happily with Winona for 30 years without benefit of wedlock, turned moralistic and insisted that Bing marry me without delay. It must have been Bing's day.

The next morning we met for 11 o'clock mass at The Mission. On the way back to Pebble Beach Bing said, "You have helped me more than you know. I didn't dare proceed with our wedding plans for fear that you might find out and leave me. Why you're the greatest woman I've ever known."

I returned his gaze with demure gravity. Was I taking these compliments under false pretenses? Well yes, but it seemed to be the only way to get any, so I patted his hand reassuringly and went on living my little white lie.

Now began my winter of discontent. The activities sounded glamorous enough: Trips to Palm Springs with Mary Henderson; singing around Jimmy Van Heusen's piano; dining at assorted restaurants such as The Sea Cove, Don the Beachcomber's, or El Patio; walking with the golfers at Thunderbird, La Quinta, or Eldorado; riding the trails around Palm Springs; big parties in Los Angeles.

I was now expected to be with Bing. As his companion I met producers like Otto Preminger, Bobby Dolan, Nunnally Johnson, Mike Todd; music people like Arthur Schwartz, Ira Gershwin, Johnny Mercer; writers like Clifford Odets and Maxwell Anderson; stars like Groucho Marx, Marlene Dietrich, Greer Garson, and Bing's *High Tor* co-star Julie Andrews. Alice and Phil Harris were close friends, who often joined us for dinners made delightful by their wit. In fact we were with too many people too damn often. I never seemed to have Bing to myself.

A precious memory from this time was an after-mass brunch at the Tamarisk Country Club. The men were preparing to play golf, and we were all stoking up on dollar pancakes. The television was broadcasting *Madame Butterfly*, and Bing was completely absorbed in the production. I watched the screen with him until, out of the corner of my eye, I saw tears coursing down his cheeks.

Bing couldn't have been overwhelmed by pity for Cho Cho San and her American lover, but Puccini's notes struck chords of empathy within him that would not be denied. What did he hear in that music that ordinary mortals missed? How could I breach the wall of reserve that forever separated him from his true emotions—and me?

My acting career was unfolding slowly but steadily with good parts in movies and TV shows, but I envied Mary Henderson her role. On Saturday, December 17th, she had married Bill Morrow. I helped Bing decorate his Palm Springs house for the event, at which he sang *I Love You Truly*, and gave the bride away.

Mary's courtship had been shorter than mine, but considerably more satisfactory since she was now named Morrow. Bill's subsequent survival must have reassured Bing because he called daily. After a family Christmas in Texas I returned to Los Angeles, where he met me at the airport and drove me to his house for supper with Lindsay.

Bing had wanted to give me a coat for Christmas, but I had told him half-seriously, "I'm sorry, I don't accept furs from men I'm just dating."

When we returned to Aunt Mary's after supper, I had yet to receive a present. Bing said, "I have your gift in the car, but I'm not going to bring it in unless you promise to accept it."

"What is it?"

"I'm not telling you, but you have to guarantee that you won't reject it."

My stomach started bubbling. At last I would have the eight-carat sparkler that all my Texas relatives had been expecting to see on an engaged girl's finger. "All right," I said meekly.

On the way back from the car Bing sounded like the Frankenstein monster. When he came into view, he looked like a pony-express rider whose horse had just died. The horn of the heavy saddle that he was dragging bore the single initial *K*.

Jennifer Jones

Judy Garland

Merle Oberon

Desert golf at Thunderbird

1956

Meanwhile a new wedding date might help. March 17th was selected to give both of us time to clear up odds and ends.

For me this meant the movies *Wild Party, Reprisal,* and *Guns of Fort Petticoat.* Bing initially sought the solitude of Palm Springs. Then he underwent eye surgery to remove a small growth in the sclera. Unfortunately this provided him with an opportunity to stretch out his convalescence until March 17th had come and gone.

Making movies became not only my occupation but also my salvation. I went from one to the next with barely an evening's pause to draw breath and listen to another refrain of "I love you and if you'll just be a bit more patient...." It was as if Bing were waiting for the right moment to tell his wife about me.

Not knowing how else to react, I pretended that I didn't care. There were scripts to learn, wardrobe fittings, hair conferences, make-up tests, and interviews. I bored Bing to tears with detailed accounts of all of them, feigning an interest that I wished I could feel.

While I was still in Tucson filming *Guns of Fort Petticoat,* Bing wrote from Palm Springs: "Lin and his pals will be down Friday for Circus Week. Big doin's I guess, and some late waitin' up nights for Daddy. You are doubtless clear-eyed, alert, and etching deathless scenes on celluloid. Well I'm off to the vet's for a spray job for my cold. No golf the way I feel. Aren't you deeply sympathetic? Will be here until Wednesday. Love, Bing."

Sympathy had I none. I just hoped that it was my co-starring with Audie Murphy that was affecting Bing's sinuses. In any event, once I was away Bing called every day. When my sister and her little boy came to visit me, he invited us all to Palm Springs.

Frances and Bill began the drive while I finished my work, caught a plane from Tucson to Phoenix, then was bumped from the Palm Springs flight. I saw that there was one to El Centro. That must be pretty close to Palm Springs. I ran for the plane, yelling over my shoulder at the reservation clerk: "Call Palm Springs and tell Bing Crosby I'll be in El Centro."

I was right in one respect. El Centro is in California, but unfortunately it sits almost

Back at Palm Springs

With my sister and her son Bill

Another unused wedding dress

astride the Mexican border. Within three minutes after my arrival, the airport was totally deserted. I waited patiently for 15 more minutes before I began to wonder vaguely about geography. There was no map handy, and of course I couldn't have read it anyway, so I just went on wondering for the three hours that it took Bing to make the drive.

He arrived on the brink of exhaustion. "Kathryn, I don't want to confuse you, but El Centro is over 100 miserable miles from Palm Springs, and I didn't get word that you were here until I reached the airport. The clerks behind the counter were still in stitches over some crazy teen-ager who'd screamed an unintelligible message. I just happened to hear the laughter and asked where the nutty adolescent had gone. To El Centro as far as they could make out. She had missed the Palm Springs plane. So then I started cursing and driving. Are you all right?"

"I am now."

After three more hours of desert driving, Bing finally got me home, so badly dehydrated that I immediately fell into the swimming pool. After Frances and Bill arrived, Bing took us to a luau in honor of Alice Faye. I unveiled the dress and matching coat that I had planned to wear for our March 17th wedding. What difference could it make now?

All was not lost, however. My sister was so surrounded by stars that she seemed to be laboring under the misapprehension that she had joined the celestial host, and like me Bill loved the swimming pool. Sunday we made a comfortable trip to Los Angeles, and then it was back to work for the erstwhile aeronaut.

Monday, May 14: "Kathryn?"

"Yes, Bing?"

"Why don't you come to Pebble Beach when you finish the picture? You'll be through in a day or two, won't you?"

"Yes, but Blake Edwards and Bob Arthur came to the set yesterday. They're doing a picture called *Mr. Cory*, and I think they want me for it."

Tuesday, May 15: They did.

Wednesday, May 16: "You mean you won't come to Pebble Beach?"

"I can't, Bing. I have to get ready for *Mr. Cory*. It begins almost immediately."

"But I'm up north all alone."

"I'm so sorry. I'm down south all alone."

"Oh no, you have those show business folks."

"Yes, and I have to do camera, hair, and make-up tests, and meet Tony Curtis."

"Well, I guess you'll never want to see me again."

"Whatever you say, dear. Good-bye."

Bing went fishing, sulked, cooled off, and finally phoned me. We agreed that after *Mr. Cory* I'd fly to the Northwest to meet Dad, Mother, and Aunt Frances, who were on a camping trip. Then we'd all head for Seattle and my family's first meeting with Bing.

As zero hour approached, my stomach churned. Would Aunt Frances blow her top as she had earlier in the year in West Columbia? All Bing needed was to have an acerbic relative of mine say, "You're much too old for Kathryn." He would flee from the room and my life.

As we waited for Mr. Right, Mother chirped like a little bird, trying to keep everything calm and easy. I lapsed into gloomy contemplation of Aunt Frances' martial air and Daddy's masonic pin, an open declaration of war to my fervent Catholic fiancé.

Suddenly the door opened and the Irish balladeer himself waltzed in. His deep windburn lent a steely glint to his eyes. Oh God, I hadn't seen him for so long, and I realized once again that I couldn't live without him. Would I ever manage to live with him? Not if this meeting didn't work out.

As I introduced Bing I realized abruptly that he was pale beneath his tan. Secure in my own two-and-twenty summers, I hadn't thought of what an ordeal it might be for a suitor to meet prospective parents-in-law of approximately his own age.

My father broke the embarrassed silence by introducing the subject of politics. Bing's anten-

"Chocolate cake is my favorite dessert in the whole world."

nae weren't working. He unwisely disclaimed all knowledge of "such a boring business."

Daddy fixed him with a penetrating stare, and I thought for a moment that all was over. Then he reluctantly acknowledged Bing's right to state an opinion, and began to question him narrowly about fishing.

Bing breathed a sigh of relief. "Yes, I like to go out for salmon. A friend of mine loans us his boat and we take a few up above Vancouver."

Both men thawed appreciably and talked of lead weights, strength of lines, rods and reels, lures and baits.

I had started to breathe again when Aunt Frances burst in apropos of nothing, "I bet you would like my German chocolate cake."

Bing fought for time to absorb this new gambit by cleaning his pipe, scraping out the bowl, filling it with a fresh bit of tobacco from the plastic pouch in his left pocket, tamping it down, lighting it with a kitchen match, and eyeing Aunt Frances through the thickening haze. "You know, Frances, chocolate cake is my favorite dessert in the whole world."

Auntie sank back mesmerized after one sentence. Why should I have worried? Bing could tame lionesses with that voice. He must view Frances as a mere house cat.

Mother was sitting on the edge of her chair, trying to look poised, and willing this meeting to go well. She felt she knew Bing because she had spoken to him over the phone. Now she wanted my father to accept him.

Slowly but surely Bing managed it. First he engineered a skillful transition from fishing to hunting. Constantly deferring to Daddy's superior experience and judgment, my Nimrod talked about the trips he'd made, the mountains he'd climbed, the shots he'd missed.

By the time we went downstairs for dinner, harmony prevailed and the men were competing only in demonstrations of solicitude toward the ladies. I'm sure I was the only one who noticed that Bing still had a slight twitch at the left corner of his mouth.

Since Bing announced that he was going fishing in Canada the next day, there was no chance for us to talk privately about a September wedding. While he tried for *les beaux saumons* up North, I went on a tamale safari to Mexico City with Mary Morrow and a friend from Texas.

Upon returning from Canada Bing phoned: "I can't wait to read the diary of your trip to Mexico. You kept one, didn't you?"

"Of course. It's somewhere in the luggage that is still lost."

"I'll be down to see you in a week or so."

"The studio said today that I might leave next week for France to do a picture with Billy Wilder."

"What?" His voice sounded deeply concerned. I wish I'd known then that he had to be afraid of losing me to become really interested.

"You can't go to Europe," he crooned in that mellifluous baritone, "You might find some Frenchman over there, and then I wouldn't see you anymore, and how could I bear that?"

"Well, darling, I don't exactly have the lead yet, but Mr. Cohn says it's a very near thing, and I'm to report for wardrobe tomorrow just in case."

"I tell you what. Why don't you come up to Hayden Lake where we can sort things out."

"Sure, if the picture doesn't come through."

"You mean you're going to let a picture stand in the way of your marriage?"

I didn't respond. What kind of body blow was that? His pictures had accounted for two of our failures to achieve connubial bliss, or at least they had been the excuses given. Bing became more adamant, petulant, possessive, but I still feared another disappointment.

Fortunately I was not forced to choose between marriage and a career. The picture fell through, and I started packing for Hayden Lake. Mary Morrow returned from Mexico just in time to help. To be sure the trousseau seemed relatively unimportant, but it was the only aspect of the situation that I could control, so I gave it my full attention.

The first spadeful of earth for the new Crosby Library

Bing's boyhood home in Spokane

As we were closing the last suitcase, Aunt Mary Banks admonished sternly, "I don't think you should go to Hayden Lake."

"This time it's set," I responded grandly. "Bing is insistent, and the documents are all in order. There is nothing but success in sight."

Mary Morrow and I flew to Seattle, then to Spokane, where we were met and driven to Hayden Lake. Father Corkery was summoned immediately, and the next day we drove to St. Aloysius Church in Spokane for wedding instructions.

Bing and I visited the house where he had lived as a little boy. He showed me the statue of St. Joseph that he had dressed in a baseball uniform the night of the big game, and introduced me to the friends of his youth.

While I studied the nuptial mass, Bing wielded a shovel to break ground for the new Crosby Library.

Upon our return to Hayden Lake Bing went golfing, and I tried water skiing with Lindsay and Mary Morrow, while Bill Morrow shouted encouragement from the shore. The next evening a call came from Gary's commanding officer. Bing was formal and noncommital, but I sensed trouble. We walked outside while he told me that Gary had gone AWOL.

Acting on a hunch, Bing put in a call to his house in Pebble Beach, and sure enough Gary answered the phone. A long conversation ensued with Bing coaxing, cajoling, and sympathizing. Eventually he elicited the whole story.

Gary had been producing, directing, and starring in USO shows. By so doing he felt that he was fulfilling his obligation to the army. Then he found out that all the missed drill, KP, shoeshining, and buckle-polishing had to be made up.

Gary couldn't stand the thought of additional rigorous military discipline with a new platoon, so he simply left. Now he was threatening to kill himself and a girl who was with him. Bing murmured to me that he sounded dead drunk, but pleaded with him for hours until Gary finally agreed to return to camp.

The next day Bing called his mother to tell her of his decision to marry a twenty-two-year-old. Then he simply listened. When he hung up, he was looking perplexed. "Mother says she won't be there when we return, that one woman is enough in a house, and if I've decided to make a fool of myself, it's my business and she won't make it hers."

With his customary resolution in the face of adversity, Bing fled to the golf course. I piled into the car with him, so he let me practice chip shots with a borrowed nine iron, while he vented his hostility on that small white ball.

When we returned, the driveway was full of reporters and photographers. We dived through the front door to apparent safety, but faces appeared at the windows. I can still see Bing standing on top of the chest in his bathroom and returning their fire.

"Are you planning to get married, Mr. Crosby?"

"Who to, anyone we know?"

"Where is Miss Grant?"

"Last I heard she was on a backpacking trip through the Bitterroot Mountains."

The reporters laughed and departed with a funny story and a picture of Bing peering out his bathroom window.

Columbia Pictures called. I was needed immediately for the lead in a picture. I turned it down. That meant I was on suspension and my last bridges had been burned. Furthermore I had given up my apartment in 1955 to live with Aunt Mary, and had now rejected her advice so firmly that I didn't dare go back.

Dinner was tasteless. Immediately thereafter Mary and Bill Morrow said they were going to take a long walk. Mrs. Lemmon swept the dishes into the kitchen, closed the door ostentatiously, and glued her ear to the keyhole.

Bing said, "I had a long talk with Father Corkery today."

"Really? So did I." ("I think Bing wants out of this commitment, Father. How can I help him?")

"Why don't we go out to the boathouse?"

Safely ensconced in our sole sanctuary, we

Entertaining at Rising River

Phil Harris and Alice Faye were in the show.

A confused spectator

sat on the vinyl seats of the motorboat. Here at last we could talk without being monitored. All I was sure of was that I would not make a scene.

"I don't know what to say, Kathryn. Things are confusing. All these letters coming in. People really seem to disapprove of the two of us."

I had recourse to tears which, like most actresses, I can produce at will, and often to good effect. "Bing, please tell me you don't love me so I can go home. That is what I should do, isn't it?"

"Maybe if we had a little more time things would work out."

"We've had all the time in the world. Just say you don't love me. Then I can quit. I've known you since I was nineteen. I'm twenty-two now. That's long enough."

My whole body was shaking with sobs, so I stopped to admire my performance. If I hadn't known better, I'd have said I was out of control. But the circumstances seemed to warrant a heroic effort, and I really had had too much easy banter, too much moonglow on the lake, too much treading water, too much unilateral love. It was time to make a home for Bing or a life for myself.

"I can't say I don't love you, Kathryn, because I do. I always have and always will."

The blue-eyed devil. He had said the one thing that would twist the knife in my heart. To my surprise and horror I found myself screaming. Somewhere back there I'd abandoned the script.

"Take me to the airport. Take me there now."

"I'll take you in the morning."

"No," I stormed. "You take me right now. If you wait until morning I won't go. I will stay with you until the bitter end and ruin both our lives."

"We can't get married now. The church is full of reporters."

"Well, what's so sinful about getting married? Let's invite them all to rejoice with us."

"For one thing, I left my hairpiece in Hollywood."

I was not amused. In fact I was wailing like a banshee and dissolving into a slobbering mess. Since I couldn't see, I don't know how Bing looked. But he sounded simply perplexed, as if an untoward fate had thrust all this confusion upon him.

"Come on, I'll take you back to the house."

Since Bing never carried a handkerchief, he couldn't offer me one. Struggling to overcome his distaste for scenes, he helped me out of the boat, guided me up the steps, and had disappeared into his own bedroom before I hit the door of mine.

Mary started up in bed, and then said simply, "Can I help?"

"No," I hiccuped, threw my dress on the floor, and hurled myself into bed, firmly resolved to weep the night through. I'd have managed it too if sleep hadn't surprised me twenty minutes later. Even so, it remains my lifetime record for an attack of insomnia.

Next morning, my plane forgotten by tacit assent, we breakfasted silently, packed the car, and drove toward Rising River. On the way Bing said, "Maybe we could zip over to Reno. You know there is no waiting requirement there. After we've finished the show at Rising River, let's double back. We want to keep our options open, you know." And lovelorn fool that I was, I nodded in agreement.

At Rising River we stayed at the fishing club. Bing tried to teach Mary and me how to use a spinning rig, and put the finishing touches on the Bing Crosby/Phil Harris Benefit Show for Mayers' Memorial Hospital, which took place at the Intermountain Fairgrounds in McArthur, California, and involved a host of other performers.

Bing functioned as both singer and comedian. His routine centered on the last-ditch struggle which Old Hollywood was waging against TV. "It doesn't kill the movies," he asserted. "It joins them in a mutual suicide pact. All Hollywood has always been united by a great brotherly bond of insanity, and now we've permitted the TV Johnnies to enter the asylum."

This time it was giggles that I couldn't control, real over-the-brink, hysterical ones. Here

With Marion Davies

Wyntoon

was Bing Crosby, idolized by millions, doing a benefit for a much-needed hospital in a little mountain town, while I was being photographed more than any of the stars on the show, and hating it because Bing did. I felt like a criminal.

Which in a way I was. Wasn't I stealing the delight of American women, the buddy of American men? Or trying to? But I wouldn't get away with it, no sirree Bob.

After the show there was a barbecue on Rising River, where most of the guests drank too much. Having no talents in that direction, I moped in a corner and buried my sorrows under platefuls of barbecued ribs, while Mary Morrow tried to prevent me from eating myself to death. Bing didn't appear at all.

Next day he took all the vaudevillians to Wyntoon, William Randolph Hearst's Bavarian village, tucked deep in the pinewoods near Mount Shasta. We inspected chalets covered with the legends of Snow White, Rose Red, and Cinderella. There was a white Victorian cottage, all gingerbread turrets and lattice, which featured beds covered by Marion Davies' patchwork quilts. As we neared it, Bing cut me from the herd, so to speak, and gently guided me into her erstwhile bedroom.

The door clicked with finality, and I shivered as my pupils contracted to adjust to the dim light. While chattering show folks passed the window, I sat on the edge of one of Miss Davies' quilts and waited.

"You look exhausted, my dear. You aren't getting enough rest."

My stiff upper lip began to tremble. I yearned for Bing to say just one magic phrase to heal my wounds, but if he continued to play cruise director, I was so tired that I would simply leave. There was, however, the little matter of acquiring accomplices. Did I want to beg a ride with the gay revelers outside, or stamp my foot and demand that Bing take me? He was presently responsible for the well-being of some fifty people who had given their time to make the hospital a reality. I'd have to take my place in line.

"I'm fine, Bing."

"This afternoon all the mob will be gone. Then there will be a chance for us to sort out our future. But damn, I've got that film to do in Pebble Beach. . . ."

He sat beside me on the bed and gently kissed the nape of my neck. My thoughts drifted. Marion Davies had been the most famous American mistress during Hollywood's 30's and 40's. Here I was in her bedroom, seemingly a more proper setting for a freshman in finishing school. How had she behaved when Hearst came calling? How much privacy could they have shared during the endless house parties here at Wyntoon, at San Simeon, and at her Santa Monica beach house?

I had heard that she had a flashing wit, a boisterous laugh, enormous charm, and a generous nature. My own heart was a shriveled flaxseed. It started to expand as Bing's mouth moved toward mine, but Marion's ghost still watched over this four-poster, so I breathed, "Dearest, your guests are waiting," and slid through his arms out the door into the noise and glare of the big cold world.

I hoped that I wasn't looking as forlorn as I felt. For the first time Bing's kisses hadn't alleviated the terrible despair in the pit of my stomach. He followed, blinking, but I was already chatting with the nearest group, so he neither pursued his earlier thoughts nor pushed me into the river.

I went back to the bunkhouse with Mary Morrow to pack for the long drive to Pebble Beach.

Once at Bing's home there, I stayed upstairs for days while he and Bill worked on a film. I listened to the crew moving in and out of the house, until I suddenly realized that I was cowering in a corner of the bedroom, and must have been doing so for hours.

Bonkersville, Kathryn.

Ah well, it was almost lunchtime. Bing would tell me what was going to happen. I went downstairs in hiking clothes and sure enough, there he was practicing putting.

"Got a game this afternoon," he said casually, if a little distantly.

Golfing at Pebble Beach

"Right," I said, feeling no twinge of envy. I'd been the golf ball long enough. I walked out of the house across the thirteenth fairway down onto the beach. Resolutely I strode along it, unaware of sea lions at play, caring naught for the giant kelp beds undulating in the waves, blind to the gulls wheeling on the wind which cooled my throbbing head.

It was people's opinions that Bing feared. All right, let's tick off what "they" thought: That I was too young for him, that I wasn't good enough for him, that I was his mistress. In the days of Mesdames Pompadour and DuBarry, mistress was a term that could be lived with and enjoyed. Neither my parents nor I could cope with it.

I had gone to Hayden Lake to marry Bing. I had abandoned my home, my employment, and my reputation. I had entrusted my fate to a masterful matinee idol, who now seemed paralyzed as a direct result.

Nonetheless I would survive, but it would be to watch Bing grow old, unable to care for him, love him, cushion the rough edges for him. Of course, Bing hadn't evinced the slightest interest in any of these things, so they remained my private regrets.

Slowly the pressure in my brain diminished. For the first time I became aware of my surroundings. I found myself bathing in the submarine colors of a glorious sunset, and suddenly it was perfectly simple: I was free, and so was Bing.

I made my way home beneath a night sky so vast that no petty human woes could trouble it. Mary rushed up to embrace me and Bing looked pale, but all he said was, "You're late for supper. Do you want some cold soup?"

"Sorry, I didn't have a watch."

In spite of Bing's pessimism, dinner was delicious. I ate ravenously while he watched me suspiciously. "These lamb chops are delicious. I'd like another with some more mint sauce please."

After eating enough for three healthy teenagers, I excused myself and phoned the airport and Columbia Pictures.

I was put through to Harry Cohn's private office, where he was going through the day's rushes.

"Mr. Cohn?"

"Yes, Miss Grant."

"I'm coming home."

There was a slight pause. "Come right to my office from the airport."

"My plane will arrive at three in the afternoon."

"I'll be expecting you."

He hung up without waiting for a response, but I had all I needed. Maybe I wasn't fired yet, or even suspended. I didn't dare call Aunt Mary, so I tried Nan Quinn, my movie stand-in. Her parents had let me share their Sunset Boulevard apartment when I was shooting at a distance from Beverly Hills. Her father had created the radio show *Fibber McGee and Molly* and the television series *Halls of Ivy*, and it was he who answered.

"You're welcome as the flowers in May, Sis."

"Thank you, Don. I'll be there about five in the afternoon."

Mary had been hovering in the background. Now she dragged me off to the bedroom.

"Bing nearly had a fit. He thought you'd run off to drown yourself, and blamed me for letting you go alone. When I told him I wasn't your keeper, I thought he was going to hit me. He's been pacing up and down the living room, and threatening to call the police."

"I took a walk. Now I'm going home."

I found Bing in his study, not occupied with his usual notes or plans, but just doodling. I sat by him and said, "I'm going home tomorrow to clean up some odds and ends." (A job, food, clothing, lodging.)

Relief flooded his face. Thank heaven this crazy girl wasn't going to scream or threaten suicide. She was calmly getting out of his life. It was more than he'd dared hope.

"I'll call you in a couple of days."

"Fine." Knowing that he'd never call, I started to leave, then turned at the door.

Back home at Columbia Pictures

"Could you drive me to the airport? I'm on the noon plane."

"Sure."

I went upstairs to pack, and saw no more of Bing. He left for the club very early the next morning. It was Leo who drove me to the Monterey airport, making cheerfully inane remarks about the weather, the beeyootiful sky, the trees, and the great show that Bing had put on for the hospital.

I carefully thought of nothing all the way home. Bing's mother's driver met me, politely carried my suitcase to the Rolls Royce, drove me to Columbia Pictures, and deposited us both in the front hall. Somehow it seemed right. Evidently this would be my new home.

Mr. Cohn's secretary led me into his inner sanctum, a long room with Oscars flanking a huge desk. For the first time since I'd been under contract he rose, walked around the desk, took my hand and said, "Miss Grant, how may I help you?"

Then I really cried.

While I was in Korea . . .

1957

I had been in my new apartment at 201-B El Camino Drive for a week before I got a phone on January 12. The installers were just leaving when it rang.

"Hello," said a voice.

My spine turned to jelly. I had returned from a USO tour of Korea and was doing fine until now.

"Who is calling please?" I asked coldly.

"This is Bing."

"Oh yes. How are you?"

"I understand you've been overseas for the Christmas holidays."

"Yes, on Johnny Grant's tour of Japan and Korea."

"I wonder if I might have some tea with you."

"Well, not today."

"Tomorrow perhaps."

"All right, but after 4."

"I'll see you around 5."

"Do you have my new address?"

"Yes."

On Sunday, January 13, I went to early mass, and spent the rest of the day preparing for Bing. I chose my black-and-white tweed skirt with a black turtle-neck sweater, the most austere things I had. I didn't want to look pretty, or to hint in any other way at how much I'd missed him.

"It will be a simple cup of tea for the last time," I lied valiantly to myself.

I filled my Japanese teapot and set it on the stove, ready to go. I placed a dish of cookies on a tray, with cups and saucers, sugar and cream. There, if that wasn't preparing for tea, I'd like to know what was.

There was little else to do. The living room contained only my new beige carpet and some bronze silk shoji pillows, flanking an ancient sofa and a nondescript coffee table.

When I opened the door Bing tried to hug me, but with an act of will worthy of an Oscar I backed away. He covered smoothly, casually observed the emptiness of the room, and murmured "So this is your apartment. You know I didn't have your number or address. I had to get them from Aunt Mary."

Travels with Phil Harris

"How well you look," I stammered, promising myself that I would deal more sternly with that perfidious breaker of promises.

"I've taken a little golf tour."

"Yes, you wrote some time in December that you were going to Cuba."

"Phil Harris and I have been on a tear. Passed through most of the southern states, and picked up some good stories along the way."

Bing rambled on comfortably, telling me about his irritation at a man honking his horn in a traffic jam, and his delight when a black woman emerged from her car, leaned over the culprit like a top sergeant and screamed, "You want to get on? Then you've got to get on over the top! That way the next bust-up will be yours, and we can all do the honking!"

He told me about the great southern restaurants where children would come out and sing the menu: "Well, we got chitlins, we got grits, and we got cornbread and collard greens, and we got roast tom turkey and candied yams, and okra and stew and pecan pie. . . ."

He told the story of his running battle with air conditioning in the Antilles. It seems his hotel was very cold, so after each day of golf in the heat and humidity of Cuba he returned to flirt with pneumonia. His pleas to the manager were fruitless, so be bought some child's bright-yellow modeling clay, and covered the air conditioning vents. This stratagem was calculated to save only his own skin, but somehow it accounted for the entire building, and Bing lived and slept comfortably the last few nights.

He reminded me of a troubadour entertaining some medieval lass, but said damsel did notice a little tarnish on his armor. He had still mentioned nothing about *her* past, and any shared future was evidently taboo.

I had been entertained previously at Hayden Lake. I rose abruptly and started toward the kitchen to rescue the whistling kettle.

Bing followed me. "Please don't go to any trouble."

"It's no trouble. I have very good tea."

I prepared some oolong and served it in a Noritake cup, both acquired in Tokyo. Then Alice and her Mad Hatter repaired to the living room to continue their tea party.

Always before by a murmur or nod, a kiss on the cheek or a touch on the forehead, Bing had hypnotically chained me to him. But while I remained, as always, delighted by his stories, I was scanning them for content this time, and finding none that concerned me.

He told me how he had shared a New Orleans hotel suite with Phil. Returning from a walk, Bing found his roommate with a group of characters, noses broken and ears cauliflowered, wearing conspicuous bulges under the armpits of their coats. He summoned Phil into the other room and said, "You have to get those mobsters out of here. We could be caught in the cross-fire."

"We can't send Benny away," Phil objected. "He just got out yesterday."

Then there was the story about their flu-induced trip to a steam room. They'd noticed a stranger shadowing them all morning. Finally he followed them into the bath where they sat swathed in percale. The intruder hesitantly edged forward, then said, "Oh Mr. Crosby, Mr. Harris, it's wonderful seeing you. I've waited years for this opportunity."

The two neophyte sheiks, whose communication was often wordless, made a simultaneous decision to prolong their victim's visit. They inquired about his life history, wife, family, and job, expressing great interest in each nervous response. Since the gentleman weighed about three-hundred pounds, and was still wearing an overcoat and muffler, he became quite red in the face.

"I'd really like to get an autograph, if you don't mind." The paper he was clutching in his left hand had wilted, and was threatening to dissolve into a wad of wood pulp. But their interest was insatiable, their interrogation endless. He was flattered, of course, so for a time he stayed.

Finally in desperation he said, "Listen, I think I'd better get out of here. Would you please sign this for me?" He held out a pencil and the very damp paper, until Bing took them

Inger Stevens

and somehow dropped the pencil between the slats of the wood floor. The stranger was verging on apoplexy. Who would believe his story without a signature?

Bing turned to Phil and asked blandly. "Do you have another pencil?"

And Phil replied on cue, "I'm sorry, Bing. I left it in my other sheet."

Much as Bing admired Phil's gift for adlibbing, I sympathized with the poor man at whose expense they'd amused themselves, and wondered glumly if I had served a similar function.

"What do you think about a little dinner this week?"

"A little dinner?"

"Yes, why don't we go out to Chasens. Thursday I believe I'm free."

"I'm not."

He looked at me blankly.

"Bing, I've been to Chasens with you. Thank you, but no thank you. Not anymore."

"Oh, all right."

He rose with some difficulty, since he had been sitting cross-legged on a pillow for half an hour. Retrieving his hat, he set it at a jaunty angle, said "See ya around," and left.

I managed to close the door behind him before my *sang-froid* thawed.

After I finished crying, I unlisted my phone number.

That didn't, however, stop the U. S. mail.

"Dear Kathryn, you were right. I shouldn't have seen you last Sunday. The visit revived old hopes and dreams which I had thought were safely interred. It'll take another couple of months to file them away again. I tried to call you a second time to find how best to get these papers to you. I thought you were leaving, you see.

"While I am writing, I'd best tell you that I look back on the past and on last summer without any bitterness or rancor—even if you can't. I guess I never did anything but make you unhappy, which in turn saddens me. But you did many, many things for me, and my memories are warm. I will always love you, Bing."

In the envelope were my birth and baptismal certificates, and the letter waiving the proclamation of banns. It was obviously an empty gesture, since if I were not going to marry Bing I would have no need for said documents. As for the couple of months it would take to get over me, I believed him and hoped I'd be equally resilient.

I was to leave in July for Spain to film *The Seventh Voyage of Sinbad.* The day before my scheduled departure, I passed by the mailroom and saw a handwriting that fairly leaped from my pigeonhole: Kathryn Grant, Columbia Studios, Gower Street, Hollywood, California. Postmarked Monterey. Return address. . .Bing Crosby, Pebble Beach, California.

I took the note to my car in the parking lot, the nearest thing to privacy at Columbia. It read, "Dear Kathryn, there is a nuisance lawsuit coming up for decision soon. Nothing that concerns you, or you and me, but I am the defendant.

"A Mr. Dahlgren, who is handling the thing for me, may want to query you on some facts, dates, etc. to establish where I was at certain times last summer. There is absolutely no chance that you will be involved in a trial, but even so I will understand if you wish to duck it. Nonetheless I promised him that I would try.

"Would you be kind enough to drop a note to 9028 Sunset, apprising me of your reaction to this proposal? Should it be negative, I will call him off. If agreeable, he can phone for an appointment. What is your number? Yours, Bing."

The next day I phoned Bing's office. "Is Mr. Dahlgren there?"

"We don't know a Mr. Dahlgren."

"Mr. Crosby called about a lawsuit."

"Mr. Crosby is in Pebble Beach. Would you like to call him there?"

"No, but he may call me here for the next hour." I left my number and hung up, demonstrating what I considered to be mature poise.

After all, Bing didn't want anything to do with me. There was no dinner invitation; he just needed to verify some incidents. That I could do. I knew that whatever Bing did or didn't do, he was always a target for a lawsuit.

Four Clams

I had heard about the accident when he had been hit by a truckload of migrant workers. They had run through a stoplight and plowed into the side of his car. They had nearly killed him and then sued him.

Bing's lawyers settled to avoid publicity. A jury trial could only hurt Bing. The people who hit him had nothing to lose; their lawyers had taken the case for a percentage of the spoils. The slogan semed to be, "Well, Bing can afford it."

Since I'd been sitting by the phone from the time I called the Crosby office, I answered on the first ring.

"Your letter arrived about the lawsuit," I babbled. "If you'll tell me the questions, I'll study them and see if I can answer them. Perhaps I could give an affidavit to Mr. Dahlgren or your lawyer tomorrow. I'm leaving town so I won't be available after that."

"I don't think there's any hurry, Kathryn," Bing drawled calmly, the tranquility in his voice slowly seeping into me. His imperturbability was so catching that we finally had a very self-possessed, untroubled exchange.

"Let me see, when are you coming back?"

"Not until the end of September."

"Then we'll just hold matters in abeyance until your return. I'll keep in touch."

Calm adieux, and suddenly it was over.

I decided to dismiss Bing and his problems from my mind. I had offered my help and he had refused it. It was time to pack my bags and try to become a movie star.

So I travelled to Denver, where I did publicity work for *3:10 to Yuma*. Thence to New York, Paris, and Spain for *The Seventh Voyage of Sinbad*.

Meanwhile Bing had been pining for me in his customary fashion, and preserving the following record for posterity:

"We left Vancouver on the yacht *Polaris* about 5:30, the evening of August 3rd. Aboard were George Rosenberg, Phil Harris, Bus Collier, and myself.

"We sailed about five or six hours that evening, putting up for the night at Pender Harbor. After making a few purchases and getting off some postcards, we continued on up the straits to Point Alexander, where we dropped hook about 10:30. It was so foggy the last couple of hours that it was necessary to proceed slowly and sound the siren intermittently.

"The next morning we were off early for the jump across Queen Charlotte Sound, and thence on up the Rivers Inlet to Kildala Bay. We arrived there about 3:30 or 4 o'clock, immediately got the boats down and the fishing gear out, and it wasn't long before we were after king salmon. I went out with Captain MacDonald's son Jerry, and caught a 58-pounder that gave such a nice fight it took me 55 minutes to boat him.

"The rain stopped on the 6th, and the next morning the fishing really improved. I left about 6:30, and was back at 10:30 with a limit of kings—the largest being 55½ pounds. I used cut herring exclusively for bait, trolling slow and letting the herring out 80 to 100 feet on one line, and just short of that on the other, using an ounce and a half of lead on one line, and two and a half on the other. It didn't seem to make any difference; the fish hit both with the same alacrity. We had lots of other strikes, and lost several giants that broke the gear.

"The other boats did equally well, so we had an over-abundance of booty to weigh and clean that night. Buster Collier's 67-pounder won the blue ribbon. He said that it gave him a prodigious battle, and cost him an hour and some change to boat it.

"We kept one of the smaller salmon for fresh steaks. Since we had room for only two of the others in the deep freeze, we filleted the rest and salted them down. When we get back to Seattle they can be smoked and shipped to California.

"It was quite a spectacle with the big knife flashing in the sun, and the huge red chunks of lovely salmon coming off in beautiful steaks. 'I wonder what Romanoff would pay to have this going on in his window,' Phil Harris mused.

"The next day the fishing was equally good, with all of the action taking place across the bay

On the dock

On the deck

from Kildala, between the old broken-down cannery and the fish boundary mark. Once the three boats from the *Polaris* were hooked up simultaneously, and all within a quarter of a mile of each other.

"On this morning I hooked a 62-pounder, my biggest catch of the trip. He acted strangely at first, striking rather tentatively, and not making much of an opening run. I thought he must be a tiny fish, and for the first 10 minutes I was wondering how to get rid of him. Then he made a couple of mild runs and sounded. Finally I pulled him in close to where he could see the boat, and then he really took off on some spectacular runs and two or three great leaps that had my heart in my mouth for fear he would shake the hook. A couple of times he had almost all my line off the spool before the boatman could turn around and chase him, enabling me to pick up the slack. It took an hour and five minutes to net him.

"By 11:30 everyone was back on the *Polaris*, where we had a big lunch and took pictures. Since we had no more barrels in which to salt the salmon, and no more room in the deep freeze, we decided to sail down to Goose Bay and have them canned. The manager of the plant put the fish on ice, and told us we could pick them up in a couple of days.

"We then went up to Bella Bella, stopping for the night at Safety Cove.

"The next afternoon we fished for cohos at Galchuck, but they were all too deep. It was necessary to use so much lead to get down to them that as sport fishing it left something to be desired.

"We returned to Bella Bella, and thence to Goose Bay to pick up our fish. The cannery workers greeted us at the dock. They were a pleasant mixture of young Chinese, Japanese, and Canadians, mostly students working at summer jobs. I sang for them before we turned in.

"The next morning, we went up to Draney Inlet. The entrance must be made at slack tide because of the heavy surf which roars from it into Rivers Inlet. We got through all right, and after an hour's run were up at the top of the Inlet, arriving about 10 o'clock. We lowered the small boats, ran up the river as far as we could go, and then packed a lunch and our trout gear to Allard Lake. It was about a 45-minute hike, straight uphill over a trail almost obliterated by fallen trees and giant boulders, a trek that I wouldn't care to attempt with a heavy pack."

"We found an old boat, which someone had constructed after hauling the planks over the hill and putting them together on the beach. Since it was the only thing to stand on—the banks being too precipitous—we bailed it out, calked it as best we could, and fished from it with spinners and flies. It was overcrowded, and we had to bail constantly to keep it afloat.

"The rain fell hard all afternoon, but in spite of sundry vicissitudes it was the best trout fishing I've ever experienced. We caught 76 fish in about two-and-a-half hours, using only one rod at a time while everyone else bailed. The trout were all native cutthroats, weighing up to two pounds.

"It is a beautiful body of water about a mile long, and I'd certainly like to return in a good boat with a kicker on the back, though it might be difficult to find a suitable campsite because of the steep banks."

Etc., etc., with lots of fish in the sea, but no mention whatsoever of one Kathryn Grant, and without even the decency to mope a little. How miserable his radiant happiness would have made me!

All of which proves once again that ignorance truly is bliss. If I'd perused that touching document immediately after it was written, I'd have been a celebrated murderess, spending the next 20 years in a penitentiary instead of in connubial bliss.

Oh well, what's sauce for the gander. . . While Bing was cruising off Canada, I was about to make landfall on the Iberian peninsula.

We began shooting our fantasy film in Granada, where I reclined on a jewel-encrusted bed in the Alhambra, my skin caressed by satin sheets. The fountains from the Lions Court splashed in the background. Technicolor lights illuminated the Moorish ceiling, while gypsies

As a princess in *The Seventh Voyage of Sinbad*

clapped out their wild rhythms from caves in the nearby mountains. In character and in person I was pampered like a princess.

From Granada we flew to the Island of Majorca. In the *Cuevas del Arta* I was rescued from the Cyclops, while miraculously dodging falling stalactites. *In propria persona* I munched crisp breakfast pastries on the balcony of a hotel suite which overlooked the blue of the Mediterranean.

When we moved north to the Costa Brava, the gold-leafed garlands of my headboard spilled and splashed upwards over two bedside closets. I was surrounded by golden fruit bowls, and vases of constantly-renewed flowers were stirred by sea breezes from the balcony.

I was full of myself, full of the fun of dining with royalty, of splashing in the warm surf and sight-seeing in the lovely village.

At twilight I watched from my balcony on life as the last of the sailboats glided toward their moorings. Tiny lights in the village mimicked those in the sky. And from the blue of the night came the strains of "I give to you and you give to me, True Love, True Love, and on and on it will always be True Love, True Love. . ."

It was the moment supreme for bawling, so I did, and right on cue. I've always wasted my best efforts offstage.

I returned to Los Angeles on Friday, September 22. A letter from Bing arrived October 2: "Dear Kathryn, Mr. Dahlgren has negotiated a satisfactory settlement of the lawsuit, and as a result it will not be necessary to bother you further. I was quite affected by your willingness to help since I rather thought you would say no, and rightfully too. I should have recalled the other times when you demonstrated your loyalty—the hospital visits, the matter we discussed on the beach—but I'm stupid. I must be or I wouldn't have lost you.

"It seems a long time since I saw you last, but you are in my thoughts every day. I've been all over the country these past months, met many people, done lots of things, but I can't forget you.

"I'm coming to L.A. in a few days and would give anything to see you and hear about your work, your life and times. Won't you drop me a note at 594 Mapleton and tell me I can phone. I miss you so much. So write, even if just to say no. Yours, Bing."

No, no, this wouldn't do. My environment was under control. I was going to be a great actress, or failing that, learn more about the real world by becoming a nurse. I had read letters as sweet as this before, if not quite so obvious. He wasn't going to entrap me again.

Now that I had almost won back my self-respect, I was going to be very mature and write the perfect letter. "To see you would be to blow warm winds on latent embers, which could do nothing but sear us both. I cringe at the thought of hurting you, and I myself am too great a coward to expose my healing heart to further pain. We must keep this book closed for both our sakes. Kathryn."

That's what I first wrote and planned to send, but when I made the mistake of trying to reread the glop, it sounded like a passage from *True Romances*.

Undecided whether to howl or throw up, I grabbed another piece of stationery and slashed. "Yes, I still love you. No, I won't see you. Kathryn."

That seemed to cover it nicely. I changed my unlisted number again.

On October 8 a letter from Los Angeles was delivered to 201 El Camino, Beverly Hills: "Dear Kathryn, please tell me why if you love me you won't see me. Honestly, I'm miserable and have been for months. I promise not to be importunate or create any complications. Love, Bing."

"Miserable" was he? But he promised not to "create any complications." Well, my life was certainly uncomplicated now. "Barren" might be a more felicitous adjective. Would I let him croon his way back into it?

Not if I didn't answer his letter.

On Sunday, October 13, the studio sent me to a hairdressers' convention. Helen Hunt created my fancy chignon, Jean-Louis loaned me an ensemble, and Muriel Davidson from

With Gary Cooper and Clark Gable, the hunting cronies Bing abandoned for the state of matrimony

publicity was there to make sure that I was chic and poised at all times.

Before I had to model Helen's coiffure, Muriel and I passed by a television set. We were just in time to catch the opening of the Edsel Show, Bing's first special. He didn't seem to be suffering. In fact, he'd never looked happier. I could feel my curls wilting.

The next day I received a note. "Dear Kathryn, I know I am a louse, but you could be a friend and answer my last letter. I only want to see you for a brief chat. I've been punished quite enough I should think. I don't want to complicate your currently well-ordered life, but I just must see you. Please! Bing."

The same day in *The Hollywood Reporter* Army Archerd observed, "Bing Crosby and George Rosenberg sky into Spokane November 3 for the Crosby Library dedication. . .Reminds us, watching the Edsel spec last Sunday, Kathy Grant's beautiful eyes filled with tears when Bing bounced on."

Two days later that little clipping arrived from Beverly Hills with Bing's card: "An apocryphal item, I'm sure, but being eager to believe it, I'm emboldened to send one more appeal to you. I'm going to the Springs tomorrow to open up the new house, but I'll be back Sunday, and I'd love to find a note here saying that you would see me. What I have to say will take only five minutes. I can't sleep, I can't do anything until I have told you what I want to say. Please do this for me. Bing."

Sunday, October 20, Bing was back in town. I had a meeting with Father Kaiser after church. Note in hand I said, "Look, he wants to see me. But I know he just wants to take me to dinner, and I have been to dinner. What should I do?"

What I really wanted was to be told, "Call him immediately. Fly to his arms. You can't let the poor man suffer."

What Father Kaiser said was, "You're doing just fine, Sis. Don't answer."

I began to feel certain reservations about Catholicism. My Baptist preacher or Methodist minister would have simply counseled kindness to man, bird, and beast. Priests, however, seemed bent on working God's will whatever the consequences to the instruments involved.

The evening of October 22 I found in my mailbox a note, which had been delivered by hand. It read, "Dearest Kathryn, I guess this will be my last letter since you won't see me. I do feel I should tell you what I want to say. I want to marry you—any time, any place you wish. I really feel this proposal deserves a personal response and, as I'm supposed to return to the Springs tomorrow, won't you please call me this evening at Crestview 55633? This is the very last thing I'll ask of you. Love, Bing."

I read the note, then reached for the phone picked it up, dialed three numbers, and hastily replaced it in its cradle.

No, he must have asked me to marry him twenty times over the last four years. I had accepted every time and nothing had happened. I'd sleep on it.

The next morning I awoke to a bright new day and picked up the phone, but not to call Bing. It was Aunt Mary who had warned me against going to Hayden Lake on that last hideous trip. Now, with my own resolve waning, I had need of her protective strength. Just let Bing try to slip by the guns of that fortress!

"Aunt Mary, I've had a letter from Bing."

"Kathryn, he's on the other line, and the poor darling sounds so sad! What have you done to him?"

So much for staunch friends where that snake in the grass was concerned!

"I'll be over in a minute. I want cream of wheat with raisins and brown sugar and butter."

"How can you think of food when that poor man is suffering so. He's still on the line, so I've got to go now."

"I understand. Good-bye."

How well I understood! I'd succumbed to those same blandishments myself more times than I cared to count.

Aunt Mary was waiting with the prescribed bowl of cereal. I ate it slowly, reflecting that I would need heavy nourishment this day.

St. Anne's in Las Vegas, the little church where we were married

"He's going to call back in ten minutes. Now what are you going to say to him?"

"I don't know."

"You've got to know. The poor man can't take any more."

"I know that I am an actress now, and that I am going to be a nurse. All my suffering was stupid. I mean, there are people in the world with real problems, and there I thought I was going to die last year just because we didn't get married. Now I'm through with all that."

"Kathryn," she moaned, "don't say such things."

"It was you who encouraged me to go into nursing. You said I thought I was too important, and that I needed to get down to work like normal people do."

"I know I said that, but can't you work for him too?"

"I can't believe this! For four years you've been warning me against Bing's snares, and now, just as I'm getting on my feet, you're enchanted."

"You know that's not true. I just didn't realize how much he cared for you. He never showed it before."

I ate stolidly. Of course Aunt Mary had babied and petted me when I was having a terrible time. There had been moments, driving on mountain curves, when I had wondered what would happen if I didn't turn the wheel.

She had lectured me constantly against yielding to depression: "Don't wear those grey sweat pants when you're feeling blue," was a typical bit of advice. "Dress in something red."

She'd taken me to the doctor's to have my thyroid checked, when I'd seemed to be sleeping day and night. I think I wanted to wake up when it was all over.

Now I was getting well. Oh God, what to do?

The phone rang again and Aunt Mary leaped for it. "Why yes, she's here having breakfast, but she wants to know. . .I mean if anything did happen, would she be able to go on with her plans to become a nurse?

"I see. And how about her movie career? You know, she's getting pretty good now. She's had leads in all her films in the last couple of years. It's amazing that she's kept up with her acting at all, while running off to Hayden Lake to get married every few months."

There was a long pause as Bing evidently tried to pass that off with a witticism. Then Aunt Mary's face became militantly triumphant: "Well, yes, I think you are right. If you are going to get married, do it immediately. I'll talk to her, and you call back in a few minutes."

She got off the phone and, like the woman she was, laid the cards on the table. By now I was curled up in her master bed, hugging a pillow, and waiting in an oddly detached way to learn my fate.

"Bing says he would like very much for you to continue your acting, and of course you are to go on with your nursing. He didn't know you were really interested in that, but he thinks it's a wonderful idea."

I climbed out of bed and put on my studio dress. "See what you can arrange. I'm going to work."

So on I drove to Gower street, wondering vaguely if what I'd needed all along was a marriage broker. If so I'd simply been a victim of cultural deprivation. We hadn't heard of them in West Columbia. But even that was no excuse for my dimwittedness in this town, where everyone was for sale and even the agents had agents.

At the studio, I checked in with talent boss Max Arnow. "There's a new picture called *Gunman's Walk* coming up in a couple of weeks. You'll work with Van Heflin, and play a half-breed. Bobby Darin and Tab Hunter are in it too."

"I'm very eager to go ahead with my hospital work," I told my tutor Lillian Barkley. "Can you make arrangements for me to start at Queen of Angels next week?"

"I've already spoken to the good sisters."

During a scene from Shakespeare, my drama coach remarked that I seemed distracted.

"I'm sorry, Benno. It was a late night."

A kiss for the bride

At about 3 p.m. I finally went down to the guard's post at the front door of Columbia and asked to borrow his telephone.

"Where in hell have you been?" I'm certain Aunt Mary had never used that word before.

"I'm at the studio."

"Not for long. We're on a 5:30 plane to Las Vegas. I'll meet you at your apartment. Just get going and don't dawdle".

I drove home on automatic pilot, idly admiring the autumn leaves and the clothes in the Wilshire shops. When I arrived, Mary was frantically pulling clothes from drawers and closets.

"I've found your white suit. You have nothing else but cocktail dresses and blue jeans. What can we do?"

"So far I've had four trousseaux and no wedding. Let's start from the other shore."

Mary was at her best ramroding the outfit, and I was content to let her perform. My own attempts at organization had invariably failed. It was a wise decision. We made it to the airport with ten minutes to spare.

In Las Vegas we registered at the Desert Inn as Mary Banks and her daughter Olive. I dined on eggs Viennese, and was reclining in a big bubble bath by the time the phone rang.

"Of course we're here," Mary cooed. "Oh no, don't tell me!" Later she informed me that Bing had been calling for hours, only to be informed by the desk that Kathryn Grant had not registered.

"I know she would love to chat with you, but she's in the bath right now and it's very late, so why don't you tell me all your plans."

I watched the bubbles pop, and listened languidly to a conversation that affected me not at all. This particular enterprise had brought me such pain that I could no longer identify with it. I wondered idly what excuse would be found to delay my marriage this time.

I was in bed at 10 and asleep at 10:02.

Meanwhile Mary was running through a checklist of my belongings: Peignoir, yes; bedroom slippers, forgotten; slacks and shirt, yes; wedding suit, just barely (an eggshell shantung lined with an impressionist print would have to do); hat of the *My Fair Lady* genre, much too formal for my odds and ends. I had also included my Spanish mantilla at the last moment, when I didn't think I could bring off the hat; matching pumps; a string of pearls; and a borrowed mink stole. That was my present trousseau in its entirety.

The plan was simple: Leo was to pick us up at 8 a.m. and drive us to the Sands Hotel.

I wonder if Bing went to the gaming tables that night, or if he had dinner with friends. Superstitiously I never asked him.

The desert dawn was clear and cold, with streaks of rose on the horizon. I dressed with fatalistic calm. No more palpitations. I had gone that route.

I put my hair up in a tight chignon, decided against the hat, snatched up the mantilla and the inevitable white gloves, and strolled with Mary into the nearly empty lobby, only to be greeted by Leo Lynn's booming, "Happy is the bride the sun shines on today."

I stopped dead in my tracks, searching the lobby to see if anyone could have avoided hearing him. "Hush, Leo," Mary said. "If we're going to do this, let's get it over with. There's been enough talking."

Leo beamed irrepressibly. It was he who had been sent to Palm Springs to pick up a few things, and when asked why Bing was going to Nevada had muttered knowingly, "He's got a little trouble with his china." (Bing's dentist was in Las Vegas.)

Only after Leo had completed the long drive to Las Vegas and delivered Bing's pinstriped suit, had the latter said, "I'm marrying Kathryn Grant in the morning. It's after midnight, but you'll have to go out and get a ring. We'll be married in the chapel at St. Ann's Church."

At 1 a.m Leo did a dry run in the car, clocking himself from the Sands Hotel to the County Courthouse, and thence to the chapel. After he found we could enter secretly by the back door, he went to one of the little all-night marriage chapels and purchased a corsage, no small feat since competition was discouraged and no one

The newlyweds' arrival in Palm Springs

was selling to outsiders. "I need the corsage for my cousin, who wants to be married here," he lied, and came away with a white orchid.

The ring that he finally unearthed God knows where was very lightly gold washed, and must have set Bing back at least six dollars.

At 8:15 we picked Bing up at the Sands Hotel. Mary and I were sitting in the back. When Bing opened her door, she started to slide out. My grip on her hand tightened, as I firmly refused to lose my security blanket. She laughed nervously and remained at her post.

Bing kissed her on the cheek, said "Good morning, Miss Grant," and slid into the front seat.

At 8:25 the County Courthouse loomed before us. Bing came around to my side of the car and helped me out. My hand must have been freezing because his seemed very warm. I dropped it, and started up steep marble steps toward a black iron door.

I stumbled slightly, and Bing took my elbow as we entered a quiet corridor and turned into the office where marriage licenses were issued.

A reporter materialized as if from thin air. "Good morning, Mr. Crosby. What are you doing here?"

I glanced at Bing as my mental computer clicked back into the 10 a.m. wardrobe fitting for *Gunman's Walk*. If I took a 9 o'clock plane I could be at the L. A. airport by 10, phone a studio driver, and arrive at Columbia Pictures only an hour late. I started marching purposefully toward the front door.

As Bing caught my arm and turned me back around, I noticed to my amazement that his face was cheerful.

"Miss Grant and I are getting married in Yerington this afternoon."

The reported yelped, "Thank you," and fled.

I didn't know whether Bing was telling the truth, but I really didn't care. He hadn't made quips about me this time. He had spoken for both of us.

I filled out the form with relative calm and walked back down those thousand courthouse steps. This time Mary sat in the front seat with Leo, and Bing joined me in the back. Ten minutes later we were at St. Anne's.

Leo drove around to a rear door framed by oleanders. We entered the vestry, where an enormous Irishman seemed as worried about his robes as I had once been about my trousseau.

"You see, Bing, I was going to Ireland. Everything was packed, and I was about to board the plane when my doctor phoned to say an embolus in my blood was apt to kick up when the plane reached altitude.

"Well, you know there's no place to land in the middle of the Atlantic. And my family certainly wouldn't want me to be carried off the plane at Shannon Airport. Their friends would think I was drunk. So I returned here just before you called yesterday. I hadn't unpacked my vestments until this morning, and they are a sorry mess."

The good father looked at me wistfully. Might I be a helpful lass with an iron? My glazed stare disillusioned him. "Well," he sighed, "a few wrinkles won't change the sacrament."

Bing laughed gaily, but I continued to observe the priest dispassionately. He filled out the certificate of marriage, added the official stamp of the church, and made two copies.

Book 57, No. 90881, State of Nevada, County of Clark, No. 352591. "This is to certify that the undersigned, Rt. Rev. John J. Ryan did on the twenty-fourth day of October A.D. 1957, join in lawful wedlock Harry L. Crosby of Los Angeles, State of California, and Olive Kathryn Grandstaff of Los Angeles, State of California, with their mutual consent, in the presence of Leo Lynn and Mrs. Guilbert Banks, who were witnesses."

I regarded Bing warily, still waiting for the moment when he would break and run. Oddly enough I wouldn't have been surprised or even hurt this time. I'd have felt only a mild concern lest he break a leg leaping over the oleanders.

But wonder of wonders he wasn't retreating. He was actually guiding me in this situation, moving me through the side door toward the altar.

Two little boys were waiting, their robes as

My new home in Palm Desert

formally starched and pressed as Monsignor Ryan's were wrinkled. The kneeler was luxuriously padded. As I sank into it I tried to pray, but discovered to my horror that I was simply catechizing the Deity:

"Can this be the right thing, Lord? I haven't seen the man for a year. Surely he's changed. I know I have. Can I still commit myself to him as completely as ever? Can I remain as calm as I am now? Will I be a good wife for Bing Crosby?"

But it was too late for misgivings; the ceremony had begun. Overwhelmed, I lapsed back into catatonia.

It was a simple mass with the addition of a few marriage prayers. Only two candles burned on the altar. There was no incense, or music other than bird song, blending with the Latin chants of the monsignor, the tinkling bells at the moment of consecration, and Bing's murmured responses.

My hands clutched Leo's wilted white orchid and the little missal that Father Corkery had given me the year before. When Bing said "With this ring I thee wed," I simply dropped them so he could place that six-dollar special on my short, square finger.

With all the years of instructions and rehearsals, I should have known what to do, but I didn't. Bing had to guide me every step of the way. He took my elbow, helped me to rise, and pulled me down when it was time to kneel. From deep in my trance I watched the altar boys glide smoothly through their tasks. So at long last this was getting married.

Dominus vobiscum.
Et cum spiritu tuo.
Ite, Missa est.
Deo gratias.

Bing gave me a peck on the cheek and it was done. We wheeled and marched into the tiny anteroom.

There, for the first time in many months, he kissed me on the lips. It was a small kiss, but at last I was free to hug him. Feeling his shoulders shaking, I backed away and saw his eyes were full of tears. Instinctively I clutched him again and turned so no one else could see.

"It's all right Bing," I whispered, desperately trying to still my own doubts. "We'll make it."

Leo intervened to say, "I don't want to disturb you, but if those reporters have gone off to Yerington, that's a five-hour drive through miserable desert. Couldn't you just give them a call?"

"There's a phone right here," boomed the monsignor.

Some of Jack Entrater's people had heard the garbled news flashes, so there were scrambled eggs and champagne for fifty by the time we had driven the fifteen minutes back to the hotel. Thus Leo, Aunt Mary, the priest, Bing, and I celebrated our nuptials with forty-five gentlemen of the press.

Bing phoned his mother while I remained serenely in shock. Could it be that I was now Mrs. Bing Crosby?

At length I called the studio to cancel my wardrobe appointment, and gathered my few belongings for the flight to Palm Springs.

"You're coming with us, aren't you Mary?" Bing asked nervously.

"No, I think you can handle it from here."

At last I was to be alone with Bing. No more chaperones and house parties. Just the two of us alone together forever.

Wrong again. We were met in Palm Springs by the mayor, with several hundred townspeople and a band playing "Here Comes the Bride." Resourcefully I simply collapsed, but after his years of running from the press and avoiding the public eye, Bing's joviality was something to see. He flaunted me as if I had suddenly been promoted to queen of the universe.

After a thousand photos, we drove ten miles past Bing's old home above the Thunderbird Country Club, turned right at Shadow Mountain, and climbed a hill to a wilderness area where we suddenly came upon four modest homes.

"On your left," announced Bing, imitating a tour guide, "is Rock of Ages. Jimmy Van

Bing's office

The dining alcove

The much-feared kitchen

Heusen has just finished that one. It takes its name from the enormous boulder at the front door."

"And here," he continued, "some hundred yards up the mountain is Della Robbia Road." This time the origin of the appellation was self-evident. A Della Robbia *Madonna and Child* was embedded in the side of the adobe wall. It was of pure porcelain, about six inches thick and three feet high.

"Where did you get that?"

"From Hearst's place at San Simeon. I've had a year to shop while you were reigning in the Alhambra. I hope you've had your fill of exotic climes."

"For a while," I smiled wanly. Dear Lord, how was I ever going to take care of a house? I'd had enough trouble with my little apartment.

The Crosby crest was embedded in the terrazo. Bing flung open a heavy, hand-carved door, picked me up, and actually carried me across the threshold.

I wondered if Bing had remembered our chat at Kathy's Cottage some centuries ago: "Certainly I would like a honeymoon later. But right after I am married I would like to go home for those precious first memories."

This then would be my future reality, a home for Mr. and Mrs. Crosby. Much as I tried to identify with it, I could think of it only as Bing's new house. He tried to dispel my obvious misgivings by showing me through it.

Cool floors of white terrazzo, burnt-orange adobe and pecky cypress, enormous sliding glass doors which brought in the desert and mountains.

Bing resumed his role as guide. "The dining table is Elizabethan. It started life as a sideboard, but Howard Lapham's cabinetmaker added a couple of inches all around and. . .uh, cut off the other melon ball."

Noting my shocked look, he biffed my cheek and continued, "It was that or eat standing up. I found this candy glass in Monterey; but the lamps, the headboard, the octagonal tables, and the urns out by the pool came from Hearst's."

He pointed through the glass doors to what seemed like driftwood chairs. "The fellow who fashioned those of manzanita also carved the altar rail for the Burney church."

I was intimidated by an armed phalanx of kitchen utensils, but the wedge-shaped office looked easy to dust, and I resolved to learn to play the piano. In spite of my terrors, Bing's hypnotic voice was wafting me into a domestic wonderland.

Then the tour ended in the bedroom with an abrupt, "These are our closets." I opened one door, then the next, and the next. All were crammed full of Bing's clothes. Tension revisited. He looked at me in honest surprise, and then allowed as how he could move some of his stuff over. And eventually he did, all of eight inches.

Dolphins cresting a wave adorned the impressive headboard of a minuscule bed. Suddenly my temples throbbed and my eyes refused to focus. It had all been a bad joke. Now the press would pop up. Fifty of Bing's friends would appear shouting "April fool," and I would be sent back to my two rooms and C-movies.

Before this could occur, Pete Petito marched in, his arms full of telegrams, flowers, presents, and a wedding cake from Alice and Phil Harris.

I laughed with relief. At last I could get into my role. I began frantically opening gifts.

"The double bed will be up in a half hour. Can you help me get this one out of here?" The men staggered off with the miserable threat to our bonds of matrimony while I hysterically arranged the flowers.

When my lord and master returned, I inquired after stationery: "I could begin writing thank-you notes."

Bing eyed me speculatively. He had long since abandoned all hope of deciphering my childish scrawl. Finally he decided to grant tentative approval and admitted that, there must be some stationery in the desk.

I set to work at the octagonal table in the living room, but I felt horribly self-conscious as

Bing's dresser at Mapleton Drive

Pete and his crew marched back and forth. "Dear Margaret, Bing and I want to thank you for your kind. . . ." Gazing into the distance I saw no garden, no lawn, no flowers; only palm trees, cactus, mesquite, and pyracantha. The swimming pool was surrounded by sand. The valley stretched away to mountains which would form the barren backdrop for what must henceforth be the drama of my life.

It was too much. I dropped my pen, moved warily into the kitchen, found a kettle, and launched my first culinary endeavor. Fortunately there were cinnamon, sugar, and butter for oven toast, the only dish of whose recipe I was reasonably certain. I found the mugs and spoons, but then stood mesmerized by the window, staring at a covey of quail scuttling past a smoke tree.

The men came into the kitchen. "Need anything else, Bing?"

"No, I'll see you tomorrow."

It was a dismissal. Pete gave us an appraising look and finally retreated.

We were alone for the first time as Mr. and Mrs., but I didn't belong here. I couldn't be Mrs. anyone, certainly not Mrs. Bing Crosby.

"Want some tea?" I suggested numbly.

Bing lifted the kettle off the burner, turned off the gas, took the mugs from my hands, and placed them on the counter top. Drawing me towards him as if we were going to dance, he said, "No, I just want you."

"Thank God," I sobbed.

Now we were one, and suddenly I knew just how life must be. From now on we would do everything together, sharing all our friends and activities.

I embarked on my domestic career on Friday, the day after our wedding. By Saturday dusting furniture had paled somewhat. I said, "Darling, I have to be at the studio on Monday, and you have to record. What if we went up early? The Royal Ballet is in town, and Margot Fonteyn is dancing *Swan Lake* Sunday night."

"Sounds interesting. I'll get you tickets."

"Won't you come too?"

"No, I have a golf game Monday morning."

"Shouldn't I stay with you?"

"Not at all."

So I drove in from Palm Springs to Los Angeles, watched Margot Fonteyn, and then found Bing's home at 594 South Mapleton, Holmby Hills.

The courtyard was lighted only by the moon. I left my headlights on for courage while I rang the bell. After an interminable wait, punctuated by screech-owl calls and mysterious movements in the shadows, I heard brisk steps marching down the hall. Georgia Hardwick, Bing's housekeeper for many years, opened the door a crack, snapped on the porch lights, and eyed me suspiciously in their glare.

Half-blinded, I turned to extinguish the car's lights and grab my one suitcase. I followed Georgia upstairs to the guest room before either of us realized that something was amiss.

"I believe I am to stay with Bing," I suggested hesitantly.

Grudgingly she led me to Bing's room. I was initially relieved at the sight of a double bed, but then I saw the monogrammed DLC on the blanket cover. A huge picture of Dixie stood on the bedside table. I felt a sudden need to unpack and establish a toehold. Pulling open the closet door, I found it full of filmy feminine nightwear.

Perhaps a hot shower would banish the cold knot in my stomach. But all the bathroom towels bore the name Dixie, And there stood still another portrait.

Suddenly I was on the set of Rebecca, complete with my very own Mrs. Danvers. I summoned her and asked if I might sleep in the room on the other side of the bath.

"That's Mrs. Senior's room," she informed me. "It was Dixie's before she died."

I thought of something Lindsay had said: "Georgia was Mom's best friend. She took care of her right to the end."

Now, I thought, she's going to take care of me, and the end may not be far away.

"Thank you, Georgia, I'm sorry to have

At home in West Columbia

awakened you in the middle of the night, but I'd forgotten to ask Bing for a key. I'll see you in the morning. What time is breakfast?"

"Mr. Crosby always eats precisely at 8 a.m. WIll that be satisfactory?"

"It sounds idyllic," I muttered, aching for her to go. After her curlers and chenille robe had disappeared around the corner, I seriously considered screaming my lungs out. No, if I made any noise Mrs. Senior would hear me from the next room. We had not met since Mary Morrow's bridal shower in March of 1956. Would she remember me? Would she forgive me for marrying Bing? Would I be able to sleep in this mausoleum?

I avoided looking at Dixie's picture as I scrubbed my face. I would find some way to make Mrs. Senior love me. That Hardwick woman, however, was something else.

I slid into the vast cold bed, and just before turning out the light, glanced up at a Russell oil of a sinister Indian hunting party. Swell, I would wake up scalped, if at all. I burrowed under the covers, firmly resolved to suffer the tortures of the damned, and awoke the next morning to greet a bright new day. I was just too young, healthy, and naturally exuberant to emulate any Rebecca, with the possible exception of the one from Sunnybrook Farm.

In early November we went to Spokane, where Bing took part in the dedication of the Crosby Library at Gonzaga University. Father Corkery was all smiles. It was as if he and the Lord had finally prevailed over the fates and the furies who had kept Bing and me apart.

What a difference a year made! Bing introduced me with pride, and I now found acceptance where all had seemed rejection before.

On November 7 Bing and I traveled to West Columbia for a proper wedding reception. Fortunately some good Samaritans had lured my schoolteacher mother out of our house and cleaned up the familiar mess. It wasn't that she had anything against housekeeping, you understand. It was just that she never got around to it. The house was never lovelier, and everyone deliberately refrained from opening closets.

Bing submitted to being touched, pummeled, cajoled, and caressed. He stood in a reception line and shook hands with everyone in the county. One elderly and slightly intoxicated dignitary was so enchanted by the whole process that he marched through the line four times, eliciting a troubled look of vague recognition from the groom on his final pass.

Bing went duck hunting the next day, and loved every moment of it. "Kathryn, your dad brought down those mallards from the stratosphere, and I did pretty well for a foreigner."

Our banker, Dooley Galloway, breathed confidentially, "Why he's just an old shoe, Kathryn, just an old shoe, and you're the smartest girl in West Columbia." (i.e. the known universe)

Not one to deny the obvious, I simply asked, "Why, Dooley?"

"Because you married Bing Crosby, that's why."

The first party at the big house in Los Angeles was held at Christmas. It juxtaposed my few friends with Bing's huge following. Amid the buffet, the Michael Burke Singers, and many funny stories, certain potential problems reared their ugly heads:

Bing's circle was at least a generation older than mine. And Mary Banks, his sole contemporary from my group, spent the evening trying to convert a bewildered Dean Martin and inebriated Ernie Kovacs to fundamentalist Christianity, while they strove desperately to imprison their exuberant vocabularies within the bounds of propriety.

But I was impervious to portents at that glorious moment. I was much too busy celebrating the end of the most decisive year in the life of a diminutive would-be actress from West Columbia to consider future problems.

Bing and his boys

1958

A year of firsts.

My first pregnancy. Bing said, a month or so after we married, "I don't know if I can give you children."

I hadn't previously discussed the matter with him. After all he had four grown sons. Moreover I was a trifle dubious about my own talent for maternity.

To be sure, most of my girl friends had children. To grow up, get married, and rear a family was the goal of every decent girl in West Columbia, Texas, but even there I'd always been an outsider. All in all I'd never felt that the world would be underpopulated without my contribution.

And here was Bing expressing his own midnight doubts, which almost immediately proved groundless. Indeed if the proof had arrived any sooner, gossips would have had recourse to their calendars.

I was wildly excited about my pregnancy. Everything was new and strange for me, and Bing acted as if it were for him too. I had been reveling in my condition for less than two months when a woman crashed into me while trying to get to my husband at the Thunderbird Country Club. I thought Bing was going to hit her.

"Madam, you just walked into my wife."

"Mr. Crosby, I wanted to know if you would attend the benefit we are giving for . . ."

"I will not have you attacking Mrs. Crosby."

He took me protectively under his wing, turned, and stalked away. She would never know how she had unsuspectingly threatened the survival of Harry Lillis Crosby Jr.

Bing opened car doors for me during that blessed time. I really seemed as one Jewish friend put it "like a sacred vessel," but better than that, I was made to feel desirable. Lured on by Bing's reinforcement, I decided to become domestic, and bravely tackled my first Virginia ham.

It was a Christmas present which we had taken to Palm Desert. Casting about for succor, I finally came across an ice bucket capacious enough to hold the thing; also some buttermilk which I poured in. I'd heard somewhere that ham could be soaked in beer, and I discovered some Olympia in the refrigerator.

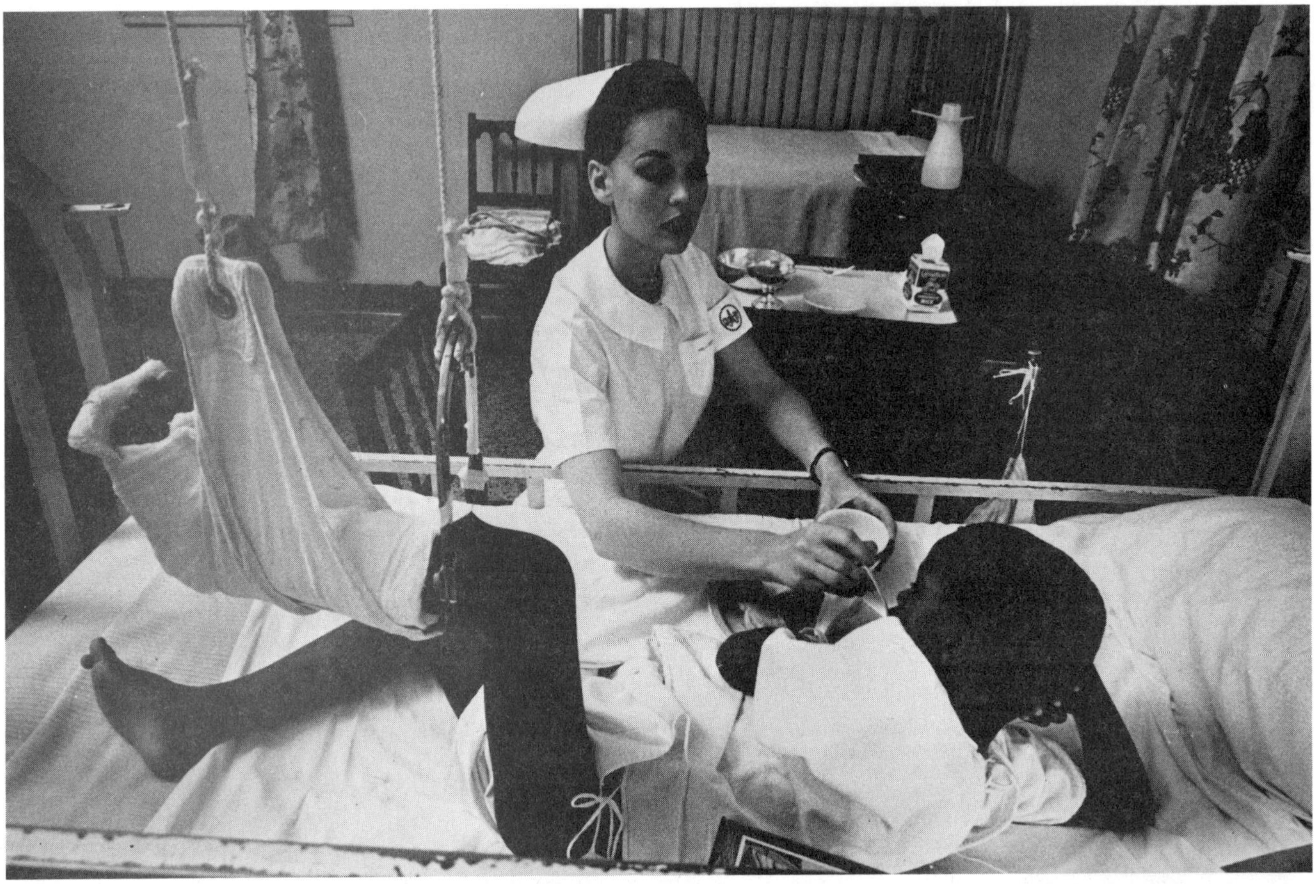

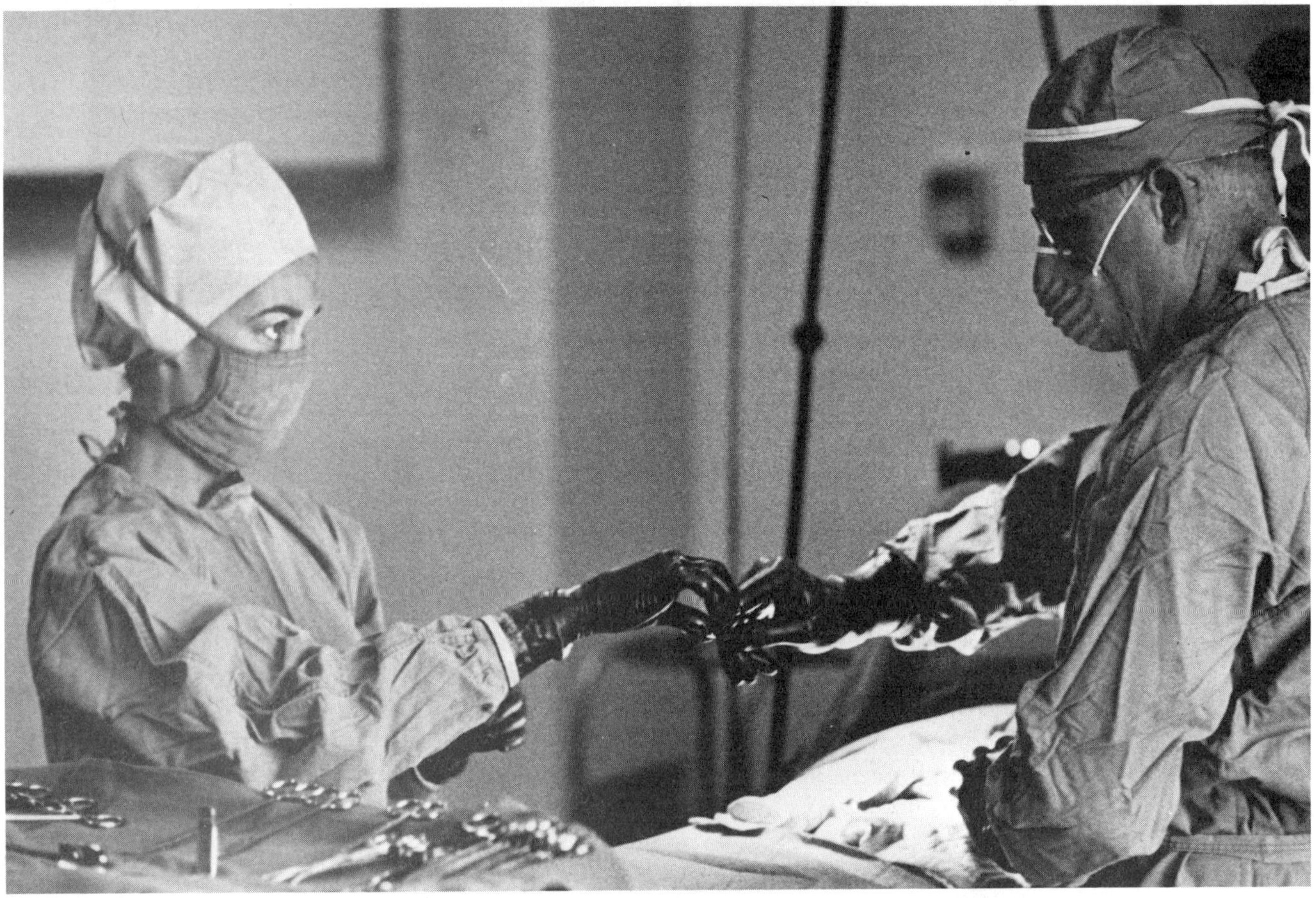

Feeding a small patient and assisting in surgery

I let the ham-buttermilk-beer combination sit for three days, at the end of which time we could have stocked Sir Alexander Fleming's experimental unit with enough molds to cure, or cause, wholesale epidemics.

Naturally Bing couldn't let me injure myself by carrying that heavy container, so he held his breath, lugged it outside, and poured off the vile fluid. He then courageously returned the ham, now bedecked with many-splendored growths. I used a Brillo pad to remove most of the muck, and consigned the remnant to the stove, but Bing's new-found gallantry had its limits, and I certainly wasn't going to risk two lives, so we never did find out how it tasted.

I had been told that pregnancy is a very healthy time of life, so I seized the opportunity to take my first golf lessons, and after many vain attempts finally learned to hit a fair drive. "If I work hard for a year or so and achieve some level of proficiency," I asked the pro, "do you think Bing would enjoy playing with me?"

"I don't know, Mrs. Crosby. I was never forced to play with a woman."

All of which cost him his future lesson fees and the potential sale of his best set of women's clubs. From then on, when Bing's game was off or he couldn't get up a match, I walked around with him and chipped and putted for him, but my balance was always changing, so I failed to make significant improvements in his score or temper.

Along with the academic side of the curriculum at Immaculate Heart College, I now embarked on the practical aspects of nursing at Queen of Angels Hospital, commuting from Palm Desert to Los Angeles.

As we were sitting by the pool, watching the desert stars do their thing, Bing remarked, "You know, you've liberated me from a whole round of boring parties. Now that I'm no longer the old bachelor of the desert, I just say 'Kathryn's in town with her nursing', or 'Kathryn's just returned from surgery and it unnerved her so that she couldn't face a big dinner party. So sorry.' "

"You're a scoundrel, you know."

"Yes," he admitted. "You must remind me to do proper penance."

In April Bing invited my sister and her husband for a visit at our Elko Ranch. It was then that I first realized that Bing didn't clearly understand that a woman is not as strong as a man—particularly when she's with child.

When we hiked in the snow his Labrador puppies knocked me down, but Bing just strode on, apparently unaware that I was being tumbled and tousled by the small brigands. I ruefully compared this lack of response to his reaction when the woman had bumped into me. But sleigh rides, the sight of jonquils in the snow, and Harry's first kick still afforded adequate compensation, so my maternal euphoria carried me smilingly through the first in a series of family crises.

Bing had been delighted with Denny's decision to settle down. But the day after the ceremony the first of his sons to wed was involved in a paternity suit. Bing was horrified, but Dennis just waited for the problem to go away, and sure enough in time things were sorted out—well after Bing had fled for his life.

"You know," he said diffidently, "every year we've gone up to Vancouver on Max Bell's yacht, the *Campana*, but I suppose I won't go this time. I shouldn't leave you now, should I?"

The wistful intonation with which he delivered the final query was worthy of an Academy Award. Fool that I was, I rose to the bait.

"Of course, my darling, you must go to Canada. You must do everything you ever did before and then some."

"Right," he chortled, "I'll call Max."

So he and his buddies, denominated *The Clams*, were off posthaste to the Far North where reporters couldn't find him, and I'd have been lonely indeed if it hadn't been for his lengthy letters:

Hotel Vancouver
British Columbia
June 1, 1958

"Dear Kathryn, Just a note before departure for *le pays du beau saumon*. Met all the chaps

The 1958 edition of The Clams

last night and had a fine dinner, after which we walked about the city until we had picked up a small following of the curious, which drove us early to bed.

"I have just returned from church and will shortly rouse my motley crew to get them to the airport, which won't be as easy as it sounds. Morrow's gear (Bill Morrow, Bing's writer), tons of it of course, which he shipped up in advance, has for some inexplicable reason been impounded by customs. It's Sunday and their warehouse is closed, but we'll have to shake out a few functionaries and see what can be done. No trip with Morrow would be normal without some complications.

"We will be back here at this hotel on the thirteenth, fourteenth, or fifteenth, depending on winds, tides, and the moods of the crew. Hope all remains serene with you. Physically, emotionally, and all ways I love you, Bing."

Yacht *Campana*
June 3, 1958

"Dearest Kathryn, So far the cruise has been a series of mishaps. Two of them before we even got aboard. Saturday night Van Heusen (Jimmy Van Heusen, the songwriter) slammed a taxi door on his index finger, lacerating it badly and breaking the bone. Collier (Buster Collier, a San Francisco friend, *bon vivant*, and early Hollywood actor) scratched his eyeball in some undetermined fashion and is now wearing a patch. I think he rather fancies himself as a romantic war correspondent. At Port Hardy crowds of villagers came down to see the Hollywood group, and a little girl fell off the pier between the yacht and the pilings. The mate jumped in and pulled her out, frightened but unhurt.

"Yesterday afternoon we anchored in a little bay fed by a rushing river. We decided to try for some trout, and went ashore in a launch towing a skiff. It's a good thing we took the latter because while we were fishing the tide went out, leaving the launch high and dry on the rocks. We had to row back to the yacht, returning for the launch this morning when the tide came back in.

"We caught some nice trout, up to a pound or so, but it was too brushy to fly-fish, so we resorted to lures. No purists in this area. Phil Harris was wearing thin rubber boots when he stepped on a sharp, broken bottle, inflicting a nasty cut on his instep. It will need stitches when we reach Prince Rupert this noon. Phil claims it's the first time he ever got in trouble with an *empty* bottle!

"The boat is comfortable and the food excellent. Harris and the cook have become quite friendly, and the Indian has a pot of beans started, with plans to add some succulent items from time to time, and promises of a very special treat for tomorrow. The cook is cooperative, but dubious about the whole enterprise.

"Mother Morrow is in good health, but he's had some heated differences of opinion with Harris about whether things should be fried or boiled. At present we are not speaking. He plugged my dictaphone into the DC socket and burned out the motor, forcing me to correspond in longhand.

"Now it's lunch time and this air does make a fellow hungry. Am going to try to be a little careful with the groceries. My chief enemy—obesity—is lurking in the gravy."

June 4, 1958

"Dear Kathryn, I wrote you yesterday from Prince Rupert, but we are leaving from Ketchikan in a few minutes to pick up some gear, so I thought I'd get off another note. Two of our invalids are on the convalescent list: Jimmy's finger annoys him, but the vet in Prince Rupert averred that it would heal if he kept the cast on. Collier's eye is practically OK. Phil's foot, however, remains very painful, so he will have penicillin shots for a few days. If he'd stay off it for a time it would doubtless heal faster, but you can't keep him down. Not a word to Alice. She'd worry unnecessarily.

"We caused a minor sensation in Prince Rupert, a town of twelve thousand souls, half of

Ready for the take-off

whom are Indian. I think we were the first show folks ever to visit the place. Fairly blocked traffic and jammed the stores. Nice people, however, and they gave us lots of good dope on where, when, and with what to fish.

"We should get some salmon today, but I'm mainly interested in locating rarely-visited lakes and streams where the trout are reputed to abound. Big scrappy rainbows and cutthroats. We'll do some snooping in Ketchikan. Maybe pick up a guide who can travel with us and show us the likeliest places.

"Yesterday morning we caught some chicken halibut, and had it poached and fried for lunch. Poached for Morrow and fried for Phil. We're going to set the crab traps tonight, and we'll also have a clam-digging detail. Peg-leg Harris will have to be straw boss.

"Here's Ketchikan. Will write again soon, and call you if I get near a phone. I miss you, Bing."

June 7, 1958

"Dearest Kathryn, We are now anchored at Bell Island, fifty miles northwest of Ketchikan. We have caught upwards of fifty salmon, fishing almost entirely in the evening. It doesn't get dark up here until midnight, and as it happens that is the low tide, which is the best time for these fish. Can you imagine fishing at midnight?

"The weather has been unbelievably beautiful—completely contrary to what I would have imagined Alaskan weather to be. Yesterday we hiked in two miles, packing a small boat and one-horse motor. Found a beautiful snow-fed lake bereft of trout.

"Collier and I travel light for these jaunts, but you should have seen Morrow toiling up the trail dragging his gear. We were too beat to bring the motor out, so someone will have to go in today and get it. It weighs a hundred and twenty-five pounds, and the trail is rough and log-strewn, with overhanging branches and mud underfoot. All this and no trout.

"Mother Harris got deep into the kitchen last night—corn bread, ribs etc. Made a large production out of it, as you know he can. The chef was somewhat less then enthusiastic, but finally damned it with faint praise.

"I feel rather derelict of my duty, leaving you alone in a house which is still strange to you, but I can only pray that your tasks are not too onerous. I miss you very much. All my love, Bing."

June 8, 1958

"Dearest Kathryn, I've always wanted to fly into a mountain lake and try some trout fishing. Yesterday my wish was gratified, but I can't say that I'm eager to repeat the experience. Four of us, excluding Morrow who pleaded the pressure of work, flew in a Grumman Goose to Humpy Lake, high up among the Alaska Mountains. We circled for an hour over, around, and between precipitous, rocky, snow-clad peaks. Then suddenly we dived through a deep pass, threaded our way between towering hills, banked a few times right and left, and landed mercifully though inexplicably on a lovely, ice-cold lake. Snow-fed, it is about eight miles long, a mile wide, and nobody knows how deep.

"We got into our waders and began whipping the banks with the spinners. Not much success for a while, and then, where a river came pouring out of a snowbank, we struck pay dirt. Almost every cast hooked a cutthroat trout. They were fat and fierce, weighing from a half pound to a pound and a half. They hit the line as if they were trying to knock it up onto the bank. What sport and what surroundings! It was just as I had always fancied it would be.

"Of course we had the usual mishaps: Collier slipped on a rock and went into the icy water up to his neck, his camera over his shoulder. After a brief period of shaking and shivering, he was back in action again, but the camera is somewhat the worse for wear.

"I hated the prospect of leaving, because I couldn't imagine how the pilot was going to get the Goose up and out of there. The feat was complicated this time by rapidly gathering clouds which were beginning to shroud the peaks. He told me that he had been flying this country for seventeen years, which should have

Catherine Harrigan Crosby

afforded some solace, but I reflected that the odds must now favor the mountains.

"Phil's palms were dripping, and I was a shaken man. After an hour spent dodging cliffs and fog, we landed back at the boat with about fifty nice trout. Believe me I took a good belt of Mr. Seagram's happy amber. Harris had of course fortified himself before, during, and after. Van Heusen, old airman that he is, affected an air of indifference betrayed only by his deathly pallor. I pray all is serene with you and with the house. Love, Bing."

All my replies have been preserved, but not a sentence will bear transcription. In retrospect they are about what one might anticipate from a pregnant young mooncalf whose idol is far away in Alaska.

One thing that I didn't discuss was my on-going relationship with my mother-in-law, which had begun with two weeks of peek-a-boo in the enormous house before we finally met.

"Mother is better in the morning," Bing had said in the evening as we sat in the library and she kept to her room.

"I think mother had a restless night," he had declared at the breakfast table while she took a tray in her suite.

I finally invited Aunt Mary for lunch, and bravely asked Georgia if Mrs. Crosby might join us. Miraculously she did.

After a piercing stare at me, she greeted Mrs. Banks cordially. During lunch I confided how grateful I was that she could manage the house, thus leaving me free to study or travel.

She accepted this tribute with dignity: "I have always felt that no house is big enough for two women, but if you need me I will stay. I moved in only to watch after the boys when their mother died."

"That brings up a delicate subject, Mrs. Crosby." I was gaining confidence and it seemed an opportune moment to mention the matter. "Dixie's pictures and monograms are everywhere. I know I didn't bring much of a dowry, but I feel surrounded."

Mrs. Senior tapped a thoughtful tattoo on the tabletop. "Don't bother about that."

Was that all? "Don't bother about that?" I stewed internally while Mrs. Crosby observed benignly to Mary, "Kathryn seems to like mature people."

"She certainly does," was the placating response. "We've been good friends for years."

Meanwhile back at the incubator black thoughts arose. I had tried to keep my frustrations in check, but now they threatened to overwhelm me. "One more week and I'm leaving," I decided. "He can come with me, or stay with her pictures, and her blanket covers, and his housekeeper who locks up the bar so my friend Nancy can't have a drink. He can continue to eat off chipped Wedgewood, or dig some whole plates out of that huge butler's pantry."

I tuned back in to hear "Yes, I had all my babies at home. Seven of them. No matter how hard Dad Crosby coaxed, I wouldn't come downstairs until I was good and ready. I took two weeks with each child. That was the only rest for a mother in those days."

Mrs. Senior talked on. She became quite friendly with Mary, and appeared to tolerate me. At least she didn't seem ready to throw me out of the house, which was surely what Bing had feared when he refrained from introductions during the first weeks.

"Come on, Mary, I'll drive you home." On the way I poured out my problems. She urged patience, and had I had any, it would indeed have been rewarded, for when I returned to the big house, the blanket cover and towels were plain. All the offending monograms and pictures had disappeared. I flew to Mrs. Senior's room and hugged her mightily.

"Kathryn," she smiled, "men just don't think of those things, so don't mention it to Bing." And indeed I never did.

As my waxing profile measured the passage of months, strange urges impelled me to transform the big house into a hive of activity. Painters, upholsterers, and restorers worked their will on it, while I arranged and rearranged all the furniture.

With Miss Nevada

With Miss France

With Miss Bremerton

By the time Bing returned home from his search for salmon, I was evidently in the grips of a full-blown nesting psychosis. After a day of observing the turmoil from the sidelines he implored, "Honey, just do me one favor. Don't buy anything else. We'll put the chairs on wires and fly them from one end of the house to the other if you just don't throw them away."

When he found me disposing of his ties he complained mildly, "But you never know when you're going to need one of those things in a period picture. I have some vintage items here."

Denny had been married on May 4. On September 25 his twin brother Phillip took the plunge. Urged on by Bing and my dawning maternal instincts, I advised my new daughter-in-law Sandy to take speech lessons. A raving beauty with black hair and eyes, high cheekbones, a perfect figure, and milk-white skin, she lost it all when she opened her mouth.

"Phillip fell in love with me this way, and this is the way I am going to stay," she declared in her strident nasal twang, so I reluctantly abandoned the field. Mothering would have to begin with smaller creatures at an earlier, more malleable stage.

My first real bouts with jealousy appeared, logically enough, when I was eight months pregnant. The first I brought on myself by agreeing to judge a beauty contest in Nevada. There I helped to choose a very pretty little girl from Sparks, who had portrayed St. Joan in the talent division, proving herself charming but a trifle raw around the edges.

"Why don't you send her to Los Angeles for a week," I suggested idiotically. "She can stay with me, see a bit of the city, and work on her poise. With a little help I'm sure she'll do very well in the *Miss America Contest*."

By the time all 105 pounds of her arrived, I was a bulgy 140. Bing made her much too welcome, and squired her to a movie premiere, where she confirmed my judgement by conducting herself beautifully.

I suddenly realized that I was now a matron of twenty-four, confronting a nubile young thing of nineteen, the magic age when Dixie had married Bing. And of course this child had to be blonde with blue eyes. I just kept repeating that I'd done it to myself.

No sooner had Miss Nevada left than Bing said, "You know, in Vancouver I too judged a contest, and the winner was a young lady named Marsha Hunter. She and her mother are coming down to Los Angeles for a visit, so I wonder if you could show them the town."

In due time Marsha and her mother arrived, and I took them to lunch. I also introduced Marsha, who said she was interested in the theater, to Columbia's drama coach Benno Schneider. Benno and I discussed the essence of Greek tragedy, while Marsha looked at the prints on the walls.

A real beauty, she did better in the Beverly Hills shops and restaurants. After a couple of days her mother confided, "I have a dental appointment in Spokane, and I'm worried about leaving Marsha at the motel. I'll be gone only a day or two so I wondered. . ."

"Marsha must remain with us," I heard myself declare firmly.

Mrs. Hunter disappeared for two weeks, after which Marsha said in her sweetest tones, "Oh, I just wish I could stay until the baby is delivered."

At this point I wished that she could have delivered the baby in my stead. I was sitting up all night so that I could get some air into my lungs, and the wretched child was interrupting my brief naps by trying to kick his way out.

Marsha was a delightful girl, and I shouldn't have been jealous. Bing must have fairly judged her to be the prettiest contestant, but I couldn't help wishing her elsewhere when I was feeling and looking like a beached whale.

No sooner had I disposed of her than a *femme fatale* from France appeared. "I'm a good friend of the dear child's parents," said Bing. "I helped them stock her little dress shop, but it all went down on the *Andrea Doria*."

"What a shame," I said, expecting to see some twelve-year-old prodigy of a designer. In point of fact, she was a sophisticated and cur-

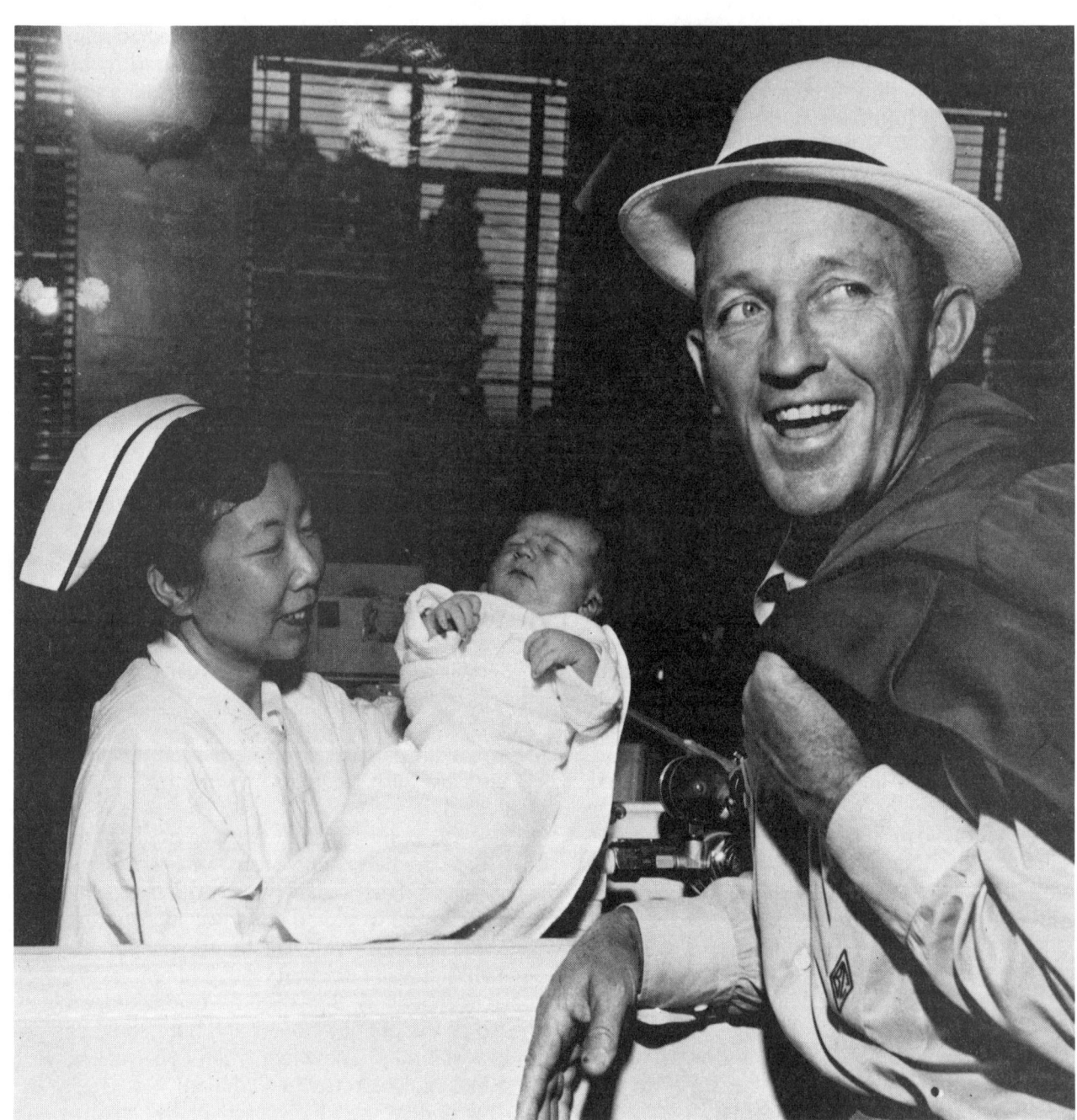
With Harry Lillis Crosby Jr.

vaceous twenty-five. Typically I invited her to supper, where she insisted on speaking her own language with Bing. Frantically I ran through my first-year French phrases and picked up most of what she said, while feigning total innocence.

"I know that Kathryn can't come to my little apartment. It is four flights up. But you must come, Bing dearest, and I will fix you a little omelet. I know how you love my omelets."

So that's what she called them. I suddenly realized that I had chanced on a picture of her in a bikini just the week before Bing returned from Alaska. It had made me sit on the floor in my muumuu and cry my fat heart out.

With only two weeks to go, I was awakened August 8 by lights flashing on and off from the ceiling. I had only recently learned that they represented two outside telephone lines and an intercom.

Since my passenger and I were unlikely to get any further sleep, I slid out of bed and staggered toward the bathroom. As I passed the bedroom door, I thought I heard a noise, which turned out to be Rose, the cook.

"I need to speak to Mr. Crosby."

"We can't disturb him, Rose. It's only six-thirty."

"Yes, but they're calling Mr. Gary from the studio. He's due at work, and I can't wake him up."

"Oh," said I officiously taking charge. "Has he had breakfast?"

"I have it right here."

I took the silver tray from her, nodded approvingly at the poached egg and toast steadfastly keeping warm under their glass bells, and marched into what had been the nursery.

I put down the tray and knocked on the door of the former nurse's bedroom, where Gary now slept.

No response, so I opened the door a crack and saw Gary lying on his stomach. "My, he's a sound sleeper," I thought innocently.

Well, I would do what my mother had always done for me. I went to the bathroom for a warm, wet washcloth, and returned to place it on the nape of his neck.

Gary rose like a vampire from his coffin, but instead of drinking my blood he flailed his arms and cursed me with virulent fluency. I dropped the cloth, backed out of the room, and closed the door, pursued by loud threats of severe bodily harm if I dared disturb him again.

"Rose, tell the studio that Gary will not come to work today."

"But I can't..."

"Yes, you can. I will not disturb Mr. Crosby, and obviously we have both failed with Gary."

"They're not gonna like this," she muttered as she retreated.

I was halfway down the hall before anger hit me so hard that I had to sit down. No one had the right to yell that way at Rose, or me, or anyone! Of course I didn't know then that Gary was dead drunk.

For reasons which I still fail to understand, it seems that people who are intoxicated have a right to do or say anything they please. But at that time I made no more allowance for Gary's drunkenness than for his extensive arsenal of epithets. I was simply furious.

As I sat raging and hugging myself, my poor over-burdened stomach began to bulge and release, bulge and release....

I no longer cared whether Gary was roused for work or not. Suddenly I had another job to do.

So it was that Harry Lillis Crosby Jr. was born two weeks early at Queen of Angels Hospital. Immediately thereafter Bing walked into the maternity room, took his son from my arms, and began delightedly crooning to him. This was a boy, and boys he understood from long experience.

"Mission accomplished," I sighed dreamily.

Ushering in the new year at Romanoff's

1959

The Tex Feldman party ushered in the new year at Romanoff's. I wore a Jean-Louis black velvet formal with a chinchilla stole, and felt that I should have been painted by John Singer Sergeant. And so should Bing in his formal attire.

This was to be an elegant year, but I should have suspected trouble when Bing couldn't find the pearl studs for his vest. "Darling," I pled, "here are some ruby ones, and some blue ones that must be sapphires, and some gold ones...."

"No, Kathryn. Don't you understand? With black tie, one must wear white studs and cuff links. Good form demands it." My husband who was seldom out of his old golfing sweater, was getting ready to put on the dog for a smooth chorus of *High Society*.

Earlier I had begun a white, leather-bound daybook with the following entry. "Dear Diary, Since my wedding on October 24, 1957 I had quite forgotten you. The beginning of a marriage is a precious string of days, each with a problem or a reward. Fortunately the joys of having Bing and our son have far outweighed the disappointments. Now I must keep a calendar lest any pleasant friendship be neglected, any warming touch be forgotten, lest this lovely life become a state of mere existence."

Now I thought back grimly on the quiet afternoon before the onslaught of party preparations, when I had penned those optimistic, organizational lines. First I had lapsed into a long visit with Bing's mother, which had left me just time to slick my long hair into a high figure eight, instead of the more elegant coiffure I had planned; next I had become involved in a bout with Harry's pablum, culminating in a battle over his refusal to burp; the climax had been Bing's quest for proper jewelry.

The solution to the last problem was a matching set of smoky-colored, genuine fake mother of pearl studs and cuff links. Leo had to run to the drug store in Westwood for those beauties, which must have dented the household budget to the tune of at least three dollars.

As I looked over the gorgeously-gowned women and formally-attired men, I reflected with weary pride that Bing was in perfect style. I was so carried away that I nearly admonished one celebrated leading man who was gauche enough to wear emerald jewelry. In my eyes

As an aerialist in *The Big Circus*

Bing was the best dancer on the floor; at dinner he was also a superb storyteller. My cup overflowed as I gathered my stole around my shoulders for a spectacular exit, reached up to smooth my hair, and knocked a tiny fistful of dried cereal from my chignon.

On January 8th shooting began on Irwin Allen's *The Big Circus*. The great aerialist Barbette had trained me to hang from a trapeze by one foot, to execute simple acrobatic stunts, and to fall into the net without fear. Rhonda Fleming, Victor Mature, Red Buttons, Gilbert Roland, Vincent Price, and Peter Lorre participated in the movie, and I was thoroughly enjoying my role when my husband summoned me to Pebble Beach on January 16th for the Eighteenth Bing Crosby Pro-Am.

I dressed to the nines in tweeds and brogans, with knotted ascot and pigskin gloves, to accompany a crooner in dark slacks, flaming tweed jacket, and shooting stick, which he waved airily and employed as a cane.

On Cypress we began following the play on the 11th hole, and stood for half an hour behind the tee at 15, watching the difficulties even the best players experienced in trying to hit the minuscule green.

As we strolled on Bing said, "Your doctor phoned."

"Why would he call you?"

There was a sparkle in Bing's eye. He actually gave me a wink.

"Dispense with the preamble," I snapped. "Is our daughter on her way?"

Employing his umbrella as a stylus, my husband wrote *y-e-s* in the white sand of the trap just to the left of the 15th green.

Throughout the afternoon and early evening, Bing hovered somewhere above the stratosphere. At a party that night he played the expansive, overwhelming lord-of-the-jungle.

Initially he had reluctantly agreed to drop by just for a minute, to show the flag and say hello. And indeed he did so, many times, to every golfer and waiter in the place, as he ate, drank, sang, told naughty stories, played host, and personally ushered every guest out until the last had left at 4 a.m., whereupon he dusted his hands in a cordially self-satisfied manner, turned to the exhausted householders and announced, "Well, I finally got rid of all those party-poopers. Now let's settle down for a bit of the bubbly and a nice chat."

After two more hours of Bing's best stories, I finally trundled him down the hill to our house in the pale light of dawn. (During the final half hour I'd had the distinct impression that he was waiting patiently for our hosts to leave.)

Then it was back to my movie set, where the elegantly-launched year began losing momentum. As I was about to climb the rope ladder to a perch high in the big top, I felt suddenly giddy, but forced myself to ascend.

The scene was filmed before I made the mistake of looking down, swayed, grabbed desperately at a rail, abandoned all further pretense of bravery, and had to be pried loose and carried away. It was my last shot for the day, so I staggered off to the car and drove very cautiously to the doctor's office.

The afternoon seemed interminable: Waiting for an examination, waiting for tests, waiting for results, and then waiting for more tests.

"Should I stay in bed tomorrow?"

"No, we have excluded the possibility of an ectopic pregnancy. If the implantation is too low, it would be better to sluff it off now. So hope for the best and check in daily."

By the 12th we knew. I jubilantly scrawled in my diary, "She lives, the wee witch."

Shortly thereafter Columbia Pictures asked me to meet Otto Preminger to discuss a possible role in *Anatomy of a Murder*. I took him a note from my physician, which stated that I was pregnant but able to work for several more months.

He envisioned no difficulties, which was nice. Neither did I, which was stupid. Bing had become bored with the problems of my career. So he cheerfully shipped me off to location in Ishpeming, Michigan, and went a-vagabonding with Bill Morrow.

I participated in a few scenes at the beginning of the film. Then I waited six weeks for my other lines. During this time Lee Remick was

Harry Lillis Jr. meets his grandfather

working all day every day, and playing with her baby in the next room nights. I went fishing with Robert Travers, studied my physiology lessons, visited with my brother's wife, wrote pleading letters home ("If you won't come, why can't Harry be with me?") and would have thrown a fit if I could have located an appreciative audience.

But no one would pay me the slightest heed. Just try playing Madame Bovary under those circumstances. It takes all the fun out of suffering.

Meanwhile from Baja California my errant husband was expressing delight in his new-found freedom in missives such as this:

"Dearest Kathryn, Here we are at Palmilla, the place described on the outside of the envelope. It is the ultimate in luxury, beautifully situated on a promontory overlooking the sea, superbly built, and tastefully furnished, with a truly excellent cuisine.

"But of course the big thing is the fishing. We went out at 10 a.m, caught three marlin, and were in port by 2:30. On the way back we ran into a school of rooster fish and caught a dozen in twenty minutes. Beautifully-colored, weighing about fifteen pounds with a sort of fan on their dorsal fin, they jump and run like mad when hooked.

"Our hotel is just thirteen miles from the tip of the peninsula on Cabo San Lucas. As you can see, we're running out of country.

"I'd love to call you, but there's absolutely no chance from here. A friend is taking this letter out. Love, Bing."

On Thursday, May 7, I finished my last scene for Mr. Preminger, climbed aboard a chartered plane, and zoomed back to Los Angeles. Bing met me and drove me home to Harry Lillis, who had grown a foot. Bing said he wanted to take me (read himself) away from all this, so we were to go fishing in Mexico.

Las Cruces, named for three crosses on an adjacent promontory, lies across a mountain range from La Paz, in Baja California. It consisted at the time of one hotel, the Rodríguez home, the Fisher home, the Lordan home (where we stayed), and assorted cabins.

There Bing introduced me to deep-sea fishing. I'd supposedly tried it once, but just so Mary Morrow and I could send our picture with a huge marlin to the boys, who were off on a salmon-fishing junket. The caption read, "How many salmon does it take to equal one 200-lb. marlin?"

On May 13 Bing and I made the almost fatal mistake of attempting to drive to La Paz. Heedless of warnings, we set forth in a borrowed jeep. We were off to a gay bouncy start, but we ran out of road after a few hundred yards, and found ourselves following deer paths and gullies.

We were remarking on the fantailed doves, prune trees, paper trees, and lovely cacti when the jeep started sputtering. At this juncture our first humans hove in sight, but Bing thought they looked like thieves, so we hicupped our way past them as far as we could. Our jeep expired at what seemed to be a fork in the non-existent road.

Bing retraced his steps to ask the brigands, who turned out to be woodcutters, "Cómo se llega a la Paz?"

"Da lo mismo," they answered. (It's all the same.)

Bing and I were equally hopeless with mechanisms. This made for a compatible but hardly symbiotic relationship. We didn't complement each other, but we did agree. When a car broke down, we walked away to pray for its speedy recovery or happy death.

This particular five-mile hike through desert heat seemed cruelly long to a would-be mother, six months pregnant with a female child who was not at all sure she wanted to go the route. I looked up and felt the wrath of the gods and the heat of the heavens upon me. If I miscarried en route, could Bing deliver the fetus without killing me? In my heart I knew he couldn't, but I kept my own counsel as we trudged along the dusty trail.

We'd managed about three miles in what we fondly hoped was the direction of La Paz when I fainted. Bing was doing his best to revive

Guess who got the big marlin.

me when a plane passed overhead. He waved his arms wildly until it circled, came in low, wiggled its wings, and took off for the La Paz airport.

It is a five-minute flight from La Paz to Las Cruces. It was three hours by a four-wheel-drive vehicle if you made it. A taxi from La Paz finally reached us after much burning of rubber and cursing in Spanish. It dropped us at the airport, whence we were flown back to Las Cruces.

The next day two mechanics in a Landrover rescued our jeep. The verdict was *agua en la gasolina*.

On Saturday, May 16, I really entered into Bing's sports life. He was, for five hours and twenty minutes, the potential holder of a well-nigh unbreakable world's record. He had hooked a thousand-pound black marlin on a ten-pound test line.

We were out with Bob and Ruth Fisher on their boat *The Volador*. The weather had been calm, with no strikes until noon. Then Bing lost three quick ones before he had a blind strike at 1:55 p.m., apparently from a shark or a wahoo. The fish didn't surface; there was just a steady pulling on the line.

The Mexican boatmen were brilliant in the use of light tackle. When a fish wanted to sound they let it, but they backed up subtly and slowly to keep the line from getting too tight. When the fish started to run, they ran along with it in a parallel line so that the angler could take up the slack. They hoped the fish would charge the boat so they could grasp it by the double leader and gaff it before it knew what had happened.

After forty minutes the fish surfaced. We saw the bubbles break off an enormous black dorsal fin, which looked like the sail of a small boat. None of the crew had seen a marlin that big in those waters. They manned battle stations, and we all settled down to watch a great sportsman in an unequal contest with a giant fish.

Nineteen times Bing had the double line almost touching his rod. The radio started sizzling as Bob Fisher called the other boats in the vicinity to join the fun. One who was already hooked up very sportingly cut his lines so there was no possibility of entanglement.

The double leader would reach the boat, Bing would back up, the boatmen with their gaffs would lean over the side; then the fish would bolt, and the whole process would repeat itself.

At 7:15 p.m. Bing moved from the back of the boat to the front, so that the lights of the *Volador* could help us keep the fish in view when it broke the surface. Just as he completed this maneuver, the marlin apparently became conscious of the fact that there was something unattractive in his jaw. He leaped, came down with his full weight on the fraying line, snapped it like the thread that it was, and greyhounded away. We followed him with the lights of the boat until he disappeared into the night, still unaware of the excitement that he had provided for some forty mortals.

Bing just collapsed, too exhausted to express his disappointment.

When we returned to the dock at Las Cruces, the mariachis were waiting to serenade us. Our whole party sat for hours under the huge desert moon, marvelling that we had been privileged to share in such a glorious defeat.

In this, my first visit, Las Cruces seemed enchanted. It was the only time that I'd ever been with Bing all day every day. I didn't have to share him with others either. The low-keyed, sporting people at the hotel and on the boat were unobtrusive, preoccupied with their own pleasures. The meals were delicious, and I didn't have to concern myself with them. I hated the thought of leaving this paradise, my first true honeymoon.

But return we did. Bing to Palm Desert, and I to Los Angeles, where I began serious work at Queen of Angels School of Nursing. I clung to my memories of our week in Las Cruces as he continued his travels, stopping briefly in Santa Barbara, Pebble Beach, and Rising River, before moving on to Denver, Seattle, Vancouver, Calgary, and anywhere else that the shooting was good or the fish were biting.

I have just calculated that Bing was home

By now The Clams had a sign, a song, and a secret password.

only 42% of the year in 1959, but in his offhand way he wrought changes in my family's life style. Mother and Dad came to California for a lengthy visit. My sister's husband, Leonard Meyer, became manager of our newly-purchased Rising River Ranch. My sister-in-law, Netta Grandstaff, traveled with me for the entire shooting of *Anatomy of a Murder*, her first stint away from home in eleven years of marriage.

Rising River Ranch
July 4, 1959

"Dear Kathryn, Leonard met me at Redding, along with Emery, Sr. (my father). There are lots of fish in the river, but the water is clear and ripple-free, a decided factor in their favor. Caught one, lost two, and released a few small ones this morning.

"Your dad has also caught some, but finds it a distinct challenge, as does everyone who comes here. He loves it though, and according to Frances Ruth (my sister) never wants to leave.

"Your mother looks better than when last I saw her. She is trying desperately to adhere to her diet. Doesn't dine with the group, but takes her hard-boiled egg and sliced tomatoes in the privacy of her digs. Too tempting, I fancy, to sit and watch us load up.

"I have been drafted to lead the 4th of July parade in Burney, astride one of Leonard's best steeds. Will call you in a day or so. Kiss Tex (our son Harry) for me. Love, Bing."

Meanwhile I was attaining heroic proportions, and making frantic, if ill-fated efforts at domesticity during my husband's brief visits home. On his way to the links one morning he discovered me pushing a sofa down the hall.

"I really like it when you putter around the house," he observed. "It's nice to have a wife who does homey things."

I, who should have been delighted at having attracted his attention, glared at him, snapped "Then you should have married Georgia," and trundled on after the sofa.

"I'll keep that in mind the next time around," Bing smiled. "For the coming weeks, however, I'm going to concentrate on fishing."

Yacht *Campana*
August 16, 1959

"Dearest, Sailing along to Vancouver and feeling very lordly, lounging in this vessel with a crew of eight, poised and ready to gratify our slightest whim. Right now we'd like some sunshine, but I doubt that they can handle that. I wish you were aboard. You would love it because the sea in this island passage is reasonably calm and the scenery is striking.

"A couple of incidents on the trip which might amuse you. Buster was showing off all his Abercrombie gear, and finally came to a package about the size of a baseball.

'What's that,' asked Morrow.

'A life preserver,' replied Collier. 'When you hit the water, you squeeze this until it inflates.'

'How long will it hold you up?'

'Until you're hoarse,' interposed Harris.

"Another time Morrow, Dick Snideman, and Crowley, who were fishing in one of the small boats, hooked onto a salmon that began racing wildly all over the ocean.

'Chase him,' cried Snideman.

'Turn right,' yelled Morrow.

'Turn left,' howled Crowley.

"The salmon ran out all the line and broke it off at the spool. You know why? Nobody was at the wheel. A colorful crowd. I have many Morrow tales which I'll relate when I get home. Enjoyed hearing your voice on the phone yesterday, and was relieved to know you are not uncomfortable. Love to mother. Bing."

Because I thought Bing wanted me to be domestic, and because I was enchanted by the children when they were small, I devoted voluminous letters to them, as if they were important events in the big world almost on a par with Bing's fish. I include this one because Remus was Bing's all-time favorite dog.

He had been a puppy in April of 1958, when Frances, Leonard, Bing, and I went to the ranch. It was he and his litter-mates who had knocked me down in the snow. Only a minuscule patch of grey above his right

Bing's idea of a maternity leave at Rising River

eyebrow distinguished him from his coal-black siblings.

August 17, 1959

"Dear Bing, The heat wave has broken and Harry has gone into his winter longies with feet. He looks more like a young seal every day. Right now he is standing by the bed, cowlick neatly combed, pompously eating a grape. Betimes he lurks behind the headboard for a short, lively game of peek-a-boo.

"Oh dear, a crisis. Your son has decided he wants an item of apparel from the rocking chair, which is just a smidgen too deep for him to reach his goal. Do you think he'd go around to the side? No, he's his father's child. He stands on one foot and then the other, screaming in pure frustration.

"Remus has destroyed our breakfast-room garden. He dug up one azalea plant four times in the same day. When Louie, Susie, Leo and I successively replanted it, he decided more drastic action was indicated. He once more lifted said azalea, carried it off, and buried it. We've not found it yet, and have perforce left that particular hole to him.

"Yesterday afternoon he had a backyard outing with his buddy HLC, Jr. Before play-time was over, he had practically taught his human to heel. And such a patient dog he is. Have no fear for Harry's health. Be concerned instead for your retriever. Harry rides him like a horse, pulls his ears, pokes his fingers up those black nostrils, and thoroughly explores the dark recesses of that soft, tender mouth, while Remus glories in every moment of it.

"Fat old Cindy has decided that her years of devoted service have qualified her for a supervisory position. She lies, head on paws, and dreams of bygone avocados. (Cindy had learned to stand on her hind legs and pluck avocados off the branches, or bump against the trunk of the tree until they fell. Understandably she had a weight problem.)

"The garden furniture was finally ordered, and in typical Grandstaff style should be finished in time for Christmas. In self-defense I can only refer you to one purportedly brindle rug, woven underwater off the mystic shores of Majorca and ordered by my betrothed for our marriage, which if memory serves arrived some two years later, and in the event was rather a pale puce.

"Your mother was delighted with the last letter, but still opens each day with the query 'Where's your old man?' Yeah, where are you? Love, Kathryn."

On Monday, August 24, I went to Elizabeth Arden's for a wash, lube, and marfax job, failing to realize, until I made the mistake of consulting my mirror, that nothing helps when you're eight months pregnant. Undeterred I put a big red bow on the door, took Harry to the airport, picked up my husband, drove him home, and informed him that he'd better love his new office, which I had redecorated and furnished with an oriental rug, a Munnings' hunting scene, and a Chinese chest, whether he wanted them or not. It had been a long, cold summer.

For the next three weeks Bing renounced his travels for golf, hunting, and his Pirates' baseball games. I played at housekeeping, fought a losing battle with a ravenous appetite, and lay like a lump on the living-room sofa much of each day.

At 7:24 p.m., September 14, 1959, Mary Frances Crosby was born, a healthy seven-pound baby girl.

Accustomed to boys, Bing had picked Harry up as casually as if he were tucking a football under his arm. He held his only daughter out in front of him at an awkward angle and asked, "But isn't she awfully red?"

"She's a perfect baby, Bing. A ten on the Apgar scale."

The proud father was ecstatic. He sat in my room all the next day holding the child, rocking her gently back and forth, and singing to her. When he thought I was asleep, he abandoned the too-rah-loo-rah-loo-rahs, for some of his own naughty parodies of famous lyrics.

Eventually I opened one jaundiced eye. "The child will pick up those improprieties. If

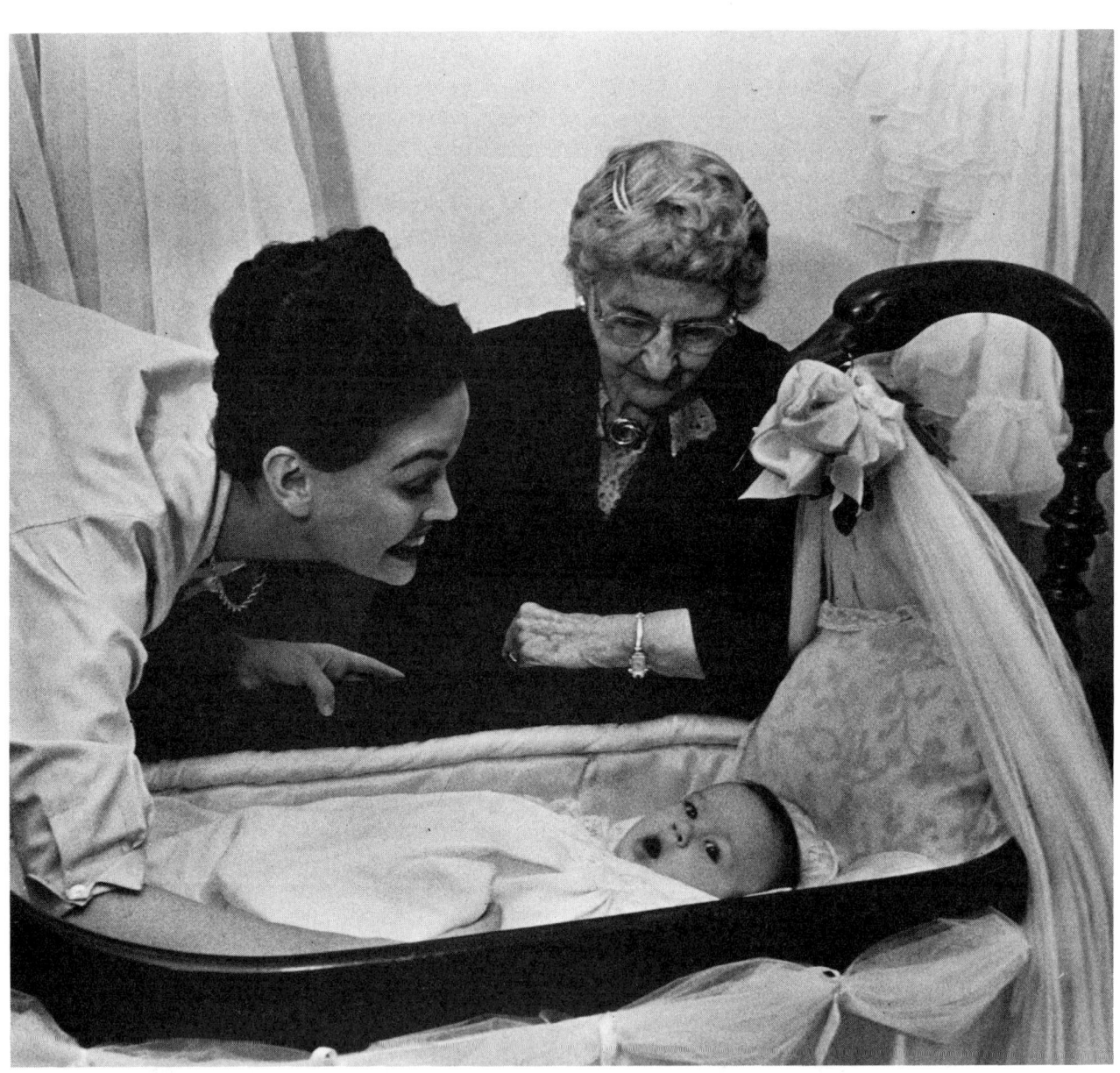
Grandmother Crosby inspects Bing's only girl child.

you don't want to sire a scarlet woman, you must set an example from the beginning." I drifted off again, secure in the knowledge that father and daughter would get along.

Though I didn't want to discuss it with Bing, I made a mental note to ask the doctor why our daughter was so ugly. Harry had been born with long black eyelashes and a full head of hair. His sister had no hair, no eyelashes, and no eyebrows either. I could only hope that nature meant her for a true blonde. In desperation a couple of weeks later, I adapted one of my falls to her small, pointed head, and painted on eyebrows. Lo and behold, suddenly there was my pretty, blue-eyed, baby girl. May all her problems be so easily resolved! My show-biz background should have taught me to be generous where the gods have proved niggardly.

Bing had his own ideas about maternity leaves. As soon as Mary Frances was comfortably settled in the competent hands of a trained nursemaid, he dragged me off to our Rising River Ranch to become an outdoor type.

On October 26, 1959, I actually shot my first goose. Amazingly enough I loved it, and Harry did too. We all played in the brisk outdoors until Phil Harris arrived and took my husband north to Weiser, Idaho, to shoot ducks, pheasant, and partridge, and then to Canada whence Bing wrote this macho mood poem on November 2:

"Dearest, Our world is a foot deep in new snow. The evergreen bows are bending low, and Remus is in his element, rolling about and snorting. We're waiting for the car to take us north into the goose, duck, and hun (Hungarian partridge) country, about a four-hour run I understand.

"We have enough warm clothes to brave the Arctic Circle, and various pheasants in the ice house in Weiser to be cleaned and plucked. I hope the blizzard abates before we have to fly through it, an experience which unnerves me and traumatizes poor Wanga (Phil Harris). A-voom! Love, Bing."

Alice Harris arrived Wednesday, November 4. We played Scrabble, made stew, and took long walks down the lane to watch the quail feed in the cover of the pines and the fields fill with newly-arrived geese."

I received a postcard on November 9. "Only four below this morning. During the night the stove (propane gas) broke down and nearly finished us. Never saw such ducks, huns, and prairie chickens. Love, Bing."

(Much later I heard of an incident occasioned by the failure of the stove. Trapped by the blizzard, the intrepid hunters were deprived of the benefits of their outdoor privy. When one neophyte sought advice and counsel on answering the call of nature in the dead of night, drowsy voices told him to use a pan.

Fully-awakened by a torrent of curses, the erstwhile sleepers abandoned their dreams for the cabin kitchen, where they found that their comrade had had the ill-fortune to choose the colander.)

The saddle that Bing had given me for Christmas in 1955 finally made its formal debut. I rode around the ranch on a quiet old horse named Idaho, delighting in the ducks at the springs and the swans on the lake.

Bing and Phil arrived November 11. We had chukkar, biscuits, and dandelion greens for supper. On Monday, November 16, we went to the big springs and I held onto Remus and listened to the din of the geese, swans, and mallards, as Bing crawled over lava rock to spy on the birds.

We were walking across the foot bridge when miraculously a huge flight of Canada geese left the lake. Remus and I crouched in the golden hay while Bing rose and downed two honkers with as many shots. Remus, professional as ever, hauled them to his master's feet.

While the rest of the party remained at the ranch, I returned to Los Angeles to make a recruitment film on nursing, reporting to headquarters as follows:

"Dearest, Your daughter eats like Casey Tibbs coming out of chute seven in the cow-milking contest. She is alert, talkative, active,

Harry Lillis Jr. learns to hunt.

beautiful, friendly, and still bow-legged. Her double chin is a new development, and oh yes, she snores.

"The film yesterday was reasonably uneventful. Gene Nelson, the very nice director, didn't get a word in edgewise. Eddy Albert lectured us on integrity, the core of the scene, kicking it around to see what we could search out, and improvising, which he did on the lawn with body English. So I improvised my part, and he read his verbatim from the teleprompter.

"This seems as good a time as any to tell you that movies are not necessary for my happiness. Particularly since I thought I was pretty bad yesterday. I have a sneaking suspicion that I would never be competent, and we simply don't have time to find out.

"Frankly I find enough satisfaction in hunting with you. As long as you want me to share your activities, my life will be completely full, but someday people all over Texas will sigh, 'She could have been another Mansfield.' C'est la bloomin' vie. Your Kathryn."

Thus I planted the basic conflict that dogged us all our days. I thought Bing wanted me to give up my career, and so did he, but every time I plunked myself down in a domestic situation he left.

Ours was not a comfortable marriage. It was one long courtship. He would disappear for long periods, and finally return for a wildly-romantic homecoming. In the back of my mind a plot was taking shape. I would escape from him into situations where he had to pursue me, and thus ensure that the magic never died.

The Crosbys, Junior and Senior

1960

A new decade. An opportunity to give Bing ten golden years. I would accept the joyous responsibility of making him happy. He would bask in the ease and grace that I demonstrated in handling our staff and entertaining his friends. No more would he say to me "Kathryn, if you'd just keep your mouth shut, people would think you almost had good sense."

No more would he look at me, wince, rise, and say to a guest, "May I get you some more wine while my wife is busy enjoying herself?" I would make everything right with Bing and his family, and there was no time like January to start.

On the 6th I gave a birthday luau for Lindsay and thirty of his friends. Trader Vic's catered it with roast pig, ti leaves, crab crêpes with sweet and sour sauce, rice, duck, fruit, fortune cookies, a huge cake, anthurium orchids, leis for the ladies, boutonnières for the men, tiki gods, and a waterfall in the dining room.

And that was just the beginning. Bing entrusted me with the delicate mission of convincing or coercing the Immaculate Heart nuns to take over his hospital at Rising River.

Feeling that I was now his consort battleship, his friend in the faith, I flew to Rising River with Mother Humiliata, Sister Columba, and Reverend Mother Regina. We stayed at the ranch, visited Wyntoon, and rode the ski lift in horrible weather. I wish the artist Caffe had seen the sisters with their wimples askew and their veils flying in the wind, clinging to each other as we rode to the top of Mount Shasta and down again. The hospital committee was eager for them to exercise their nursing expertise. In return local citizens would build a convent, and enlarge the facilities sufficiently to make them cost-efficient.

On the 23rd of January I gave a baby shower for an expectant friend. Mike Romanoff planned the menu: grapefruit basket, sole mousse with wine sauce, artichoke hearts filled with spinach, pineapple sherbet, petits fours. There was an enormous stork on the hall table, delivering a centerpiece full of tulips, snapdragons, camellias, delphiniums, and roses.

Oddly enough Bing had escaped to Pebble Beach. I was pretty full of myself when I joined him there. I'd engineered two successful occa-

Our house on the 13th fairway at Pebble Beach

sions in two weeks, and now there was just time to change and accompany our house guests to Admiral Yeoman's cocktail party and buffet. I dressed ultra-conservatively in high neck and long sleeves, and Bing nodded casual approval.

When we arrived I stole a quick glance at him. The picture was worth a thousand words. His eyes, almost colorless in the bright light of the foyer, had opened wide in surprise, closed in intense scrutiny, then narrowed still more in concentration, as if he were trying to wish something away. The tips of his ears were beet red.

The Beverly Hills designer Jax was famous at the time for slacks that wouldn't fit anyone with the slightest ounce of avoirdupois on her derrière; and for chic man-tailored suits, with one-button jackets and straight skirts slit on the side. These were worn with sleeveless, turtleneck, silk blouses to compensate for the tuxedo-front effect.

In the middle of the cocktail party stood Dennis with his new bride Patricia, the warmest, friendliest girl I've ever known. At the moment, however, her large heart was all too visible, because she had generously elected to wear her Jax suit without the blouse.

Obviously entranced, Dennis was keeping Pat supplied with ginger ale. She, who never drank hard liquor, was intoxicated with the attention she was receiving. With her spectacular figure and golden hair peek-a-booing over one eye in the style that Veronica Lake had popularized, she made every other woman in the room pale into insignificance.

Everyone except Bing enjoyed her display tremendously. We ate two canapes and left, arriving home just in time to witness an exchange in the front room.

Sandra was brandishing the fire tongs and howling at Phillip, who was giggling in high good humor and teasing her. Leo and the cook were standing on the other side of the room, watching the contest as if it were a championship tennis match.

"Now stop it, both of you," I screamed.

They were so startled by my dog-trainer's voice that Sandra yielded up her weapon as if I were her mother. "He won't tell us where Lindsay is, and Barbara's broken-hearted," she sobbed.

"You and Phillip get to bed."

"Barbara is half-crazy. She ran outside to find Lindsay or drown herself."

"I'll find her and fix that up. You and Phillip say good night."

He tittered, put his arm around his wife, and guided her upstairs. I marched outside, wondering vaguely why I was fated to handle the problems of far-more-experienced women a head taller than I.

I called for Barbara from the front door, but my voice was lost in the wind, so I walked around the house and stood on the balcony overlooking the ocean, but then my shouts were drowned in the sound of the waves.

Nothing.

I tried the other side of the house. After a long search I finally heard what sounded like faint chanting, and there sat Barbara in an enormous garbage can. She had drunk too much wine, Lindsay had disappeared, and she was babbling about throwing herself into the ocean if she could just manage to stand up.

I helped her to bed, feeling suddenly like an elderly matron faced with Halloweeners or college fraternity pranks, and reflecting that Bing's friends at Pebble Beach were people of substance and considerable reserve. The older generation would not be amused by the flashiness of Hollywood as exemplified by Pat and Dennis, the brawling Irish drunks in the Phillip Crosby household, or the besotten distress of Lindsay's fiancée over his disappearance.

"Don't worry, Lindsay will be back soon," I soothed as I tucked Barbara in. "He's safe and sound, or the police would have called. Even if he weren't, your hysterics wouldn't help."

When I finally tiptoed into our bedroom, Bing glared at me accusingly. As our glances met we silently agreed that it was all my fault.

"You mean Lindsay wants to marry that girl? Why she's not stable. Imagine waiting for

Dixie's father with his four grandchildren and their wives: Gary and Barbara, Dennis and Pat, Phillip and Sandra, Lindsay and Barbara

Godot in a garbage can just because a fellow checks out."

Trying to make light of it I said, "Darling, you consider me stable only because you've never checked the garbage cans after your disappearances. You'll never know, will you?"

My attempt at levity fell on deaf ears. "I don't want him to get married. He's much too young. I'm going to have lunch with him next week and talk him out of all that nonsense."

"Let's not worry about it now," I sighed, bowed beneath the awesome task of mothering the whole world.

These were all innocents, I reflected, and while I was less than certain of my own recently-acquired social graces, I had just experienced the efficacy of my Attila-the-Hun attack. I might not be much, but I was all we had. Determinedly I calmed Bing until he finally went to sleep.

After considerable indecisive soul-searching, he finally set a luncheon date for a fatherly chat with Lindsay: "I'll simply make it clear that he's much too young for marriage; that he and his brothers are all ill-prepared to support wives and care for families."

"I'm sure you will, dear," I remarked absently, as I mentally started planning Lindsay's wedding.

We would this time, I decided, stage the formal ceremony that I had longed for. It would be performed at St. Paul's Catholic Church in Westwood. Afterwards we'd hold an enormous reception at Holmby Hills.

Fortunately for all concerned Bing had to leave for location on February 1. While Blake Edwards was directing him in *High Time*, I huddled with Lindsay's intended and prepared for a February 6 wedding.

Somehow Bing's mother got wind of my plans, and suddenly announced that she could not permit Lindsay to get married. Rather than tackle the matter head-on, I replied irrelevantly that I was giving her a 90th birthday party on February 7. I then began frantically phoning her children to invite them to both ceremonies. Most were delighted, but Bing's sister Catherine replied, "I won't come unless Ted is included. This has gone on long enough."

"I'm new in the family. Who's Ted?"

"He is the brother to whom Bing hasn't spoken for thirty years."

"Do you have Ted's phone number? Let me call him."

Ted said he would love to come. "It is time we all met," he added smoothly.

"Yes, isn't it," blithely assented Olive Kathryn Grandstaff Grant Crosby, MRS., BFA, Incipient RN, Incipient Credentialed Teacher, and Perennial April Fool.

When Bing phoned on February 5 to tell me what plane he'd arrive on the following day, I mentioned casually that we would be having a wedding and a birthday party, and that the whole family was coming: Everett, Catherine, Bob, Larry, Ted, and Mary Rose. (Cleverly throwing Ted's name into the midst of the pack so that it might escape immediate notice.)

Contrary to my expectation, it served as a lightning rod. Mother and son were forgotten in the ensuing explosion.

"You did what? Kathryn, some things aren't to be meddled with, and that's one of them. You had no right to ask that man to my home. He did something that I can never forgive. I have not discussed it with you, and I don't intend to, but you had no right." He slammed down the phone.

That was twice that I had been screamed at unjustly by a Crosby. The first time, some part of my mind knew that Gary wasn't dealing with me personally. He was screaming at the world, and I just happened to be around. I doubt that he was ever conscious of the fact that I was the recipient of his drunken curses.

But this time I was definitely the target. I had overstepped all bounds, meddling in Bing's family business and intruding into an area where I had no authority. I had displeased him enormously, and there was no way out. I drowned my sorrows in preparation for the parties.

That same night I held a wedding-rehearsal dinner at Perino's for which Gary played host.

Catherine Harrigan Crosby, surrounded by her seven living children and assorted spouses at her 90th birthday party

I hope it went well. Through it all I sat in a daze, wrapped in horrible forebodings.

The next morning I attended 6:30 mass, then inspected the house to reassure myself that the battleground was spotless. I was dressed to the nines in my favorite beige ensemble, with a three-quarter length coat, mink cuffs, and mink cloche hat, ready to drive to the wedding when a taxi pulled up in front of the house.

"Kathryn, what are you doing?"

"I'm just leaving for the church. Would you like to go with me?"

Bing looked at me strangely. "It's two o'clock in the afternoon. You did remember that my plane was arriving at 11:30?"

"Plane?" I inquired blankly. Oh yes, before he had screamed at me Bing had made it quite clear that I was to pick him up at the airport. Thereafter I'd blanked out on the entire conversation. He now became so preoccupied with trying to understand my weird behavior that he hardly noticed the drive to St. Paul's church or the subsequent ceremony.

Barbara and Lindsay had taken charge of the guest list, and though some of Bing's show-business friends were invited, most of the young people were strangers to me. The house was full of picture taking, and other taking: From the hall powder room alone we lost flowers, perfume, vases, combs and brushes, guest towels, soaps, picture frames, silver bonbon dishes, lipsticks, boxes of powder, eyebrow pencils, mascara, rouge, Murine, and the mirrored Kleenex boxes. But I seemed to have regained my still-bemused husband, so the price was right.

On Sunday, February 7, Catherine Harrigan Crosby, her seven children, and their respective spouses attended 11 o'clock mass. Back at the house, the Queen Mother hauled me upstairs and announced in accents worthy of Elizabeth I, "I'm not going down there. That man is in the living room."

I must have been participating in Bing's state of shock because I asked innocently, "What man?"

"Ted. His behavior brought on my husband's death. I will not speak to him."

Inspired by her regal demeanor, I in turn drew myself up to my full five feet four (half an inch taller than my adversary) and proclaimed, "Mrs. Crosby, that man is your son, so you are coming down to the living room. You remain the head of this house, and you will behave like the lady that you are."

She looked at me appraisingly and finally negotiated. "All right, but I won't talk to him."

I gave her the last word and my good right arm as we majestically descended the stairs. No sooner had we entered the living room than the front doorbell rang. Doubtless another ostracized relative. And I had to keep my lion-tamer act going!

"God help me," I groaned as I raced disaster to the door. After a few moments of silent but fervent prayer, I finally flung the portal wide and faced a curious *deus ex machina* in the form of a portly cherub, who turned out to be Father Patrick Payton, originator of *The Rosary Hour*.

"God love ya, Kathryn. It seems you've had a wedding in the family, so I wanted to drop by and say hello to everybody. And is Mrs. Senior really ninety years old today?"

We walked down the hall. Yesterday's lilies of the valley had been changed to bright red roses. Starting at dawn my friends from *Flower Fashions* had wound them up the stairway, placed long-stemmed ones in enormous vases on the table in the front hall, and filled the living room with them.

Drawing his inspiration from his favorite flower, my savior faced the assembled fighting Crosbys and beamed, "Well, God bless ya all. It's wonderful to join ya on such a happy occasion. Everybody on your knees now. We will say a decade of the rosary."

After a moment's stunned silence the family hit the deck. As the murmur of prayers rose heavenward, I could feel the unity of childhood returning to hitherto-estranged siblings. My own prayers were idiosyncratic: "Don't let Mrs. Senior blow up. Don't let Bing freeze me out for meddling. Please help me replace the stolen

Playing hooky at The Winter Olympics

With *High Time* co-star Nicole Maurey

powder-room furnishings before Bing notices, and if that doesn't use up all my credits. . . ."

At the end of the rosary we found that we were all holding hands. Lindsay's marriage was now his problem. Mrs. Senior had forgotten him and all other children but her own. After all she had reared five sons and two daughters. They constituted her contribution to the world, and now, at 90, she was finally prepared to rest on it. Bing meanwhile was in the throes of some sort of religious illumination that I wouldn't have dreamed of disturbing.

Father Payton disappeared as simply and as quickly as he had come, and we never heard from him again. In retrospect I'm sure he was a particularly fortunate aspect of my guardian angel.

For the next few days he must have been active in various other guises, because Bing accepted the wedding as a *fait accompli* and returned to location without a further word about Ted, Mrs. Senior purred like a kitten, and the newlyweds were ecstatic.

I opened in *King Lear* at Immaculate Heart College on February 18. On February 20 Bing simply jumped ship and went to Squaw Valley with Buster and Stevie Collier. I thought that if he were going to go somewhere he should have come home to watch me emote, but apparently he preferred the Winter Olympics to my amateurish histrionics.

On Tuesday Bing returned to the set of *High Time*, and Blake Edwards took him to task in front of the assembled company. "That's the least professional thing I can imagine. We were all waiting to work on Saturday. You have wasted three days for the entire cast and crew. Why didn't you at least come back so we could shoot on Monday?"

Bing's innocent blue eyes gazed soulfully back at his director: "But Blake, there I was trapped in a broom closet with twenty-nine gypsies and a hot guitar. What could I do?" The star shrugged his shoulders and slouched back to his canvas chair to await the next scene.

Blake confided, "I've been a writer all my life, and that is the single funniest line I've ever heard. Imagine! 'Trapped in a broom closet with twenty-nine gypsies and a hot guitar.' It defused me completely, and sent the whole company right back to work."

Bing's absence afforded me an opportunity to conspire with his sons' wives to form a family social circle. Previously I had availed myself of every opportunity to escape from the burden of preparing meals. Hence each trip for Bing had meant instant weight loss for Kathryn.

But now Sandy, Pat, and I began organizing a new pattern of Crosby living, starting with Sundays at home. On the first one after Bing's return, Sandy and Phil arrived bright and early with asparagus and beans. Pat and Dennis brought salad and French bread. I fixed a ham. Harland Svare, a friend of the boys, joined us with a date and a football. Gary brought the ice cream. Harry, Mary Frances, Dennis Jr., and Phillip's daughter Dixie Lee tumbled around in the sunny back yard with half-a-dozen delighted Labradors.

Bing basked in one of the lawn chairs, threw a few footballs, and seemed happy in his new role of resident patriarch, demonstrating an easy rapport with all his children and grandchildren. Thus I was all the more surprised when my supposedly newly-domesticated spouse suddenly announced that the party was over, and that he was leaving immediately. While the clan scattered, I packed posthaste and shared the drive to Palm Desert, where he practiced golf for two days and visited with Phil Harris and Alice Faye.

On the way back, he brought up the subject of household expenses in general and florist's bills in particular. I had to admit that I had exceeded all limits in the wildly extravagant mood of the wedding and birthday parties. Contritely I promised to mend my ways, and started immediately by skimping on our menus.

At first Bing accepted his Spartan fare without comment, but after I served Nicole Morey, his leading lady in *High Time*, a shrimp creole that would have disgraced a TV dinner, he finally exploded.

When I noted that Nicole had been so

Pat, Sandra, and little Dixie Lee Crosby

The winners of the Pro-Am at the Seminole Country Club

wrapped up in him that she would have cheerfully ingested rattlesnake topped with fried ants, he departed in high dudgeon for New York, leaving me to play hostess at another Sunday gathering, which it was now too late to cancel.

When he returned, it was only to face another crisis: "You know what's happening, don't you? That radical Ronald Reagan has called our first actors' strike. There's now no way to finish the movie."

"Yes, but it will soon be over. Then you'll all go back to work."

"Perhaps, but I can't stand all this waiting around. Let's head for Palm Beach, Jamaica, the Masters, whatever."

My mind, which had been wondering vaguely if there might be a call for scab labor after all the real actors had walked out, suddenly snapped to attention. My husband had definitely employed the plural form *Let's*. What was mere thespian glory compared to this? In a trice I was stuffing suitcases with anything handy.

Too late! Bing was already at the door, muttering something about "going on ahead to get things organized."

Nothing daunted I clung to that blessed plural, even stretching it a bit to make it include Harry, who flew off to Florida with me to catch up with Bing and watch him team with Gardner Dickinson to win the Pro-Am at the Seminole Country Club.

This called for a celebration at Chris Dunphy's, who admitted, while serving "an amusing little wine," that he'd hidden the good stuff in the cellar. Perhaps, but not from my Nimrod, who ferreted it out so successfully that we were soon translated to the Celebrity Room, with Bing promoted to featured member of the Marshall Grant Quintet. His consort, who was born drunk, joined him in *Sometimes I'm Happy*, until the precarious duet was mercifully drowned in a session of deep-down jazz that led to some mad twirling about the floor and lasted till 6 a.m.

When I awoke the following afternoon, Bing was already off to the links. As I stumbled out the front door of the bridal suite, I heard an ominous click behind me.

"Strange," I thought. "That lock wasn't set."

Gazing blearily through the slats of the Venetian blinds, I discovered the source of the problem. My first-born had given the initial evidence of what would later prove to be a phenomenal mechanical aptitude, by tottering to the door after me and resolutely turning the lock.

No problem. I would simply coax him to turn it back. And coax I did while Harry practiced throwing glasses, smashing lamps, and coyly playing peek-a-boo, all the while smiling angelically in serene security, proof against my threats of reprisal.

Finally six good men and true disassembled the door, and I initiated operation cleanup, meanwhile prophesying a dim future for my diminutive psychopath.

"Just wait till I get you alone," I muttered, but all in vain because Harry had taken the elementary precaution of leaving with the workmen. So when I finally caught up with him, he was safely surrounded by fresh admirers.

Thence to Round Hill, a development in Jamaica some 20 minutes from Montego Bay. There Harry seized his opportunity while his old used mother was luxuriating on the beach. Abandoning the sand for the good and sufficient reason that it tickled his toes, he observed a passing ebony lady with a basket on her head. He approached her with his most winsomely famished expression, was rewarded with a banana, and immediately embarked upon a career of mendicancy which led inevitably to other ladies with larger baskets.

When I finally caught up with him, he was rolling in the dust and loudly lamenting the agonies which an unjust Providence had visited upon him. Surrounding him were the skins of a dozen tropical fruits which, like the dusky circle of attendant Jamaicans, served as mute witnesses of his sundry crimes.

Vocal they became, however, (the Jamaicans, not the fruit skins) when his unworthy

Golfing with Jamaican hosts and Bill Paley, who is on the right

mother appeared on the scene, and then departed in some haste, burdened down with the shame of being unable to feed or guard such an engaging child. And that time he really did get it, collywobbles or no.

Bill Paley of CBS had discovered Bing and given him his first radio contract. His gorgeous wife Barbara, the pride of *Women's Wear Daily*, invited us to a Jamaican beach party which featured suckling pig and Lillian Hellman. I was, of course, fascinated by the aging playwright, but my husband's highly-developed moral sense was offended by the presence of her young lover. So I hung upon her every word at one end of the long picnic table, while he spent the evening at the other end, flirting with the exotic Mrs. Pringle, wife of Round Hill's developer.

It was on Jamaica that I had my first confrontation with Bing's heretofore secret vice. Since I blush to introduce it, let him reveal all in the following words from his diary:

Monday, March 28, 1960

"Beautiful day, fair round, 77 with two lost balls. After lunch a full tour of residential sites. Believe I'll buy lots 2 and 8, right on the beach without too much surf."

Notations like this were to haunt me for 20 years of marriage. Bing travelled constantly, and every trip had its inevitable sequel of plot plans, architects' drawings, contracts of sale, and visits from starry-eyed realtors.

Imagine, if you will, what all this meant to a would-be housekeeper, who with all the will in the world had yet to dust the furniture, replace the ruined rugs, or paint the walls of her principal residence in Los Angeles, not to mention totally-neglected second, third, and fourth homes in Palm Desert, Pebble Beach, and Rising River. Why oh why had she married a raving housophiliac?

Fortunately for all concerned, the elements came to my rescue like the proverbial marines. Witness this entry in Bing's diary on March 30, the day of our departure from Jamaica:

"Beautiful morning, but the same could have been said of yesterday, whose waning hours brought the most terrifying downpour I've ever seen or imagined. A raging torrent cascaded down the road to Round Hill and tore out 30 feet of lovely, sandy beach. Apparently you can be watching the Jamaican waves one moment, and be part of them the next."

Exit one helpless helpmate, breathing an enormous sigh of relief. In point of fact our exodus had been precipitated by a macabre incident involving a cuckolded husband, who surprised his wife and her lover in the rented Princess Lichtenstein's cottage the preceding afternoon. As it later transpired, the lothario, an airlines representative, had been dallying amorously and recklessly all over the North Jamaican coast.

On this occasion he had courted not only a dusky local lovely, but also imminent peril to life and limb. The severe beating which the powerful husband administered sent its victim straightway to the hospital.

While the whole colony was buzzing with excitement that evening, Bing was expressing his disgust with gossips and sympathy for the betrayed husband. When the latter drove off a cliff during the night, my prudish bigger half decided to remove me from the snares of decadent Jamaican society.

Our next stop was the Masters golf tournament, during which we stayed in Aiken, South Carolina, some 30 miles from Augusta. The antebellum tone of society there made me regret my immediate forebears' translation from Southeast to Southwest. The practical results were that I was always in doubt as to which of six spoons to use, and couldn't ride to hounds worth a lick. I just wasn't at home in a world of liveried butlers and shad-roe mousse, and it showed, damn it, it showed.

Determined to make Bing proud of me, or in any event less ashamed, I spent long afternoons learning just how to spoon in tea leaves or take a spirited hunter over a hurdle. I must admit, however, that to this day polo remains something of a mystery to me.

Meanwhile Bing, who had hardly been born to the purple himself, chatted with these

Checking Arnold Palmer's round on the scoreboard at the Masters

scions of "the best families" as casually as he would with the boys in Phil Harris's band, while in spite of my lip service to decorum, I remained breathless at the sight of Mr. Ambrose Clarke, who had refused to let the streets of Aiken be paved lest they spoil his horses' hooves, descending regally from his coach and four.

We returned to the 20th century only for the Masters itself, where our friends split up to follow their favorites, most of them joining the galleries of Hogan, Snead, Julius Boros, Gary Player, or the chubby twenty-year-old amateur champion, a new face named Jack Nicklaus. But Bing, who had put all his money on Arnold Palmer, asssured me that only Ken Venturi could threaten his favorite, and it was they whom we followed right through the last day when Palmer, with one of his miraculous finishes, edged out Venturi by a single stroke.

And now the time has come to disclose still another of the Crosby family's guilty secrets, which I have kept locked within my breast lo these many years. Wild horses couldn't have torn it from me during Bing's lifetime, but now I need no longer change the names in my narrative to protect the guilty, and confession, so they say, is good for the soul.

Without further preamble here is the bitter truth. Crooning was just a sideline for my husband. We actually lived off his golf winnings, which he derived mainly from hustling based on his own game, which was invariably superlative when the chips were down, but also from his uncanny knack for picking winners at occasions like the Masters. A sadder but wiser accomplice, I now understood the true reason for the glum looks that accompanied our departure with all the loot.

Back home in Los Angeles, I busily drowned the Scotch in Bing's drinks, burned his lamb chops, steamed his asparagus within an inch of its life, detinned his fruit salad, and served the results on a TV tray, while he watched the fights, and his two children nodded off to sleep on the big down cushions of the sofa.

It was a scene to warm the cockles of a mother's heart, but it seemed slightly less efficacious with fathers. In any event the one who concerned me most abandoned my new drill for Palm Springs ere 48 hours had passed. Was he simply proof against all the charms of domesticity, or did the coward fear ptomaine?

The next day I ruined five consecutive plates of E-coli bacteria in the lab at Immaculate Heart. "Is something troubling you?" Sister Damian Marie inquired.

Why hadn't I thought of it myself? This was definitely the time to seek counsel from a spiritual adviser, however incongruous it might seem to do so over a Bunsen burner. "It's my husband," I told her. "He packed and left for Palm Springs yesterday without a parting word."

"Had you done something to offend him?"

I reflected on how my parting instructions to the housekeeper had resulted in the removal of the gold finish from our antique lamps. "Clean as a whistle now," she'd remarked proudly.

A thousand other peccadillos crossed my mind in rapid succession. "Yes," I admitted, "it's just possible that I did."

"Well, then, you must fly straight off to see him. After all, it's Saturday and you don't have to slave away here."

I grabbed the first plane out, and arrived in Palm Springs just after noon. Leo drove me to the house where, having forgotten to pack my textbooks, I listened to records and practiced piano until 4 p.m., a time when Bing should certainly have arrived home. Worried at his absence, I phoned Thunderbird and was informed in icy tones that Mr. Crosby was in *The Snake Pit*, the inner sanctum where male golfers played cards after their rounds.

"Well, call him out."

"Is this an emergency, Madame?"

"If you don't get him right now, it's going to be."

After an eternity of waiting I finally heard Bing's very annoyed voice, and affected a casual tone: "What took you so long?"

"I finally had a winning hand."

Bing's shots were looking very odd.

"Oh, had you been losing?"

"Yes, my streak of recent disasters at the gaming tables would indicate that I'm due to be all-too-lucky in love."

"If you'll just drop all that nonsense and come home, I think I can practically guarantee it."

"Sorry, I need to practice my golf."

"But I flew down here just to surprise you."

"And you succeeded beyond your wildest expectations."

"Great. What would you like me to fix for dinner?"

"I'm a patient man, but there are limits to even my endurance." He hung up.

Bing finally arrived at 8, and took me out to a grim and silent dinner. In the absence of entertainment, I made domestic notes: "Hubby doesn't like surprises, and at the moment is less than fond of wife, her cooking, her idle chatter, perhaps even her agile brain. Nonetheless she will persevere."

And so it was that I passed up a wonderful opportunity to rush back to Los Angeles.

After 7:30 mass the next morning we had breakfast at Eldorado, where I spent the rest of the day somberly watching Bing hit thousands of balls off the practice tee. For the first five or six hours I was sunk so deep in my private misery that I took no notice of external reality. When I finally emerged from my cocoon, I remarked to my surprise that Bing's shots were looking very odd. They were flying high, low, left, right, and indeed in every direction except that of the flag at which he was presumably aiming.

On closer inspection, I observed that the lovely, effortless rhythm of his swing had disintegrated into a wild sway away from the ball, followed by a desperate and ineffective lunge in its general direction. At long last I had penetrated directly into the heart of the mystery. For the first time since I had known him, Bing's golf game was off.

Deprived of its center, his life had lost all meaning. Until normalcy could be restored, such peripheral phenomena as food, drink, women, children, and career were felt only as intolerable annoyances which served to distract a man from the true purpose of life. Paranoid as I was, I had attributed to my experience an importance which it simply didn't possess. Certain that I was the hub of Bing's world, I had assumed that if he was angry, it must be with me.

First things first. I had learned the grim lesson that a mere woman cannot compete with golf for a man's affections. (Though Bing did confide once, in a moment of supreme tenderness, that he liked me better than basketball.) Relieved but saddened, I summoned Leo to drive me to the airport. So much for advice from celibate nuns on marital problems. All the consolations of religion would never compete with one sub-par round. Ah well, back to the biology lab.

And there I remained until May 2 when Bing returned from Palm Springs. He seemed to have forgotten that it was his birthday, but I had ordered an enormous global map of the world from Neiman Marcus for his study. I wrapped it before rushing off to school. On my return I decorated a huge birthday cake, filled the house with flowers, and supervised the preparation of a sumptuous repast, which I was careful not to ruin with any finishing touches from my own delicate little hands.

Since I didn't know where Bing was, I could only await his arrival—which I eagerly did from 5 p.m. to 6, 7, 8, 9, 10, and finally 11, at which point I left his cake on the table in the front hall, with a note indicating that he would find his birthday dinner in the oven. I never did learn where he'd been. After the failure of my unanticipated visit to Palm Springs, I suppose I should have known enough not to undertake a surprise party. I resolved in the future to warn him well in advance of the advent of his birthday.

Contrary to the adage, for a time thereafter the path of true love did seem to run smooth, perhaps because Bing was spending his days on the set of *High Time* while I destroyed specimens and apparatus in the bacteriology lab. I did wonder occasionally whether he just

La belle Bing trips the light fantastic.

might not be hinting at something when he spoke of "poor abandoned infants" as I waved my books at our cherubs and dashed for the door, but I was much too busy for morbid introspective brooding.

One evening Bing invited me to join him on the set, observing enigmatically that I might find it colorful. I arrived in blue jeans, only to discover that the cast was in evening gowns and tuxedos. Feeling embarrassed amid all the elegance, I was stumbling about the elaborately-decorated stage looking for an exit, when I chanced upon the moon of my delight, supposedly involved in a fraternity initiation stunt. While I watched he finished shooting, took his place in a camp chair, crossed his legs, and lit his pipe.

A familiar scene, nicht wahr? Nein, meine Herren, for the legs were clad in gorgeous nylons, the derrière in the canvas seat was wearing a hoop skirt, the torso was half covered with an off-the-shoulder, full-busted bodice, and the blue eyes peered forth from under absurd false eyelashes and a long, blond wig. From time to time America's sweetheart absently waved the pipe smoke away with a perfectly darling fan. The gays had queued up three ranks deep, but Bing seemed happily oblivious of all but his own discomfort.

"How in hell do you stand these waist-pincher things?" he offered in lieu of greeting.

"*Cincher*, dearest," I corrected as I wiped the tears from my eyes.

He waved an evening paper. "And this just hit the streets. What will mother say?" He pointed to a front-page study of *la belle Bing* in full drag.

Personally I couldn't wait to find out, so I relieved him of the publication, lit out for home, and raced upstairs to say good night to Mrs. Senior.

"Have you seen the evening paper?" was my opening ploy.

"I never bother with the silly thing."

"Well, here's a picture that might interest you. Take a good look."

Obediently she held the paper up to a strong light and studied it attentively. Finally she nodded solemnly and observed, "You're quite right. I think I used to know this woman."

On Friday morning, May 27, Bing remarked at breakfast, "You've been staying at school later and later these past weeks."

"I'm trying to get through bacteriology as fast as possible. This way I can do two or three experiments a day."

"Well, see that you're home and ready to leave for Santa Barbara at 3 this afternoon."

"Yes, dear," I purred. I do so love strong, masterful men, especially when they tell me just what I want to hear.

Before leaving for school I was packed to the gunwales, and organized within an inch of my spiked heels, but as it transpired I blew it anyway.

I came screeching up to the back of the house at exactly 3:21. Since this constituted a genuine triumph for anyone with my time sense, I at first refused to believe that the taillights which I saw disappearing down the front drive belonged to Bing's Rolls. Forced to accept the evidence of my eyes, I then tried to chase the car, following it all the way down to Wilshire before losing it in afternoon traffic and finally recognizing my defeat.

Returning home, I crawled slowly up the stairs to my bedroom, gazed somberly at the neatly-packed bags in the corner, shed my skirt and sweater on the floor, crawled in under the covers, and howled.

When I paused long enough to hear myself think, I envisioned chartering a plane for Santa Barbara and greeting Bing on his arrival, but this couldn't fail to be an expensive shock for a man who hated surprises. Speaking of which, I am sure it will come as a great revelation to you that I have no vocation for tragedy. My grief is not of the type that sweeps nations in its wake. When I mourn my nose runs, my eyes swell shut, I sniffle horribly, and I become very, very tired.

I was certain that I had ruined my entire future life, and I was soberly reflecting upon this fact, and envisioning myself coolly and authoritatively cutting Bing to ribbons if he called to

An early duet with Mary Frances

apologize, when I was awakened briefly by the sound of my own snoring. Bravely facing the fact that, when it comes to *hauteur*, I am something of a Labrador puppy, I rolled over and hid my head beneath the pillow.

It was some hours later that the phone roused me and I answered before I was fully awake: "Hello darling, I followed you all the way to Westwood."

"You're always late, and I had to get in a practice round at the Valley Club."

"Of course, dearest," I yawned.

There was a lengthy pause while Bing waited for the inevitable explosion, a cutting remark, or perhaps even an excuse. He was rewarded for this tactical blunder by a gentle, contented snore.

"Have I wakened you?" he asked in disbelief, since the time was still only late afternoon.

No answer.

"Have I wakened you?" he shouted at the top of his lungs.

"Um hum."

"Somehow I get the feeling that I'm talking in your sleep. I guess I'll call back later."

As an inveterate insomniac, Bing had a religious reverence for repose, which conquered whatever resentment he may have felt at my snoring in his ear. But he had received a clear insight into the impossibility of competing with Morpheus for his inamorata's attention.

An hour later Bing tried again. The eleventh ring actually awakened me, and I managed to concentrate long enough to hear the words "I've arranged for Leo to drive you here."

"Fine," I agreed blearily. "Make it late tomorrow morning."

Bing played well in the tournament the next day, we danced divinely at the club that night, and I carefully refrained from asking why he had left me in the lurch. He never did explain his behavior, but I knew when I was well off.

Shooting on *High Time* concluded on June 15. Now that his work was done, Bing was delighted with the prospect of Mexico. I was equally excited but without due cause, for he flew south of the border without me.

Returning three weeks later, tanned, laughing, rested, and enormously pleased with himself, he observed that the children were healthy, his mother was doing a splendid job of managing the house unaided, and his wife was very much at loose ends. "Want to go to Canada?" he asked dubiously.

Consolidating my gain before he thought to retract the offer, I determined to earn my passage. "Shall I pack for you, dear?"

Bing jumped as if an accompanist had chosen the wrong key. I could see that he was already regretting his impetuous offer. "Nothing for me and very little for you," he snapped, "and this time we leave promptly."

That we did in a friend's private plane, which flew us directly to Calgary, where an enormous crowd waited at the airport to cheer Bing while the loudspeakers played *Where the Blue of the Night meets the Gold of the Day*. The next hours passed in a blur of excitement as we rode in the parade, played games on the midway, thrilled to the action in the rodeo, and watched our host's horse win at the races.

Then we drove off to Banff Springs with Phil Harris and Alice Faye in a convertible with the top down. Since I wore my hair in a chignon, I was able to ignore the tempest and appreciate the scenery, but Alice's initially beautifully coifed blonde hairdo soon looked as if it had been prepared in a Mixmaster.

Once again I envisioned a honeymoon in a world apart, and predictably I was again consigned to the role of golf widow. Left to my own devices, I repaired to the local zoo, where I contemplated the brown bears, mountain goats, and native varieties of deer, and inquired about conditions of employment, offering as my motivation the fact that one could get so much closer to animals than to certain humans.

Back in Calgary I shouted myself hoarse at the chuck-wagon races, while Bing received an elegant bronze sculpture by Charles Beale and sang *It had to be You* to the assembled multitude. I walked in on the second chorus, which he sang directly to me to the delight of the throng.

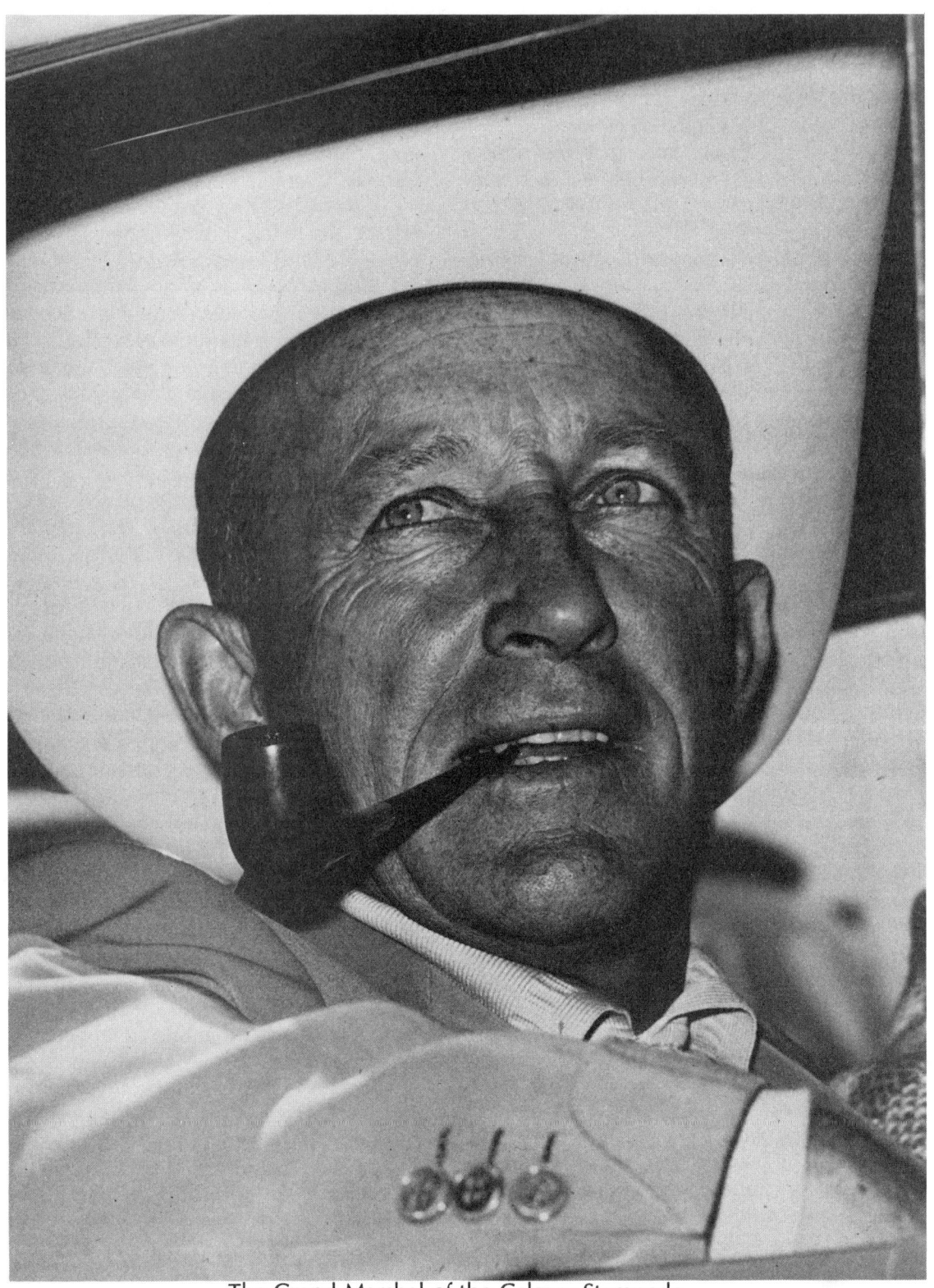
The Grand Marshal of the Calgary Stampede

For a time I thought I'd pinned my butterfly, but upon our return to the States Bing forsook the joys of domesticity for the Bohemian Grove, his ranch at Rising River, and finally the charms of salmon fishing in the country around Seattle.

When he finally phoned, he mentioned in an aside toward the end of the conversation that we were going to the Olympics in Rome.

"But I'm supposed to start my nurse's training in September."

"We're going to Rome."

"I'll ask for a leave of absence."

The Franciscan sisters would cheerfully have mailed Olive Kathryn Grandstaff back to West Columbia, but of course they could refuse nothing to "Father O'Malley." So they decided that I might be able to catch up with my class with some extra work and tutoring.

I also turned down a movie for Columbia which would have paid $50,000, a considerable sum for a contract player in those days. "My husband," I loftily informed the studio, "is taking me away from all this."

At the time said husband was writing letters of this ilk: "Wonderful weather, but miserable salmon fishing. Lots of clams, crabs, halibut, cod, and bass, but no salmon. We have visited our favorite haunts, sent the planes spotting up and down the coast, bribed the natives, all to no avail. Even the commercial fishermen are in bad shape this year. They are denouncing the Russians and Japanese for depleting the fish supply in the Aleutians."

What woman could be blamed for abandoning the snares and delusions of worldly grandeur for a man whose prose could scale such romantic heights? Forsaking his faithless fish, he finally returned to whisk me off to Europe.

Studio tours had offered my only previous experience with organized travel. Columbia Pictures had trained me to show up in hairdressing at 6 a.m., and spend the ensuing twelve hours following precise, direct orders. The assistant director told me where to go, the script told me what to say, and the director told me how to say it. The union determined when I should eat, and the studio driver deposited me at my hotel.

Bing, on the other hand, was fortunate that he could sing, because he would never have qualified for a post as tour guide. He relied completely on travel agents to make all arrangements, somehow osmosed them himself, and communicated nothing at all. As a consequence I was faced with constant surprises involving taxis, plane and hotel reservations, apartment rentals, tickets for the theater, golf games, hunting trips, luncheon and dinner dates. Bing had indicated that it wouldn't be dull, and that was one promise that he really kept.

We received a thunderous welcome on our arrival in London, and were greeted warmly by the British press. We were then swept off to a suite at Claridge's, where I somehow felt that I should be reading a script and memorizing my lines. Instead of rushing off to wardrobe, my chore on this trip was to unpack for Bing and accompany him to his tailor's.

Our pictures were taken for an album cover. We toured Buckingham Palace, watched the changing of the guard with a group of other tourists, wandered through Westminster Abbey, St James, and Berkeley Square, and finally visited Bing's friend, Ambassador Whitney.

Unfortunately, upon our return a photographer caught Bing practicing chip shots into the brass cuspidor in the hall outside the door. While Claridge's allowed us to conclude our visit, never again did they have available space when Bing applied for a room reservation.

Bing had always enjoyed hawk-like vision, but now, at the age of 56, his arms had suddenly become too short for close work. He hated the thought of glasses, and had hitherto avoided them, but the problem became acute on a trip. The unaccustomed noises in strange hotel rooms aggravated his lifelong insomnia, so he habitually lay awake till 3 a.m., reading and listening to my heavy breathing.

He finally decided that the solution might lie in a pair of spectacles with Ben Franklin-style

Before Buckingham Palace

half lenses, which would permit him to see his fingernails without detriment to his excellent distance vision.

After a lengthy search involving half the optometrists in London, Bing arrived with just the pair he wanted, and promptly lost them. He returned to the source, bought another pair, and lost them.

By the time the third pair arrived I was becoming familiar with the drill, and had the good sense to keep an eye on him. It became apparent that the problem was more psychological than physical. He didn't have the habit of glasses, hated the things, and absent-mindedly removed them and dropped them at any opportunity. Not regarding himself as a wearer of spectacles, he couldn't imagine that they were his, and simply abandoned them.

I resolved the problem by attaching them around his neck with an elastic cord, a stopgap solution which made Bing protest that he felt like a little boy whose mother had tied his mittens on.

Upon our return home I purchased 30 pairs of spectacles to his prescription, and scattered them throughout his several houses, so that help was always at hand when he needed it. This worked well enough on his own premises, but he never did acquire the habit of carrying glasses, and was constantly at a loss for them when we traveled. I finally adopted the expedient of tucking them into the glove compartments of his various cars and carrying them in my purses.

On September 2 we landed in Rome. Terrified by the wild assaults of Italian newsmen, I promptly decided that the proper position for a Latin wife was behind her husband, preferably about 30 feet behind. To my amazement, Bing laughingly rose to the occasion with a splendid TV speech in an idiolect of his own invention based on Jesuit Latin, which he obviously considered to be simply old Italian. I, who had been feeling useless, had thought that I might at least serve as an interpreter on the basis of my Spanish, and now even that faint hope went aglimmering.

Random chance vouchsafed us an apartment that was a cool, white, marble haven from the noisy activity of the Roman streets, a welcome contrast to the excitement of the games. While Bing went off to see some of the running events, I unpacked, explained the necessity of silence to the bewildered household staff in my inimitable Spanish, and unearthed and consigned to the garden several potentially noisy crickets. I further discovered that by closing the bedroom shutters I could achieve total darkness, and congratulated myself upon being a paragon of a wife, the answer to any insomniac's prayer.

I have been told that I shall doubtless miss the last trump if the Deity has the ill luck to schedule the Second Coming in the wee hours of the morning, but the subsequent 6 a.m. explosion knocked even me right out of bed. Staggering windowward, I bumped into another blind clawing creature, and together we finally managed to fling open the wooden shutters. In the first light of a lovely Italian dawn we solemnly watched the campanile, not ten yards away, peal out the Angelus for all of Rome.

When it was over, I could tell that Bing's lips were moving, but couldn't distinguish a word that he said. As I slowly recovered my hearing, I found that he was repeating with patient firmness, his deep bass morning tones rumbling through the soprano of bird song, "Kathryn, as you know I am a very light sleeper. I never close my eyes before 2 a.m. on a trip, and I must have quiet in the morning."

I was so dazed that I promised to see to it, and had a wild vision of myself swinging from a clapper and howling, "The Angelus shall not ring this morn."

After gazing in dismay at what the establishment called breakfast, Bing diffidently suggested grocery shopping. I assented with alacrity. Here was my opportunity to demonstrate just what a little Heloise of a housewife he really had. I had finally found my role in life: I would be interpreter and purchasing agent for Bing Crosby Enterprises in Rome.

"Tomate, por favor."

Three coins in the fountain

A blank stare from the fat, bald proprietor of the small grocery store.

"Jugo de manzana," spoken slowly and clearly as to a deficient child.

An expectant smile from fatso, but no resultant activity. Great Jupiter, chief deity of all the Roman pantheon, had I failed again?

Bing's pained look showed that it was no more than he had expected. It was obviously time for his number, so he stepped on stage with some more Jesuit Latin.

A look of mild apprehension crossed our host's face, and I wondered vaguely what Bing might have said.

Nothing daunted, my brave hubby now tried his own private brand of French, salted with a few English words in a peculiar Southern accent. To this day I am unaware of what lay behind his reasoning, and can only suppose that he had a vague association of romantic Latins and tropic climes. In any event he fared worse than I, for he was rewarded by a look of frank alarm which made me fear that we might soon be explaining ourselves to the police.

Casting desperately about, my eye lit upon a pyramid of cans with gorgeous ripe tomatoes on the labels. Victory! I seized the top one, searched out the legend on the back, and crowed, "It's *pomodoro!*"

Suddenly Bing and I were little children in a candy store. We raced about looking for familiar pictures, and bought enough canned goods to last a year. On the way home I even determined that apple juice was *succo di mele*.

I have my faults, and sometimes I even acknowledge them, but I did not engage our chauffeur. It was in a bar that Bing had stumbled across the only Italian drunk or courageous enough to claim that he could drive the enormous complimentary station wagon which had been shipped over for our use by the Oldsmobile Division of General Motors. After the first trial run, it looked as if someone had been breaking it in with an axe.

On the way back from Wilma Rudolph's splendid victories, we crashed spectacularly into the back of an inoffensive truck. After much shouting and exchanging of identifications, we resumed our lethal pace until I finally plucked up sufficient courage to remonstrate with our maniac's employer.

"You have a wife and children and a house in the country," I began. "You're too young to die."

"It's hard to find a good driver in Italy. They just don't understand hydromatics over here."

"Are they all blind, deaf, and suicidal?"

"Why can't you be a good sport like Stevie?" (A girl from San Francisco who was riding with us.)

"Sport my ass!" snorted our chic friend. "I'm smiling only because I just figured out three foolproof ways to murder that crazy son-of-a-bitch before he finally does me in."

I returned to the fray. "I know that this car is too large for the Roman streets, so I can understand our difficulties in traffic jams, and even an occasional dent or scrape, but the way this man attacks parked cars on both sides of the road, we'll soon have no fenders left to crease. This morning, when Stevie and I taxied to meet you, the whole trip took only ten minutes. It's half an hour when we're lucky with our wonderful guide."

As usual Bing acknowledged the truth of my complaints with bemused equanimity, just as he accepted the terrible knocking in the engine after he had paid for the highest-test Italian gasoline. Face-to-face confrontations with offensive employees didn't suit his style. I too would probably have remained silent if the villain hadn't lurched into traffic with a jolt the day before, when I was juggling an armload of packages and had only one leg in the car.

And so we spent yet another week riding to our deaths through the lovely streets of Rome, and gaily cheered Livio Berruti to Italy's first gold medal. On Sunday I solemnly awarded us purple hearts and insisted on a day of rest and recreation, which we celebrated by a long, leisurely walking tour through the city. On September 9 Monsignor Ryan, the Secretary of State for the Vatican, guided us through the Sistine Chapel and Vatican City.

At the Vatican

Il Ristorante Bing Crosby in Florence

After an audience with Pope John XXIII Bing wrote to his mother: "The pope is a wonderful man with a fine sense of humor, who treats visitors as if they're all from his home town. He had something personal to say to each of the twenty people at our audience, blessed us all, and sent you a special message which I will convey when we arrive. On September 20 he is going to say his rosary for your intentions. Don't forget the date."

On September 12 we piled our luggage into the enormous station wagon for a trip to Sienna. Somehow I had thought that we would abandon our Roman driver in his lair, but he materialized suddenly and settled behind the wheel. Since my husband simply looked embarrassed, I finally lost control and drove the maniac from the car with a spate of Spanish curses that I hadn't thought I knew.

When Bing grumbled, I told him that we owed it to our children. On a cross-country drive, with no parked cars to inhibit him, that fool was sure to drive us all off a cliff.

It was a fortunate decision because the Oldsmobile proved too wide to enter the narrow streets of Sienna, and I'm sure that we would never have convinced our erstwhile cicerone to skirt the town.

Arriving in Florence, we searched for and eventually found the fabled Ristorante Bing Crosby. Of course Bing was photographed, and we were all served too many free drinks. To my amazement Bing found some golfing buddies there, and repaired to the local course to win their money. He later admitted that he had seen several golf balls competing for primacy on each tee, and had achieved a modicum of success only by shutting one eye and swinging at the middle one. Meanwhile I tried shakily to visit the Ponte Vecchio, the old bridge covered with shops, but had to give it up and nap in the car.

We arrived in Venice on September 16. By moonlight it seemed a fairy city but somehow, betrayed by all those gondolas in the movies, we hadn't reckoned with mechanized transport. It was true that no automobiles were allowed on the island, but the vaporettos sounded like powerful motorcycles.

All night long Bing padded around our room in the Gritti Hotel like a caged panther. Of course all this is hearsay on my part, at least until 4 a.m. when, overcome by envy of my happy snores, he finally shook me awake. There he stood cursing progress, his matinee-idol profile silhouetted in the moonlight from our tall windows, his little kewpie-doll curls standing up on the back of his neck. I joined him and we both stared silently out at the moon-drenched canal, whence the evil summer smells had disappeared, washed seaward by the freshening autumn waves.

"How could anything so beautiful be so goddam noisy?" Father O'Malley groused.

"We'll move in the morning. Surely the hotel has rooms facing away from the canal."

"Oh it has, Kathryn, indeed it has," Bing howled like a madman above the roar of a couple of passing motor launches. "Those are the rooms that face the church!"

"Well, let's sleep until the Angelus rings at 6," I counseled. And that's just what one of us did.

We whiled away the next morning sightseeing in St. Mark's square, tried to nap in our room after lunch, and finally, as a futile protest against the vaporettos, spent the afternoon and evening traversing the canals in a real gondola. As night fell, our craft metamorphosed into a time machine which returned us to the 16th century. In the feeble moonglow the modern embellishments faded into the shadows, and only the eternal stone buildings remained. The pulse of the sea was everywhere, and even our whispers were ageless echoes of the voices of millions of lovers who had plied these canals, distilled between the walls of time in casks of long ago.

"And I hear they've got a tricky little golf course on Lido Isle," Bing appended.

The next day we joined the noisemakers, hiring a motorboat to seek Torcello Isle. We passed five small islands which Bing identified as Murano, "where they make the famous

Embarking in one of the cursed vaporettos

crystal." He, who was hungry, refused to stop, to slow down, or to let me dive overboard and swim ashore. Instead we ingested calories that we didn't need at Torcello, visited two churches and a museum, and raced back past Murano again.

For the next few days Bing played golf in the rain while I stared out into it, gained 8 pounds relieving my boredom with food, and dreamed of starring in Roman movies. At long last I made a list of my grievances and presented them to Bing at dinner time.

He listened without a word until I had finished my pronunciamiento and then remarked, "If you really want sympathy, hold out your little lame brain. Better still, look it up in the dictionary. You will find it under *simp*—that's *s-i-m-p*."

But my diatribe had driven him out of Venice. On September 20 we motored to Treviso, where we lunched and of course Bing discovered a golf course. For a time it seemed that I had succeeded only in forcing him to play in a less interesting environment, but fortunately for me the course was short, Bing's shots were long, and he finally drove into the foursome ahead of us.

Since we didn't know what the local penalty might be, we fled all the way to Velden, where we stayed at a charming inn and Bing of course won money at the nearby casino. I, who knew nothing of games of chance, had expected something like Las Vegas, and was surprised to be ushered into a quiet room with a few card tables, where gambling was accomplished in hushed tones with great solemnity. I suppose that for the connoisseurs the drama lay in wagering amounts of money that they couldn't afford to lose.

Having swept through the pear orchards of Northern Italy, the passes of the Alps, and the forest of Velden, we now arrived at the Sacher Hotel, opposite the Opera House in Vienna, and occupied one of the suites where Austrian royalty once kept their favorite ballerinas.

For a week we attended every performance of the opera, and Bing trailed clouds of glory. Thanks to his incredible ear for music, he was moved to ecstasy by performances that I found simply loud and unintelligible.

Then we were off to Mittersill to stay with Princess Honeychile Wilder, the proud possessor of Austria's most lurid vocabulary. She greeted my husband with "Hi, you *unmentionable, unprintable, adorable obscenity!*"

Bing turned beet-red, choked, presented me, and finally managed to gasp out. "How have you been?"

"Oh, still trying to get a little *obscenity*. Remember, that's what you told me life's all about." She continued, as Bing flirted with apoplexy, "Have you seen Bob, that magnificent *blankety-blank-blank-blank?*"

Honey had worked for Bob Hope on his radio show until she was cashiered for getting more laughs than he did. That was how she had wound up with a prince and a castle at Mittersill. Obviously her marriage had failed to put a damper on the mule-skinner dialect that she had learned as a child in Tiger, Georgia.

Dinner that night was formal, with some twenty princes, barons, dukes, and earls about the table, but Honey's language remained undiminished in scope and vigor.

I'm sure that the pope would have been sorry to hear it, but September 28 was the height of the tour for Bing. Finishing with a brilliant series of sub-par holes, he dominated the annual Mittersill Invitational Golf Tournament, winning first prizes for both low net and low gross.

He had attained such an acute pitch of limited excellence that the rest of the trip had to savor of anticlimax. My diary makes much of a silly incident in a shop in Kitzbühel. While we were being fitted for loden coats and hunting attire, a baby in her mother's arms started yowling her head off.

Bing's distaste for loud noise led him to test a peculiar remedy. He put his face up close to the child's and started singing an Irish lullaby, while imprudently waving his finger before her face in time to the music.

All the singing was to no avail. Faced with

Princess Honeychile Wilder Hohenlohe with Prince Alfie Auersburg, Sunny's husband

Princess Sunny Auersburg, who later married Klaus von Bulow, and became the subject of a celebrated trial.

Winning the Mittersill Invitational

stiff competition, the infant simply redoubled her efforts. But the finger was something else again. As Bing rashly brought it close to her lips, she suddenly thrust her head forward and bit it. With saucer-blue eyes still streaming, she thoughtfully munched on it while Bing's tooraloora-looras were soon punctuated by sobs and ouches. We were then surrounded by a huge crowd, who I'm sure derived considerably more satisfaction from the spectacle than did the performing vocalist.

As soon as he had recovered from this experience, Bing recurred to the old theme of "Why don't we build a house here?" I had no choice but to pack him off to Paris before we were drowned in a flood of architects' drawings.

There we stayed in the Trianon Palace Hotel, sightseeing and shopping each day, and listening to Bing's Pirates play in the World Series at night.

On the evening of the final game we dined at a friend's house while we listened to Armed Forces Radio. When Mazeroski came to bat in the ninth inning, the meal was over and Bing had started to fix himself a drink. He picked up an unopened bottle of Scotch just as his hero laid into the ball.

The bottle dropped from Bing's numbed fingers and the Scotch ran into the fireplace. Flames sprang up and threatened to engulf the room. All the while he was doing his version of an Apache war dance and screaming "We win ten to nine. We win ten to nine!"

I helped our hostess extinguish the flames while she murmured something about men who turn destructive when excited. Since our popularity seemed to be on the wane, we left for the Ritz Bar, Fouquet's, and finally an enormous victory bash sponsored by Monsieur Dubonnet. All in all a great evening, but no rival for Bing's triumph at Mittersill.

We arrived home to find that Bing's oldest son Gary had married on September 6, without requesting his father's approval or indeed apprising him of the event. Everyone but me seemed to be in doubt as to what the paternal reaction would be. While the family waited in trepidation, Bing, with his wonted Spartan fortitude, fled first to Palm Springs, and thence to his ranch. Try as I would, I couldn't lure him back for another father-of-the-groom party.

Finally I gave up trying, packed up the two children, and joined Bing at the ranch. There he shot and Remus retrieved our Thanksgiving Canada goose, and we all participated in a snowy Currier and Ives print.

I returned to Los Angeles to continue my nurse's training, while Bing continued to skulk at the ranch until a golf tournament finally lured him back to Palm Springs. After which he had to come home to record *A Christmas Sing With Bing*. Fresh out of excuses, he finally agreed to meet Gary at Chasen's Restaurant on December 19.

Fortunately Barbara, Gary's new wife, took over before father and son could get started. A slender, statuesque blonde with bright blue eyes, she had been the loveliest show girl in Las Vegas. Instinctively she seemed to realize that Bing couldn't stand people who were in awe of him. She was so charmingly at her ease that Bing soon relaxed too. Within an hour he was literally eating tidbits out of her hand.

It would have been hard for anyone to resist the newlyweds. They were obviously united by that strong physical and emotional bond which a later generation was to denominate "great chemistry." I was gratified to see how their delight in one another lifted Bing's spirits, but in the midst of all this good cheer I was suddenly depressed and jealous. Why couldn't I make Bing as happy as Barbara obviously made Gary?

Numerous answers came to mind. I was certainly not an elegant hostess like my own sister, or a sparkling personality like Barbara. For the first time Bing had taken me on long trips with him this year, but I had felt ignorant and awkward in the presence of Southern and European aristocracy.

I now wanted just a little piece of the younger Crosbys' magic carpet, so that I too

The newlyweds, Gary and Barbara

could be the make-believe princess I had portrayed on film. My present situation had all the ingredients of a fairy tale, but it remained amazingly difficult to assemble them properly. Still there had to be a way. Mentally I started making my New Year's resolutions.

At Cypress Point with Wheeler Farish, Harvey Ward, and Francis Brown

1961

This years's diary opens with a fervent prayer: "Dear God, please help me to take control of my life. Teach me the necessary knack of mounting my white horse and riding it off in all directions."

Just as I was at least thinking of getting organized, Bing decided that he wanted another baby. My mounting paranoia made me darkly suspicious. Was this a plot to prevent me from accompanying him on his European travels and fishing and hunting trips? Would it permit him to say with a clear conscience, "I'm sorry, but my wife can't do that picture because she's expecting again." Barefoot, pregnant, and chained to the bed. Was that how he wanted me?

I spent the first week of January in the desert with Bing and his friends, feeling guilty about our abandoned children. On the 9th Leo drove me back to Los Angeles and nursery duty at 7 a.m., community health at noon, volunteer work for the Brail Institute and Fire Prevention all afternoon, and finally an evening show of domesticity in repairing battered furniture and worn-out rugs. Slowly I was replacing the remnants of carpeting that had survived the North Hollywood fire but been irreparably damaged by dogs and teenagers.

Meanwhile, safe from my cooking, Bing was lunching and dining wherever he played his golf. Since he was the only one in our household who could prepare a decent breakfast, his culinary problems had been fully resolved.

Still needing to be needed, I decided to surprise Bing by removing a slight stain from his white silk pajamas. I knew that such delicate work must be done by hand, so I gently placed them in a bowl of Clorox, and glumly watched them dissolve before my eyes.

Enough of that. Bing would never discard his favorite sports clothes, so I would mend the alpaca sweater that was going at one elbow. On closer inspection I found that the other sleeve had been repaired some years before by a lady who could sew. Since there was no point in rushing into battle all-unarmed, I sadly replaced the garment in his drawer, and set about refinishing our much-abused piano.

I went to Abell's on Beverly Boulevard to inquire about the proper stains, varnishes, or

With the Hearsts and the Morrows at San Simeon

It wasn't Bing's first trip to San Simeon.

Or his second.

whatever. Far off in a back corner my eye caught a gleam of blond veneer. "What's that?" I asked curiously.

"Just a rental piece that the movie studios use."

"Let's see what it looks like."

Dave Abell moved a few larger objects away from the most beautiful piano I'd ever seen. "What movies was it used in?" I asked cautiously, trying not to drool over the gorgeous wood and intricate carvings.

"The last ones were *Rapsody* and *High Society*. If you like I can get a list of the others."

"Never mind. Would you consider a swap?"

For reasons that I still don't understand, he traded me his seven-foot 1890 Erard, with its keyboard in perfect pitch, for my battered five-foot 1930 Steinway, with its idiosyncratic engravings of *E flat* and *Phillip* on the front. In subsequent years Bing never tired of telling the story of how for once his dingbat had outsmarted the experts.

From Palm Springs Bing went straight to Pebble Beach to prepare for the Crosby Golf Tournament. If he couldn't stop me from studying nursing, he certainly wasn't going to hang around and watch. An insomniac, who has finally started knitting up the raveled sleeve of care at 3 a.m., doesn't appreciate being awakened at 5 by an apparition in a white uniform.

The situation didn't improve at the other end of the day, when meals were delayed until all hours by my unpredictably late arrival. There is, of course, no way of saying when an emergency operation will end. Once Bing had greeted me suspiciously at the front door when I arrived at 9 p.m.

"Where in hell have you been?" he demanded darkly.

"Shooting pool with the fellows."

Rebuffed but reassured he rejoined, "That's nice. Win any money?"

"I took the whole pot."

Bing hated my work so much that he never asked how it was going, but he was genuinely concerned when I drove home alone at night. He didn't like risks that he considered useless, and of course he felt that my true place was in the house, awaiting his return. I hoped that the Crosby would afford an opportunity for a reunion on neutral ground.

When I arrived at Pebble Beach, Bing, who was at sixes and sevens, suggested a drive to San Simeon. As it turned out, we not only explored the castle thoroughly, but also acquired many of its treasures. We both loved beautiful old things, and were as happy as children selecting them and deciding where they would fit in our houses.

Bing reminisced about the great days of the past when he had often been a castle guest. He had taken long walks with William Randolph Hearst, exchanging thoughts on what was beautiful and important in the world.

"Randolph coveted rooms as women covet pearls," Bing said. "He would remove the entire inner paneling and store it. The best ones are still lovingly preserved in pine boxes in a warehouse on the East River in New York."

On the drive back from San Simeon my acquisitive soul kept recurring to the thought of uncrating some of those panels and installing them in a house of our own one day.

In retrospect I regret that I shared so little of the responsibility for the annual Bing Crosby Golf Tournament at Pebble Beach, an event which now fascinates me. Throughout the week of the tournament Bing was concerned about the weather, the conditions of the course, the pairings, the sponsors, the galleries, and the TV shows, while I simply waited outside a world I did not understand.

My big moment came when it was all over and I spirited Bing away to Cypress Point Club, where we could wander around with a band of miniature deer, bark back at the sea lions, and laugh at the wheeling, screaming gulls before returning to Los Angeles.

Meanwhile Dennis, Phillip, Lindsay, and their wives were staying at our house in Palm Desert, since the boys' act was booked at the ChiChi Night Club. On February 3 we joined

The campaigners

them, and I had a delightful time with the girls, who were all about my age. Bing seemed disappointed that I failed to take charge of the group, but I was hopelessly miscast as the evil stepmother since all the sons' wives were far better managers, cooks and housekeepers than I.

On February 7 Bing took the children to Squaw Valley. I obtained time off from my studies to join them on February 10 for our first vacation in the snow.

While Bing worked out with the other experts, the children and I tried the bunny hill. They caught on immediately, and even I experienced no difficulty in assuming the proper stance, but there were no hills in West Columbia, so I have always mistaken gentle slopes for steep precipices.

When my great moment arrived, I took the tow rope up, and then froze in terror as Bing and his friends shouted encouragement from the bottom of the hill.

Since it became apparent that I would never budge under my own power, Bing finally sent up a guide to take me by the hand and lead me down. Terribly ashamed, I removed my skis forever, but I still found a use for one piece of equipment. Bing had been trying to cover his embarrassment by making me the butt of a series of funny but cruel jokes. Urged on by the cheers of a considerable crowd, I did my level best to shish-kebab him with a ski pole.

On the 19th of February some friends from Argentina invited Bing to visit them in Patagonia. When I realized that he was preparing to go alone, I decided that the role of Penelope no longer suited me. "Together or not at all," was my ultimatum.

Seeing no alternative, Bing reluctantly agreed to let me accompany him, but I was fresh out of excuses to escape from school. After devoting considerable thought to the matter, I finally decided to have recourse to my histrionic talents. As I listened to the lecturer I deemed most susceptible, I filled my mind with sad, sad thoughts. Sure enough, huge tears ran from my eyes and streamed down my cheeks. Since I sat in the front row and managed my feat in total silence, none of my classmates suspected anything, but the instructor got the full benefit of a performance that might have won me an Oscar if only I'd had a smidgen of talent to go with it.

At the end of class I answered the instructor's concerned queries with my own version of a nervous breakdown. Within two hours I was free from all courses, with a physician's recommendation for a long vacation.

I raced to the nearest phone and informed my mate that the deed was done, only to hear him drawl, "I meant to tell you that I've decided not to go to Argentina after all. There is just too much excitement for me in those Latin homes. They race around the ranch all day and then eat all evening, hold a late party, and start dancing on the tables at midnight."

"Olé" I shouted, swinging into a chorus of "Down Argentine Way."

"Sorry, but I'm too tired to put up with any more of that sort of thing."

Bing hung up, but he had inadvertently put his finger on a big bone of contention between us. As a consequence of the thirty-year age gap, he had already done all the things that I wanted to do.

I ripped up my ticket to Argentina, ran back to class, sat very straight in my seat, paid strict attention, and took notes furiously. As an acting job it wasn't a patch on my previous performance, but at least the furious part had a ring of truth.

I had, however, played my previous role not wisely but well. Throughout the rest of my nurse's training, the slightest expression of emotion from me elicited nervous glances from my instructors.

I soon found a way to make Bing regret the cancellation of our trip to Patagonia. On March 2 my father, who had been teaching government and American History in high school, filed for the Senate race in Texas. As he explained over the phone, "It costs only 150 dollars, and it will be a fine way to teach my students what's really involved in practical politics."

The benefactor who bought the orphanage

Bing was aghast at the news. "Tell him to drop it," he snapped.

"How can I? Nobody tells my father what to do, least of all me."

"Then stay out of it."

"That's not the Texas way. When I was a little girl I always went out on election day and told everybody I met, 'Vote for my daddy for county commissioner. You know he's the right man for the job.' "

Bing was livid. Even more than he hated politics, he detested the idea of my being exposed to public criticism while begging for votes. He declared that if I wouldn't stay home he wouldn't either, and set off for the Bahamas by way of Palm Beach.

It was now that my bogus breakdown stood me in good stead. My request for a month's leave of absence was immediately granted, and I began zigzagging across Texas with my parents, reveling in the glory of the southwestern springtime. On April 4 John Tower won the senatorial seat. My father had finished 8th in a field of 71.

When I returned to Los Angeles, Bing himself a recent arrival, met me at the door. He had personally diagnosed a passing complaint of Harry's as epilepsy. He now demanded that I quit nursing and tend to my children, and announced that he was off alone to Mexico. Grimly I returned to my nursing classes, resolved to make up for lost time, but fearful of Bing's reaction to my mutinous conduct.

To my immense relief, when Bing returned at the end of the month he seemed blissfully oblivious of my shortcomings as a wife and mother. He spoke enthusiastically of the weather, the fishing, and the possibility of building in Las Cruces. He didn't even seem to notice that I had dispatched his mother and the entire household staff to Palm Desert so that I could be alone and get some studying done. I'll append a sample of his new Mexican stories:

"When I emerged from a shop in La Paz, I saw a priest talking to my driver."

"Money?" I ventured. I was only a convert, but I had quickly grasped the basic tenets of Catholicism.

"Well, yes, but at least it was for a novel cause. Do you remember the big white building on the mountainside that we used to pass on the way into town?"

"The one with all the pillars and arches? Doesn't it belong to a rich woman?"

Bing gazed upon me with his customary mixture of compassion and amusement. "It certainly does, and as a member of the landed aristocracy she is referred to as *Madame* in all circles of society. Her home, or rather house, has a lovely dining room and many, many bedrooms."

"How do you know so much?" I inquired suspiciously. "Have you been researching local customs?"

"The priest told me all about it. He wants me to buy it for an orphanage. There is an order of nuns who have agreed to work with him if they can just find a suitable building."

The result was the *Colina de la Cruz*, where children between the ages of five and sixteen were housed, fed, clothed, and educated in both academic subjects and vocational skills. Suddenly the starving creatures were transported to a world of plenty, where there were no fences and no locks on the doors. The resultant *algeria* led to lots of dancing and singing, but somehow the mansion never regained its former place in the hearts of the town's gallants, many of whom still harbor a smoldering resentment toward Bing and all his works.

When Bing finished his story, he started immediately for the wood pile. "Isn't it a bit warm for a fire?" I asked.

Bing studied the matter thoughtfully for an absurdly long time. Then he replied simply, "But that was always my job. Larry fed the chickens, Catherine and Mary Rose set the table and did the dishes, Everett, Ted, and Bob did the chores, and mother fixed dinner."

Well at least I understood now, and I resolved never again to complain when my impractical mate offered me the benefit of the only

Palmilla

household task that he knew how to perform.

Now that I think of it, he did have one other talent that we put to great use when the children were small. Whenever they seemed querulous in the evening, he simply sang them a lullaby, which invariably put them to sleep.

Of course we never did run a controlled experiment. As their mother's children, it might well be that they would have dropped off anyway, and the lullaby had no more effect than hurricanes or earthquakes have on my repose. Somehow it seems sad that we will never know the truth of the matter.

There was only one good thing about a serious hunt for a new building site. Since there was no denying the fact that I was intimately involved, I got to go along. On May 10 we flew to La Paz, and found that we had to go through a minute customs inspection because we had hitched a ride with lettuce exporters.

The next day we cruised down the coast and docked at Palmilla on the very tip of the peninsula. I enjoyed visiting San José Del Cabo, whence shark fins were being shipped to Japan to be made into soup that would be served in San Francisco, but I hated the thought of building a house in this remote spot and then trying to find excuses to live in it.

While Bing was selecting a beautifully-tooled leather saddle for Harry to grow into, I thought the matter through and made my plans. As he walked resolutely along the shore, surveying the lay of the land with practiced eye, I moved off behind some friendly dunes and began my version of a Hopi rain dance.

Right on cue, the gods of my far-off Indian forebears rushed to my assistance. By noon black clouds were scuttling across the horizon. By 2 p.m. we were experiencing a big blow. Before evening waves were crashing wildly against the rocks, and boats were torn from their moorings.

"This place does seem to have a bit more weather than Las Cruces," I suggested mildly. "And as sure as my name is Colleen O'Grandstaff and I'm in league with the devil, it will continue to have," I muttered beneath my breath.

By the next morning the force of the storm had abated, but as we left the harbor at 5:30 a.m. high waves were still crashing against the cliffs to the left and right of Palmilla. "Imagine the children caught in that," I suggested, recalling that rocky cliffs and strong undertows had clinched Bing's decision to sell the Pebble Beach home shortly after Mary Frances was born.

I renewed my incantations, and sure enough by 9:30 we had to take refuge in Los Frailes. Being marooned with Bing was my version of paradise. We anchored in the lee of some big rocks, made our way ashore, and hiked to a nearby ranch. There the tenant farmers invited us to join them in a lunch of chicken, rice, tortillas, and refried beans. Afterwards we inspected the spread on which they ran fifty head of cattle, and couldn't help comparing their simple, apparently happy life with the complicated mess in which we habitually found ourselves.

They made everything themselves, using leather strips from their own cattle as bedsprings, and thatch for the roof of their hut. Fish dried on a line, and busy chickens were everywhere.

We decided to contribute by fishing on the beach. Bing caught several huge cabrilla with which we repaid our friends' hospitality, and then a smaller one which we fried over a fire on the beach for ourselves.

Much to my delight we were marooned all the next day too, but Bing continued to catch enough fish to keep us going.

When the storm continued into the third day I began to think that, not knowing my own strength, perhaps I had exaggerated a trifle in my initial efforts. Since the charms of the simple life were beginning to pale, I concentrated hard on reversing my incantations.

As it transpired, I had whomped up so powerful a spell that it took me a full 24 hours to counteract it, but by the following morning the storm had abated sufficiently to permit us to

Fishing with Remus

Look who caught one.

Oh well, it must have been easy.

leave. I was then punished for my crime by a terrible bout of seasickness, which lasted all the way to Las Cruces.

Once back on *terra firma*, I swore a solemn oath never to tread a deck again. Now that I had rescued us from architects for the nonce, it was time to get back to Los Angeles. I had been warned that if I didn't resume my courses faithfully this time, I would be dismissed from the nursing program for good.

I had long since learned that my studies were unacceptable as an excuse, so I invoked the well-being of the children. Bing started to mutter something about their being safer without the ministrations of Calamity Jane, but then realized that he had to be consistent in demanding the wife and mother bit from me, so he bade me a reluctant farewell, obviously suspecting that our babies were just a cover for more of my clandestine activities.

How right he was! With the hope of catching up while he was out of town, I doubled my academic load, so that I was steadily occupied at Queen of Angels Hospital from 7 in the morning until 10 at night. My classmates thought I was crazy, but for me nursing had the charm of forbidden fruit. As an interesting sidelight, a routine nurse's physical unearthed the reason for my seasickness. I decided that it would be a boy, and that his name would be Nathaniel.

On June 2, I staggered in from the hospital at about midnight to find Bing in his office reading through three weeks' mail. After congratulating me on my close supervision of the children, he informed me that he had found just the place for a new home in Las Cruces. Indeed the seed of crime bears bitter fruit.

I sneaked away the next morning for my final exam in, ironically enough, labor and delivery. One might have thought that I already had the hang of that. Meanwhile, as often happened, Bing caught the flu upon returning to civilization from a relatively germ-free outdoor environment, so for the next few days I did my nursing at home.

When it came to any sort of crisis, Bing was not a fighter, but a runner. Once he was helpless in bed, Gary was the first to arrive and take advantage of the golden opportunity. After he emerged from his father's bedroom, he told everyone in the kitchen his troubles while he attacked the refrigerator. We assured him that he was exaggerating his difficulties with his wife, but it was apparent that he hadn't eaten for days.

Two nights later Gary phoned for help. He couldn't awaken Barbara, and was sure that she had taken an overdose of sleeping tablets. I called the doctor while Bing staggered up from his sickbed to accompany me to the valley.

Barbara did seem to be sleeping very soundly, but I had had no experience with patients in coma so I limited myself to taking her pulse, which seemed strong and regular, and observing her respiration until the doctor arrived. Meanwhile Bing sat in the living room with Gary, while the latter continued to pour out his troubles and drink what looked like water. Years later, after his successful cure, he informed us that it had been straight vodka.

The doctor instructed us to let Barbara sleep off the overdose, which was not sufficient to endanger her life. The next day, however, we faced a more serious crisis. Barbara had locked herself in the bathroom, and was threatening suicide. I responded immediately in my role of Nurse Jane Fuzzy Wuzzy and somehow, following the manual to the letter, I was able to talk her into opening the door. As I led her back to bed, she remained calm and was soon fast asleep.

Suddenly three men and a nurse rushed in the front door, seized Barbara, crammed her into a strait jacket, and carried her off on a stretcher. Meanwhile she was screaming, biting, and kicking like a madwoman. I would have too. She and Gary had all our sympathy. We didn't know then that Barbara's main problem was sleeplessness, aggravated by his continual drinking bouts.

I caught Bing's flu, and it was he who had the chore of following through with Barbara's doctors. To his surprise they informed him that she was in good physical and mental condition,

On the road again

but in bad need of rest. After a few days of sleep in a quiet hospital she would be right as rain.

When I recovered I followed Bing up to the ranch, where I mounted a last-ditch assault on the culinary arts. I had always loved to read gourmet cookbooks, but my viewpoint had been that of a passive consumer. Now I resolved to cater to the enormous appetites stemming from fresh air and hard work.

Our own Rising River offered some of the best trout fishing in the world, and Bing took full advantage of it. I tried every conceivable fish dish, but Bing said that his favorite was trout-a-la-floor smaché. Whenever old butter-fingers let it drop, she simply told herself, "That's perfectly all right, Kathryn. Just bring in the other trout." Then she put it back on the platter and served it with a smile.

For a change from fish I prepared ham à la mimosa for Sunday dinner. Lacking a slicer I tried to cut and roll the little cornucopias by hand. I then stuffed them with a cream cheese mousse and glazed the results.

It took an entire day, on which the temperature never dropped below 105. By the time Bing returned from the river banks with five more slimy monsters for me to gut and scale, I was so queasy that I just sat and sulked while the family and guests tried to eat. No one said it was the most beautiful dish ever seen, but shortly thereafter everyone did become horribly ill.

When Bing had finally emptied out his stomach and recovered his fighting spirit, he explained patiently that he couldn't have me poisoning his children and guests.

I in turn made a momentous decision which I communicated to him succinctly. I was not a cook, I would never become one, and I no longer cared how, when, or where anyone ate. In a pinch I would open a can of soup and make do with it, and my next of kin had best be prepared to imitate me.

On our return from the ranch Bing suddenly announced that he was leaving for London to film *The Road to Hong Kong* with Bob Hope.

I waited expectantly. When no specific invitation seemed to be forthcoming, I decided to finesse this hand. "How exciting! You can show me all the parts of London that we missed the last time. What a delight it will be to live in England!"

"I'm going alone."

"But I have to go along and take care of you."

"You're in no condition to take care of anyone."

Since my pregnancy made me feel awkward and inept, that finished it. I clumped upstairs and spent my usual five minutes crying myself to sleep. But on awakening I deviated from my normal pattern. For me sleep has always been gloriously therapeutic. However dismal the preceding day, I greet the dawn drowsy but suffused with well-being. This morning found me wide awake and furiously plotting revenge.

I would burn his fishing rods and his golf bags, and lock him out of the house. I would hide his pipes and feed the dogs his slippers. I would pour glue into his luggage and ship it to Afghanistan, I would, I would.

What I actually did was call Lillian Barkley, the friendly PhD who had tutored me through my courses and exams at the University of Texas. "He won't let me travel with him," I hiccuped. "I can't live with him in London. In my condition I have to stay at home. Who put me in my condition?"

Dr. Barkley waited philosophically for a pause in the wowling. Then she asked very quietly, "Did you know that the twins were premature? They weighed only a couple of pounds each at birth, and their survival was in doubt for some months."

"No," I gulped. With incredible naiveté for a nurse, I had simply assumed that all Dixie's babies had been as blissfully healthy as my own.

"At the time Dixie had been trying to do too much for Bing, and I know that he felt very guilty about it."

"Well, why couldn't he tell me? Why can't he ever give me a straight reason for anything?"

"It might be that he doesn't want to worry you. By the way, when he mentioned his con-

Cranbourne Court

cern about your driving at night across the desert to the hospital, did it change your behavior in any way?"

"Not a bit."

"Well, consider your failings throughout the day, and unlock the bedroom door at night."

"I have to sleep in the nursery with the children."

"Then leave a sweet note on your pillow."

Since Lillian's death I have taken to praying to saints. During her lifetime I didn't need them. She maintained a cool, objective view of my family, while remaining wholly outside of it, refusing even to meet the other members. Now that I think of it, perhaps her acquaintance with one member was quite enough.

The following day was a Sunday, so Bing and I were off to 8 o'clock mass. We must have presented what seemed like a united front, though I admit that I drew well back when he received communion, lest with the proverbial inaccuracy of celestial artillery the lightning bolt meant for his black soul might just strike an innocent bystander. I had followed Lillian's prescription to the letter, but I hadn't forgiven his beastly behavior.

Monday morning I was up at 5 a.m. to dispatch my sister's family and our own Mary Frances to the ranch. When I returned, Bing, always surly when robbed of sleep, had already left the house with golf gear. Muttering maledictions I finished packing his suitcases and had them moved to the station wagon.

When Bing returned from his round of golf, he found Harry dressed in a neat little suit and his mother swathed in the least hideous of her pregnancy tents. "Never you mind," I thought as we drove into the airport. "You can forget your worries about this new baby, because if you're going to leave me to take care of it alone, from now on I'll consider it to be all mine."

As I held Harry up to him at the plane, Bing actually had a tear in his eye. I had none. When Harry tried to ask, "Daddy, when do we come?" I whirled him about and said, "Look at the big bird, darling!"

When Bing said, "I'll call you," I smiled sardonically.

What I wanted to say was, "Don't bother. You have just taken leave of your wife, child, and child-to-be forever," but I bit my tongue. Dr. Barkley had given me my orders, and I was following them to the letter. A treacherous knave was abandoning his hideous, huge-bellied wife to her own devices, and there seemed to be no one else to call his attention to his foul misdeed, but I remained silent as a tomb.

Just before he disappeared through the doorway of the plane, Bing turned and blew us a much-photographed kiss. Harry sent one right back, but I hurled only choice Texas expletives through my still-smiling lips.

On Wednesday, July 19, I learned for the nth time why it was wiser to follow Dr. Barkley's behests than my own dubious inclinations. Henceforth I would simply do and die, asking questions later if at all, for my errant husband phoned with incredible news: Right from the plane he had joined Dolores Hope and a real estate agent in looking for a place for his family to live. "I've seen only one home which is large enough, but it's a long way from the studio, and it has no garden for you and Harry to play in. We do have lots of leads, however, so I should soon find exactly what we need."

On August 3 Harry and I were, as he phrased it, "off to Yurrup."

Bing had finally decided that we would share Cranbourne Court with Bob Hope and his family. Originally Lord Duveen's country house, it had an enormous square entrance hall, with a surrounding second-floor gallery leading to the bedrooms. Downstairs the formal dining room, sitting room, and drawing room were all on the same Brobdingnagian scale. I hastened to assure myself that we had a proper nursery for Harry, and numberless bedrooms for ourselves and guests. The bathrooms were something of an afterthought, and far down the hall, but that's par for the course in British country houses.

Speaking of which, we were conveniently

Tea break at Shepperton

close to Sunningdale golf course, Ascot race track, and Shepperton studios. What else could a man ask of life?

Best of all, from my point of view, were our four built-in baby-sitters: to wit Tony, Linda, Nora, and Kelly Hope, who were all eager, willing, and able. Wonderful children, they delighted in spoiling Harry rotten. Eileen Taylor, an Irish girl who had been with the Hope family for many years, followed Bing's orders to the letter, and really tried to fatten our wiry son. She coaxed him to eat gobs of oatmeal with double cream and sugar, but finally reported despondently, "It's no good, really. Just comes out the other end."

During the first few days Bing played croquet in the yard with Harry, and spent hours walking in the garden with me. I was astonished to find that his knowledge of English homes and gardens was encyclopedic, and I encouraged him to show it off until I realized to my horror that, tempted by unusually balmy summer weather, he was considering buying one.

Fortunately shooting began on the picture and temporarily distracted him. We fell into a pattern in which Dolores and I joined Bing and Bob for an enormous breakfast at about 7, waved them good-bye at the door, and spent the entire day touring, shopping, and in my case eating.

The men finished work at 4 in the afternoon, raced off to one of the many good golf courses in the area, and played a full round in the long British twilight. Then we met them at an English pub, where Bing could have a pint while I stuffed myself with sausage rolls.

Friday was our date night. The men joined us in town for dinner at the Savoy Grill, followed by a play or a party. Hardly able to believe my good fortune, I was surprised to find that Dolores shared my sentiments. "I haven't seen this much of Bob since we were married," she confessed wistfully.

On August 25 we visited Nice for a long weekend. Despite my now advanced state of pregnancy, I took Harry to the Cap Ferrat beach, where I waded balloon-like in my pink, candy-striped tent dress, and tried not to notice the lovely mermaids disporting themselves in their brief bikinis.

On Sunday Bing was photographed playing golf with Joseph Kennedy, leading Lindsay to voice a practical suggestion in his next letter: "Why don't you wager your yacht against his? After all, what have you got to lose?"

That evening we had a drink with David Niven, Gregory Peck, and their wives before Bing donned full evening dress to take me to Casa Madrid. Our chauffeur saluted as he whipped open the door of the rented Rolls, and Bing in his grandest manner swept me up to the portal, where a doorman dressed like a Gilbert and Sullivan major general inquired frostily after our reservations.

"I am Bing Crosby," my husband announced loftily.

"That is not my problem, monsieur. If you have no reservation, we have no place for you."

Bing was furious, but half way down the mountain I induced him to stop at a little inn called La Ferme. There we sat under a grape arbor drenched in moonlight, devoured huge bowls of salad and plates of sausage and paté, with fruit for dessert, and envied no man.

Back to London for the orgy scene before Bing and Bob replaced the monkeys that were to be sent to the moon. At the witching hour of 4 p.m. Bing was still lying on a chaise and eating grapes while his brow was fanned by scantily-attired harem cuties, and Bob was sharing the sybaritic environment and having his toenails painted. When the head gaffer pulled the light switch, everyone broke for the front of the studio, Bing and Bob in the lead and headed for golf.

In sharp contrast to the scene which they had just left, the locker room at the nearest course had a naked light bulb in the ceiling and a few nails on the wall. As the erstwhile sybarites were madly changing clothes, hurling trousers in one direction and shirts in another, and grabbing for spiked shoes, two Colonel Blimps walked in and stared in consternation at all the American-style commotion. Suddenly

Dolores Hope and gravid friend in Florence

one of them froze. He was gazing at the ten twinkling toes of Bob's still-naked feet.

Finally Bob became aware of the silence, looked up, then down at his brilliant toenails, and finally up again in mute appeal. It was the first time that anyone had ever seen Hope speechless.

The climax came when the larger of the colonels moved over to Bing and asked in a whisper that must have reached the first tee, "Mr. Crosby, is your friend with the ballet?"

Not wishing to push our luck, Dolores and I took a week off to travel through Italy with Father Brooks, the Hope family chaplain. It was not customary at the time for ever-so-pregnant Italian women to appear in public. It was only later that Dolores, our only Italian speaker, informed me of the adverse comments occasioned by a priest openly escorting his gravid girl friend.

The combination of Father Brooks' clerical habit and Dolores' contacts in high places not only gained us access to a public audience with Pope John, but also allowed us to pass through the priests' entry behind the high altar. In my bright mantilla and wheat-colored duster, I must have resembled an ice-cream sundae as I emerged to find myself facing the expectant multitude.

Terrified by the sea of faces and unprepared for the role of pope, I collapsed upon the nearest seat available, from which I was immediately expelled by Dolores who hissed desperately, "Kathryn, that's the cardinal's chair." Sadly I lurched after her and attempted unsuccessfully to submerge my many-splendored self in a sea of black robes.

It was understandable that we had not been able to reach our men during the working week, but there should have been someone answering the phone during the weekend. I became more and more frantic while Dolores placidly explained, "You'll get used to it. For the first 15 years or so I worried all the time when Bob was away."

Finally I reached an unidentified female voice, who announced airily that the men of the house were "gone for the weekend."

Upon our arrival home, while Dolores looked on compassionately, I unsuccessfully tried to pin down two all-too-innocent-looking males, who repeatedly backed each other's stories of having been home all weekend with no knowledge of any sultry answering service.

As soon as Bing had finished shooting, he took off for Ireland, where his biggest fan had interviewed hundreds of prospective nannies, and decided that one Bridget Brennan would be the most suitable. Bing was hesitant until he discovered that she was the best left-handed woman golfer in Erin; whereupon he hired her on the spot. I heartily recommend this somewhat arbitrary selection process if you're ever looking for a nursemaid with a brilliant mechanical bent.

Meanwhile I was interviewing potential butlers. To my mind the pick of the litter was a hopelessly over-qualified young man named Alan Fisher, who had started his life of service at the age of fourteen as a footman in Buckingham Palace. He had served as butler to Princess Elizabeth before her accession to the throne, and thereafter to the Duchess of Windsor.

Since I hadn't the faintest idea of what a butler did, I had checked such books as were available, and had succeeded only in ascertaining the proper nomenclature: I was to call him by his last name. Resolutely I demanded, "Fisher, what do you do in a home?"

Nothing daunted, he gazed at me with wide brown eyes, smiled jovially, and replied, "Whatever needs to be done, Mrs. Crosby."

Little did either of us suspect at the time that the poor man and his wife were destined to spend some fifteen years desperately doing just that for what must often have seemed to be an ungrateful horde, before returning to his native isle to manage the household of the newly-wed Prince Charles and Princess Diana.

On October 4 Harry and I flew home to await the blessed event. Characteristically I handed him to a stewardess, keeled over, and

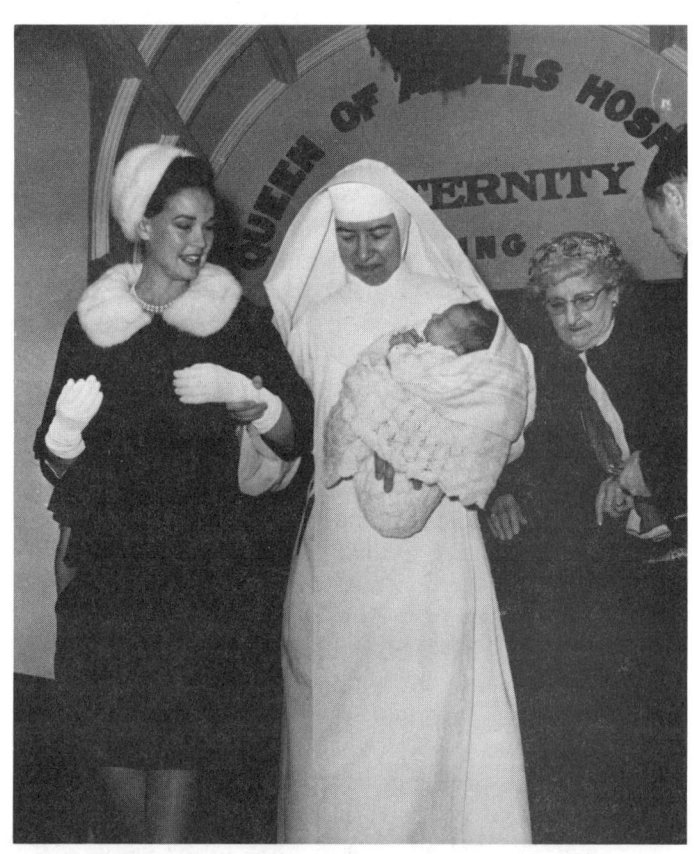

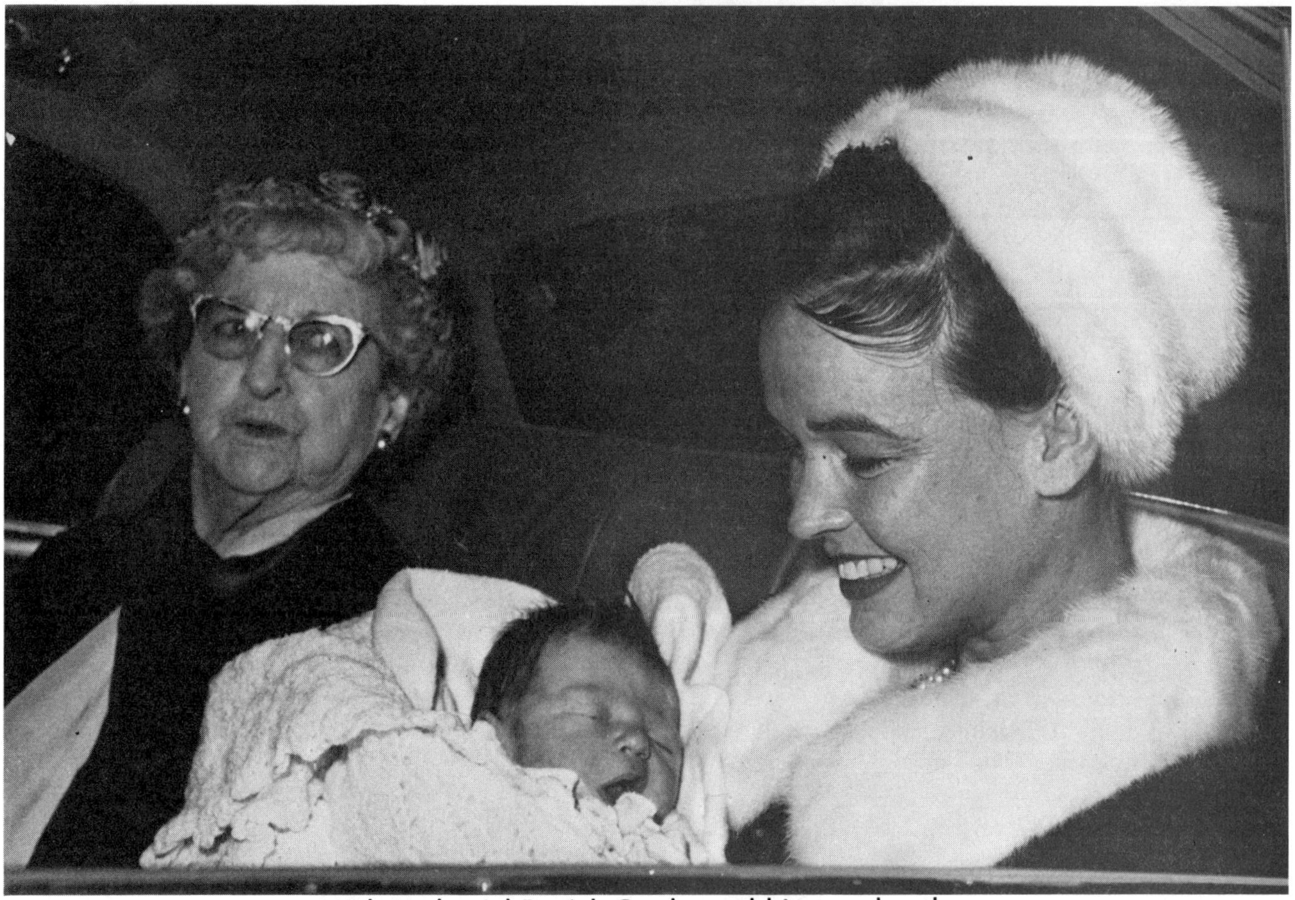

With Nathaniel Patrick Crosby and his grandmother

slept straight through. I haven't the slightest notion of how he passed the time, but he was bright-eyed and bushy-tailed on arrival.

At 10:57 on the night of October 29, Nathaniel Patrick Crosby was born. At 9 pounds 2½ ounces, he was the biggest baby in the nursery.

Bing, who had remained in England, was ecstatic at the news. He had always been sensitive about his own slight stature, and had hated to see it repeated in his sons. Previously my only solution to the dilemma had been the suggestion that he divorce the runt of the litter and marry my statuesque sister, a proposal which I'd withdrawn immediately when I saw the gleam in his eye.

Day after day Bing called for reassurance that Nathaniel was doing fine. A hater of telephones, he had always insisted that if you can't get your business done in two minutes, you should write a letter. Now he continued to correspond by mail, but he also made a great nuisance of himself by calling the hospital every day, and insisting on speaking for hours over a bad overseas line.

Bing arrived from England on November 16, gloated over Nathaniel for a couple of days, and then drove Harry and me to the ranch for what he termed "post-natal rest and recreation." The English translation was cooking, making beds, cleaning house, and helping with the outdoor chores.

Bing and I were usually awakened at about midnight by a small visitor from the next room, who crawled between us and settled down. One night, just as we were going back to sleep, a swan calling for its mate swept low over the house.

"Isn't it lovely?" murmured Bing sleepily.

"Yes, daddy," said Harry, cuddling in closer to his father's furry chest. And that I thought should have been our swan song.

But it wasn't. Instead of returning home, Bing decided the next day that I was to become his hunting companion. "You're a little puny since Nathaniel," he offered as his excuse.

Poor trusting innocent that I was, I should have noted that he lacked a native boy with a drum. For a special treat he sent me hiking through the lava, with orders to shoo out every duck that I saw lurking in the underbrush. He bagged several mallards, and I got a bad case of sore feet.

My complaints led to a promotion to Great White Hunter. In this role I was dangerous to man and beast, but harmed no birds until the last moment when, walking down the lane near the house, I finally nailed two quail. This was patently illegal because the lane quail counted as home covey, but as Phil Harris insisted, "You can't let them inbreed. They'll come out with one eye right in the middle of their foreheads." Incestuous or no, they were fine for breakfast.

We returned from the free and easy life of the ranch to participate in the rituals of the San Francisco social season. After a lunch with Phyllis Tucker, the original sponsor of the Cotillion, we donned formal dress for Abigail Folger's debut ball. Certainly no one at that gala event could possibly have anticipated that the lovely girl would be murdered by Charles Manson's cultists a decade later.

Just as we entered the grand ballroom of the Palace Hotel, Bing slipped to the floor in agony. A physician appeared, his tongue heavy with champagne, but his diagnostic abilities unimpaired. "It looks like kidney stones," he decided. "I'll call an ambulance."

I spent a terrified night at Bing's side in the hospital. It was the first time that I'd ever seen him give in to pain and groan in unremitting agony. Finally a combination of antispasmodic drugs and strong narcotics brought blessed oblivion.

By the next day the medication had controlled the spasm to a point where Bing could walk again. We flew back to Los Angeles, where my pathetic attempts at Christmas cheer were dampened by Bing's inability to participate, and overshadowed by the fear of imminent major surgery.

La Casa Crosby at Las Cruces

1962

We started the new year with Bing in the hospital. On January 3 he was released for two hours to attend Nathaniel's christening, but tests had revealed stones in both kidneys. Since a human must have at least one functioning kidney, there was no way to operate on both of them simultaneously.

On Friday, January 6, four stones were removed from Bing's left kidney. For the next few days he endured the pain without complaint, but by Tuesday he was obviously tired of having me hovering about. Over the baked eggs that I had brought him for breakfast he talked at length about the house he was building on a hill in Las Cruces.

"Why don't you go down and furnish it?" he began, and then suddenly clutched at the tubes in his side and asked me to leave.

I did so, but I made the mistake of returning that evening with chicken crêpes, only to find that Bing couldn't eat. "Please leave now and don't bring me any breakfast," he begged. "I'm going to try to sleep later in the morning."

Even when heavily sedated Bing maintained his own peculiar schedule of sleeping. They could knock him out for only about 4 hours, after which he would awake, read for a while, and even write a few notes. About 5 a.m. came the merciful second sleep, which lasted until as late as 8 if no one awakened him. Disturbing him was the most serious crime against his health, and I with my classes, nursing, and morning calls for makeup, had been guilty of it from the beginning of our marriage.

As I was finally to learn, Bing was as exhausted from the strain of being brave as I was from being cheerful. We both needed to drop our respective roles and get offstage for a time. So I endured a final lecture about the exchange rate of dollars to pesos and the peculiarities of Mexican banks, to which I was much too tired and distressed to listen, and took off in our new Aero Commander for Baja California.

Once settled in a cabaña in Las Cruces, I drove out to the future Casa Crosby. I hadn't quite believed in it, and was amazed to find a white stucco structure, with a red tile roof and a sweeping view of the sea, in this deserted spot in a country where things happened slowly if at all. I, who had taken two years to get a living

The family minus Nathaniel at Las Cruces

where father and daughter performed a novel birdbath ballet

room painted white, couldn't understand how Bing had conjured up a whole house in a matter of months. Now it was my job to furnish it from the stores in La Paz, Taxco, and Mexico City.

The project nearly cost me my life. Swooping in for a landing at Taxco, I noticed at the very last second that an almost invisible barbed-wire fence stretched across the middle of the runway. The pilot gunned the engine and we just cleared it. Short of fuel we had to land anyway, and did so precariously on a bare hillside. I later learned that an indignant farmer, whom the government had failed to pay for his expropriated land, had simply reclaimed it.

Spending like a drunken sailor on a six-hour pass, I accumulated within a matter of days all the necessary hardware for doors and windows, together with the entire contents of a going establishment: to wit, stove, refrigerator, freezer, tables, chairs, toilets, sinks, and more beds than we could possibly use. "Mission accomplished," I sighed happily.

Flushed with success, I flew back to get Bing out of the hospital. He still needed frequent checkups, so we had to stay in Los Angeles until February 1, when I was able to remove him to the slower-paced vacation atmosphere of Palm Springs, the serenity of which was shattered by news of a suicide attempt by Lindsay's eight-months-pregnant wife Barbara, which had led to the loss of the child. With characteristic fortitude Bing cowered in Palm Springs while I took charge of the baby's funeral and burial, and dealt with a frantic Lindsay, who was suffering from feelings of guilt which subsequently necessitated lengthy psychological treatment.

Since a number of other family problems loomed on the immediate horizon, I bundled Bing into the Aero Commander and shipped him off to the tranquility of Las Cruces, which in turn was disturbed by a series of threatening communications. The first note was from Taxco, stating simply that my check had bounced. Then a series of bad checks flooded in from La Paz. Finally Rodríguez came in from monitoring the ship-to-shore news to announce that Bing's wife was in serious trouble.

"Oh God, I told her to stay away from that hospital," Bing wailed. "What has she done now?"

"What hospital?" asked Rod in some bewilderment. "All I heard is that she has written hot checks all over Mexico, and the police now have an all-points bulletin out for her."

So my poor sick husband had to climb into the plane and retrace my route, checkbook in hand. The worst of my problems derived from the fact that I had made some purchases at the federal Monte de Piedad, and the Mexican government took a dim view of forgers and swindlers.

To further complicate the matter, the police had failed to identify me with Bing, and had been pursuing a mythical "Caterina Crosbyng." They gave Bing a long lecture on the criminal aspects of writing checks with insufficient funds to back them, and didn't seem to lend much credence to his story that his wife couldn't tell dollars from pesos.

The owners of the private establishments were more reasonable, largely because my fault in this instance lay only in having signed my totally unauthorized name to Bing's perfectly good checks.

Meanwhile, back at the house, the contractor had heard of bouncing checks and stopped all work. Bing had to return to goad, wheedle, coerce, and bribe the various craftsmen and sub-contractors into completing their appointed tasks.

Blissfully ignorant of all the trouble I had caused, I set our Palm Desert house in order for President Kennedy's March 22-25 visit, and then raced back to Los Angeles and more nursing. Taking full advantage of the Aero Commander, I thenceforth continued my school work during the week, and commuted to Las Cruces on weekends.

Our suicidal pilot permitted me to fly the plane, a relatively simple feat on the surface of it since I had naught to do but follow the peninsula, keeping the water on my left and land on my right, and not forgetting to turn in at La Paz. I actually logged over a hundred hours of cross-

Heading for the hotel. On the return trip, Mary Frances moved over onto Bing's lap and the accident occurred.

country flying, and managed several hair-raising landings and takeoffs in the sharp thermal drafts at Mexicali before I mistakenly essayed my first and last stall. Reality dropped out from under me, my stomach pasted itself against my esophagus, and I abandoned the junior birdman bit for life.

By the beginning of May, Bing was well enough to do some recording in Los Angeles. When he returned, he resumed fishing with a vengeance. On May 9 he records that, "Between 6:30 and 2:30 p.m. we actually hooked 21 marlin. Of course the big ones got away, but this time we had an excuse because Jack was running the boat. He's a good captain and a fair-to-middling cook, but he has a lot to learn about fighting fish. When the biggest marlin pulled the bait off the outrigger and hooked himself, Jack, thinking it was his job to set the hook, raced off in the other direction. Of course the monster took bait, line, and rod, and went dancing off to tell Davy Jones about it. I lost another rod when, on a double hookup, I told Alfonso to break his fish off. He did it with such gusto that he broke the rod too."

A series of friends arrived to celebrate Bing's return to health. When I flew down with Rosemary Clooney on the 25th, she mentioned her fears for her children when the car door had flown open the week before. "Our children always wear their safety belts," I thought smugly.

We returned from a swim at the hotel with Mary Frances on Bing's lap "helping him drive," Harry in the wicker seat to his right, and Rosie and me in the back of the little Renault beach wagon. Our conveyance lacked not only seat belts but also doors, and the sandy road was a series of deep ruts and bumps. In a scene that appeared to have been filmed in slow motion, Bing turned a corner to the left just as Harry stood up to gesture to me. I saw the child tumble over the side of the car, and felt an ominous bump as Bing jammed on the brake, leaped out dumping Mary Frances into the sand, and raced for Harry.

For reasons of her own, Rosie climbed over me and across Bing's front seat to grab up Mary Frances and walk her away from the accident. Meanwhile I scrambled out over Harry's wicker basket, and fell into the sand almost on top of a small crumpled heap which, thanks be to God, was shrieking its lungs out, my first indication that we hadn't run over Harry's head.

The face that he turned up to the light was smeared with blood from an eye that was full of sand and obviously seriously injured. I was so horrified that I didn't notice until much later that one arm was badly bruised and covered with tire marks.

I picked Harry up and jumped back into the car. In less than five minutes he was lying on top of the counter in my bathroom, while I bathed the eye as best I could. As we flew to the hospital in La Paz, Harry repeated again and again, "I'm sorry that I let go, daddy. I won't do it anymore."

Miraculously a taxi was waiting for us at the La Paz airport. We embarked on a nightmarish search for a doctor, found the old clinic closed, and raced on to the new one, which had yet to open. Inquiring frantically for the addresses of physicians, we finally located a Dr. Von Borstel.

In a perfect vicious circle, he in turn led us straight back to the old clinic. Bing huddled in the patio, I scrubbed for surgery, and the doctor started cleaning the debris from Harry's eye.

It was only then that we learned that the eyeball had been scratched but not punctured. We washed it carefully with saline solution, and then I held a screaming child while the doctor sutured a long gash that ran through the eyebrow.

"Can't we get any more of that dirt out?"

"It's too deeply imbedded, but it will grow out in time. The same is true of the sand in the abrasion under the eye."

Harry was so glad that the operation was over that he sat patiently through the X-rays. There was no skull fracture and no sign of concussion. An X-ray of his bruised arm showed only a chipped elbow from the time when he'd fallen near the pool, and poor Bing had thought he was having an epileptic seizure.

Abelardo Rodriguez, bush pilot par excellence

I now realized that Harry was in a state of post-operative shock, which was acting as an anesthetic. At the same time I saw the immediate value of having the right male ego model. When his father came in, he immediately adopted Bing's attitude of feeling no pain, and even insisted that he had felt none during the entire procedure.

Bing and I spent the night with Harry in the obsolete clinic. At midnight we were amazed to hear the buzz of an airplane. La Paz was strictly a daylight field with no facilities for night landings, but 10 minutes later Rod Rodriguez strode in.

"What's happened?" he demanded. "Everyone at the hotel is waiting for news."

"He's going to be just fine." And then to Harry, who had stirred restively: "Go to sleep, darling, it's all right."

"One eye is already closed, mommy."

Like everything else, the mosquito netting had been moved to the new clinic. I brushed frantically at the clouds of insects, but my poor child was deserving of a better guardian. I fell asleep in the very act of complaining that, after so much pain, it was only fair that the mosquitoes should leave him alone.

Harry roused me at about 2 a.m., and said simply "Bathroom."

When Bing carried him in and turned on the light, the walls and ceiling moved. But Harry, who had yet to reach his fourth birthday, wasn't going to show fear of mere cockroaches in front of his daddy.

The next morning Rosie and I threw a few things together and took off for Los Angeles with Harry. U.S. customs had been forewarned, so they didn't even make a token search of our luggage, limiting themselves to asking, "Is there anything we can do to help?"

In Los Angeles our pediatrician met the plane and whisked Harry to Children's Hospital. X-rays were taken, and the wound was reexamined and cleaned. This time Harry was out of shock, into pain, and safe from his father's disapproving stare, so he howled with terror and begged me to take him home. Instead the physicians ostracized his weeping mother.

By the time I reached 594 Mapleton I had concocted a plan to kidnap my much-abused child. I would have carried it out too, had I not passed out as soon as I sat down to consider the details.

I awoke the next morning, possessed of my customary strength and ill-humor, and ready to make a fight of it, but when I reached the hospital I found that as usual I was rushing into battle where no battle was. Harry had charmed both nurses and patients, and now absolutely refused to leave his new friends. It wasn't until the 30th that I finally prevailed upon him to depart with me.

"I have to take care of my sister and brother," he explained with great dignity, and marched out to the car, huge black eye still sealed shut but exhibiting no permanent damage.

In the wee hours of the morning on June 4th Bing arrived in Los Angeles, saw me in my nursing uniform, and suddenly rolled all his fears for Harry, his concerns about his own health, and his generalized Irish guilt into a ball and hurled them at the duck-footed shoes, the white dacron dress, and the starched hat marked Q of A. I gathered from his remarks that I was derelict in my duties as wife and mother.

Resolved to placate Bing I raced home at noon, only to find that he had gone golfing five minutes after the conclusion of his matutinal diatribe. At dinner and throughout the following day he remained grimly silent, sallying forth in the evening without a word of explanation.

On Wednesday I pointedly cut my classes, babysat, cleaned the house, and cooked, while Bing sulked in his office. At last I forced my way in for a chat, in the course of which he stated that I was incompetent as a housekeeper and unavailable as a parent, and that consequently my children were undisciplined. Whereupon he left for the airport and boarded our plane for Las Cruces.

Stung by the truth of much that Bing had said, I embarked upon a new career as a wall-to-wall mother. Resolutely I spirited the children

Aerial view of our Las Cruces home

off to the ranch to see their new surprise from daddy, four Welsh ponies named Susie, Story, Roman Lavender, and Jasper. My cherubs enjoyed themselves enormously while I whomped up some of my inimitable culinary creations, hoped that they were resistant to botulism, and favored them with what must have been the wildest bedtime stories in the history of English oral literature.

So much for motherhood. Now for my other neglected role as winsome wife. Resolutely I flew to Las Cruces to win back my Latin lover. If it's true that the way to a man's heart is through his stomach, I can see why I had such difficulty in traversing a blocked tunnel. With more than a little help from a stout Mexican cook, and a full day's effort over a not-so-hot stove, since the gas pressure was way down, I concocted an enormous meal that I considered downright edible.

Bing tasted each dish warily, manifesting open suspicion of my motives and skills, but the effect was well-nigh miraculous. As we sat outside, listening to the ball game on Armed Forces Radio and watching the shining standards of the sky glide across the heavens, he uttered no further word of criticism. In fact no sounds at all were forthcoming until the majesty of the night was finally interrupted by a gentle snore. Eureka! Where the strongest hypnotics had failed, my cooking had succeeded in anaesthetizing my insomniac. Who said the age of miracles was dead?

As I finally learned the next day, Bing's outburst in Los Angeles had really had very little to do with me. Once again I had mistakenly assumed that I was the center of his universe. The fact was that he had not yet recovered his strength from one operation, knew that he needed another, and was facing a series of other problems that I had known nothing about.

There was a nasty paradox here. I spent my life seeking out problems and giving advice that no one wanted. Bing, who hid from people and their problems in the farthest corners of the known world, was continually having them thrust upon him.

He resented this because he didn't want to be a meddler, and he didn't fancy a wife who wanted nothing else. My nurse's uniform had symbolized my enormous need to poke my nose into others' lives and resolve their difficulties.

Specifically I had been trying to mediate between Phillip and Sandra, suggesting none too tactfully to the former that it was not cricket to throw a five-months-pregnant wife down a flight of stairs, even if it was simply the conclusion of a playful wrestling match. I shuddered now as I recalled how Sandra had stated flatly, "You're no help. I want Bing to tell Phillip how to treat me."

Just for the intellectual exercise, I tried my best to imagine Bing sitting down to discuss her domestic affairs with Sandra, and then lecturing Phil on becoming a model husband.

The shuddering continued as I reflected on how I'd been helping Gary. He had phoned a number of times, trying to lure Bing into inspecting the new house that he had found in the valley for his family. He had hoped that Bing would not only approve of it, but also loan him the money to buy it.

My interest in the project had been tolerated only because I might be able to put in a good word with dad. Not one to miss an opportunity, I had of course favored Bing with many thousands of words on the subject, while he simply shook his head at the impossiblity of explaining to me how many times he had already traveled the same road.

Thus Bing's demands that I become involved with home and children were really simply pleas for peace. A rough translation might have been, "Will you please stop causing so damn much trouble in the outside world."

By June 22 Bing was obviously recovering his strength and feeling better about life in general. He appeared in the library, where I was arranging books, and asked that I come to his office.

Five minutes later I dashed upstairs muttering, "What have I done now?" and feeling as if I'd been sent to the principal. I was totally

The Crosbys and the Waynes arrive in Hawaii to keep a date with destiny

and that unlikely femme fatale, my mother Olive.

unprepared for, "How about a little trip to Hawaii?"

Not being one to look a gift horse in the mouth, I simply asked "When?"

"The 28th."

"With whom?"

"Harry and Mary Frances—and why not your mother if your dad will let her go?"

All this was new and wondrous strange, so I rushed in to consolidate the territory on my mother's behalf. "He'll let her go all right, and she'll be a great help with the children."

And so it was that our little caravan came to the Coco Palms Hotel in Kauai for early pit barbecue, late lava tub baths, and fragrant frangipani blossoms under a tropic moon.

Bing had an infinite capacity for leisure, and this was a perfect place for him to rest. I had always found it much harder to turn off the invisible loudspeakers in the walls that demand constant maximizing, so I salved my conscience by reading Michener's *Hawaii* and harkening back to ancient days of glory, so that I could explain the torch-lighting ceremony and the sounds of the conch shell to our delighted children.

Mother was the beauty in our family, and here in a muumuu, with black waves cascading to her waist, she put the loveliest of the native girls to shame. After a day of swimming with the children, Bing invited John and Pilar Wayne for a late-afternoon mai-tai.

Now mother was a strict Baptist who had never touched alcohol, but she found these "fruit punches" delicious, so we said nothing to disillusion her. "That was so refreshing that I think I'll have another," she told John Wayne, who dutifully fetched her another, and another, and another, and true knight of the saddle that he was, joined her each time.

By the fifth round of mai-tais mother and the duke were busily holding each other up, while she explained that he had always been her ideal of American manhood, and he insisted that she was the cutest little thing on the beach.

Shortly thereafter the thing between them became too big for mere talk, so they launched into a gloriously off-key duet rendition of "Oh the moon shines tonight on pretty Redwing. . .the breeze is sighing. . .the nightbirds crying. . .far, oh, far beneath the sky her brave is sleeping. . .while Redwing's weeping her heart away."

Obviously feeling that the melody was in desperate need of surgery, Bing made a half-hearted attempt to join in, but was immediately and unanimously rejected on the grounds that he obviously had no feeling for music. Nothing personal, you understand.

This could have gone on forever, and it almost did, but Bing and I finally managed to save my mother's virtue, and possibly her life, by pushing her off in one direction, while a furious Latin lovely dragged her husband off in the other. I never did learn what happened to Big John, but my mother, a true Grandstaff, passed blissfully into never-never land, where she remained for the next 12 hours. Upon awakening she complained of a slight headache, exhibited a ravenous appetite, and to all appearances had completely forgotten her erstwhile attempt to wreck the Waynes' happy home.

On July 2 Bing received a phone call from a psychiatrist at St. John's Hospital, who insisted that he commit Lindsay. This was just the sort of thing that Bing found hardest to deal with. His face went gray and the lines of sorrow deepened. I was desperate to take over for him, and make the decision by simply saying *yes*, but of course I had no rights in the matter.

After over an hour on the phone Bing finally said abruptly "No, I can't do it," and hung up. At least he had made a decision not to decide, but I hated to see worries about the family haunt him even in our Pacific paradise.

We stayed on and continued to go through the motions. Bing played golf daily while I ate litchi nuts off the trees and watched the children, who had learned to swim before they could walk, playing in the surf like little seals.

On July 19 we made the grave error of returning to civilization. The cook quit, the children all got sick, Bing had trouble with his

The younger members of the Crosby clan visit Disneyland.

teeth and his family, and I bought a ticket back to Hawaii.

All four of Bing's grown sons were having serious problems, of which he would tell me nothing for fear that I might jump in with both feet. So he suffered in silence and I went wild with frustration. It was a vicious circle. My meddling had cost me my husband's confidences, which in turn prevented me from further meddling. It seemed a high price to pay for being such a busybody.

With no other lives to run, I concentrated on my poor children, and spent days overpreparing Harry for his eye repair. When I took him into surgery at St. Joseph's, he understood precisely what his rights and my duties were, and insisted that I bring a whole library of books that I'd promised to read to him. He conducted himself so beautifully in surgery, laughing as he went under anesthesia and recovered from it, that the doctor said I could take him right home.

At this point the laughter stopped. I had on my hands a furious child, who had been exhaustively prepared for the role of martyr and was determined to play it. "Mama," he demanded, "you promised to read all those books to me first."

This in front of an admiring gallery of doctors and nurses, obviously questioning the quality of the home life of a child who was so desperate to remain in the hospital. After much strenuous debate, my first-born agreed reluctantly to accompany me on the condition that his daddy read him all the books.

"Of course he will, darling," I lied diplomatically, and thus finally made my embarrassed way out of there.

On the 29th of July Bing escaped from family pressures the only way he knew how by boarding a plane for Biarritz. His first letter back was devoted entirely to Harry and the type of direction that I should give him.

". . .The vital thing is that he should never know that he is being taught. We can't just tell a youngster what is right and wrong. More can be accomplished by example, by illuminating the principle that those who do right, who work, who have worthwhile aspirations, are happy and successful.

"This fall he must spend lots of time with other boys of his age, learning to adjust. It will provide him with an understanding of others, and of their rights and privileges. Do look after him. . ."

Bing's second letter contained a graphic description of Biarritz, and concluded with the following note about his friend Chris Dunphy: "Chris has upset the American community by assuming the position of my social secretary. His latest edict is 'Fork in hand at 8:15 or we don't show.' Last night Duree Shevlin remonstrated 'But Chris, *my servants* haven't eaten by then.' "

In his third letter Bing was back to golf, describing how Catherine La Coste, former French women's champion, had managed to beat him. He appended another note about Chris Dunphy: "He has chosen Sir Charles Abraham, who fancies himself a backgammon player, as his particular pigeon. Chris nurses him along carefully, but occasionally Sir Charles will make such a gaff that Chris insists, 'I can't let you do that, sir. It's just too horrible.' Chris has won all his expenses here, and I hope Sir Charles will write them off as lessons from an expert."

Bing was obviously getting back into the carefree, vagabond life that he loved. My great moment came when he interrupted his description of it to invite me to join him. He closed that letter with the following tribute to my financial wizardry: "Get five hundred dollars in cash before you leave. The rate of exchange for new francs is very simple: Five for one dollar, ten for two dollars, fifty for ten dollars, one hundred for twenty dollars." Evidently the debacle in Mexico was forgiven but not forgotten.

The last letter prepared the village idiot for life among the *crème de la crème:* "My chauffeur will meet you at the plane at Nice in a silver Rolls, and drive you to our cabaña at Eden Roc, where we swam with the Kennedys last year. You will need two or three dinner dresses, luncheon things, a bathing suit, a walking outfit, a

With self-appointed social secretary Chris Dunphy

warm coat, whatever is appropriate for the bullfights, and some celebrity T-shirts for a girl of fourteen."

The last item was a bit puzzling, but even I could manage the rest. On August 9 I bundled my mother, Mary Frances, and Harry into a plane for Paris, where we indulged in a bit of sight-seeing before I sent the others on to Nice and Cannes, while I proceeded to a rendezvous with Bing and trouble at Biarritz.

Both were immediately apparent upon arrival. Bing was tanned, smiling, and looking his very best, particularly with the ravishing creature on his arm, who, as it transpired, was destined to fill out those T-shirts.

And not in any teen-age fashion either. Some 21 summers had been well spent in accumulating her quite fantastic curves. Apparently I was to have another brush with Bing's fatal weakness for French charmers.

And so winsomely did she sweep me off to see an enormous gray stone palace, with the straightforward tiled-roof architecture of all the huge houses in Biarritz, and so terrified was I that Bing would carry through his announced intention of buying the damned place, that it took some hours before I could bring the subject around to her ostensible function in my life.

"I am to be the new nursemaid," Janine announced firmly, "I have grown tired of the stewardess life with Air France, and your wonderful husband said he wants the children to grow up speaking French."

I'd just bet he did. I had quietly noted in the interim that his own French had improved markedly during the past weeks. They do say that practice makes perfect.

"Besides," Bing announced ingenuously, "you have all your school work and nursing courses to finish, so this way the children can stay in Biarritz, and learn French, and have someone to take care of them."

"And not only the children," I reflected glumly. Well, I had asked for it, but however just my fate, this old used mother wasn't going to be retired to Los Angeles while her husband set up his real home in Biarritz. I determined that Little Miss Air France would have to go back to stewardessing, but the matter would take some study.

And study I did throughout the next days as our mobile *ménage à trois* moved through a round of cocktails and dinner parties, at which my rival outdid me at every turn. When Tommy Shevlin came rushing in to apologize for being late "because he had just been swimming with Sir," she explained loftily that the poor man meant Don Carlos, the pretender to the Spanish throne.

She was also the first to mention that Duree Shevlin had been secretly married to Jack Kennedy long before Jacqueline appeared on the scene, a rumor which was to surface shortly in the press and never to be denied by the redoubtable Duree, who simply laughed and said, "Let him deny it."

Meanwhile I was familiarizing myself with the French words for strychnine and arsenic, but help was waiting in the wings, as anyone but a poor blind mother would have known. On August 25 we abandoned the hotel in Biarritz, where Bing with a superb show of competence and magnanimity tipped the maids, the porter, and the doorman, and ushered our luggage safely into the van, forgetting only one tiny detail. Somehow in his haste to impress Janine he had neglected to pay the hotel bill, so we were pursued to the airport by an indignant assistant manager.

Having pronounced my bathing suit perfectly dreadful, Janine next expressed surprise at the fact that I couldn't get into the one that she had loaned me, at least without risking arrest. I smiled, ate my liver, and tactfully pointed out to Bing that after all we had hired Bridget Brennan as the children's nurse.

"She's now a full-time nanny for Nathaniel," Bing snapped, "and besides she doesn't speak a word of French."

After breakfast on the terrace, we wound our way down the tortuous mountain road to the cabaña at Eden Roc. There our nursemaid first met her new charges, and pronounced herself absolutely *enchantée* with their charm-

217

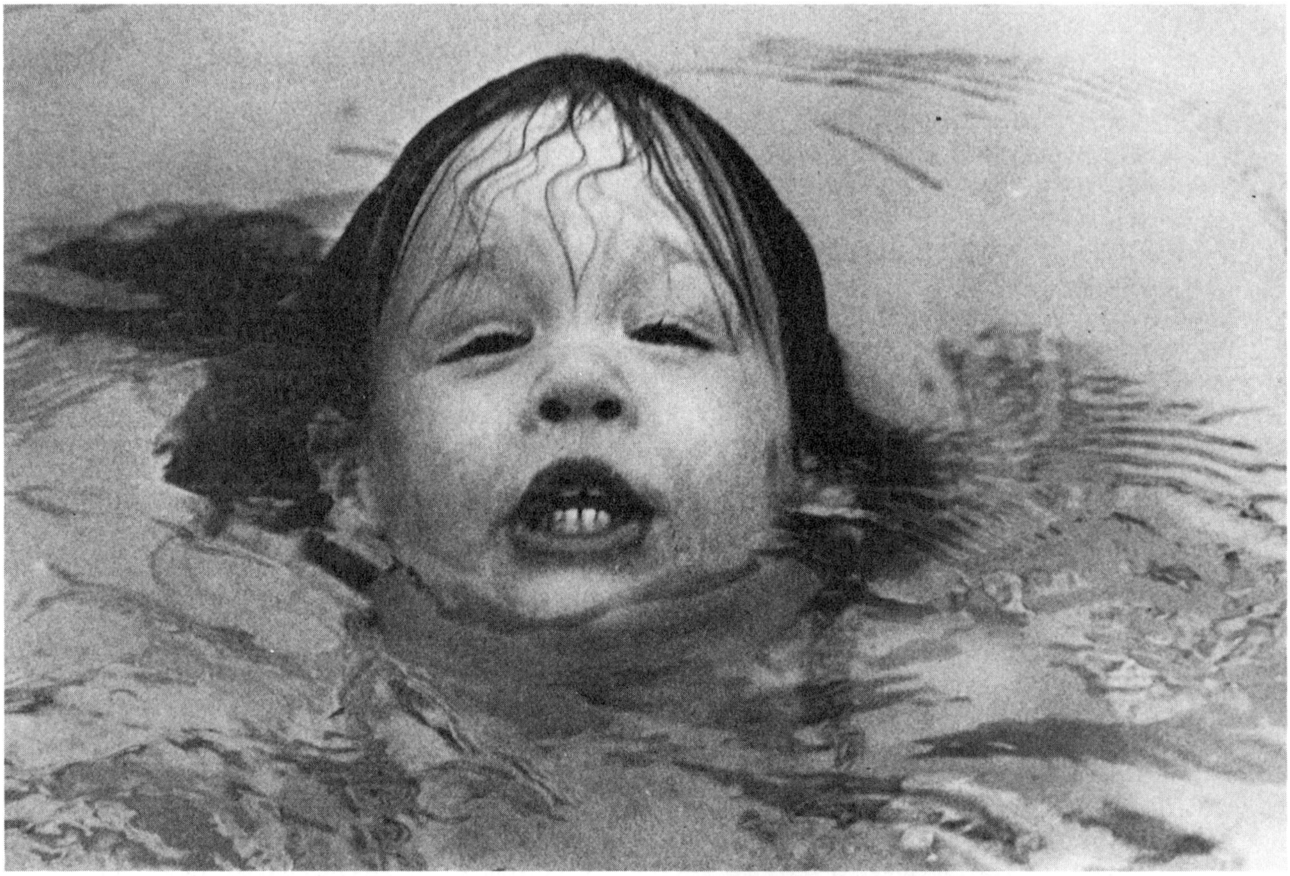

The littlest mermaid hits the water.

And brother Harry is not far behind.

A momentary pause at Eden Roc

ing demeanor. Then the tots set off resolutely for a swim, and I watched Janine trying to guide them toward the wading pool, where children below the age of ten were safely paddling about in their life preservers.

Gazing far up beyond this secure retreat, Mary Frances, who at the age of two had been the youngest child to win her Red-Cross swimming certificate, spied a twelve-foot diving board, perched on a precipice above the Mediterranean. With a shriek of unholy glee, she was up the cliff like a monkey and hurling herself off into the sea, with Harry, not to be outdone by a mere girl, right behind her. Mary's shrieks were nothing compared to those of Janine, who as we now learned couldn't swim and was terrified of the water.

My first impulse was to race to her aid, but an unseen hand restrained me. A slight ray of hope had suddenly appeared in the Egyptian blackness of my psyche. My revenge would have a subtle oriental flavor. I would simply leave them to each other.

It was some hours later when the children tired of sporting in the waves and pronounced themselves famished. We repaired to the elegant French restaurant at Eden Roc, where I once again refrained from disciplinary measures as my little bundles of energy ripped the buffet to pieces, while a desperate and exhausted French girl trailed in their wake shouting vainly *Mais non, Attendez*, and finally *Au secours!*

But there was no help for the wicked. For the first time in a week it was I who was sitting poised and cool at Bing's side, eating with renewed appetite while he hissed uncomfortably, "Can't you teach her to do something with those kids?"

"Doubtless she'll get the hang of it," I smiled airily, failing to mention the fact that if she did she would be a long step ahead of me.

Right after lunch the children decided to go exploring in the Alpes Maritimes. Up the steep mountain trails they raced like goats, with Janine's high heels scrambling somewhat less agilely behind them. They returned at dinnertime with wondrous tales of adventures, which Bing tried to check with Janine, who curiously enough was unavailable, having pled a sick headache and taken to her bed.

The next day Mary Frances continued her diving exhibition, and Janine was actually showing signs of adjusting to it, when Harry decided to imitate the water skiers. He had had his fourth birthday only two weeks before, and was still much too light to hold the skis in position, so he took fall after fall as Janine tried to shout warnings from the shore over the sound of the boat's motor, and he waved cheerfully back at her.

Then there were delightful side trips to the Picasso Museum, to the Matisse Chapel, to tour the U.S.S. Enterprise, to picnic on Ste. Marguerite Island, and to the finest restaurants in the area. I was never lovelier, remaining self-possessed and *tres chic* at Bing's side, while Janine sought to preserve renowned French landmarks from imminent destruction.

All in vain. Harry's surface charm masked a devilish bent for mischief, and Mary Frances had been a hellion from the day she was born. They rioted, climbed, tumbled, and rolled about formal restaurants like miniature whirlwinds, with a desperate nanny trailing in their wake at ever-greater distances.

Finally we returned from purchasing pottery in Vallauris to find them wrestling in the dust, with Harry doing his level best to tear Mary Frances' hair out by the roots, while she stoutly whaled away at his midsection. Janine had obviously abandoned the field. She was leaning against the Rolls with a glazed look and complaining to the chauffeur, "*Mais ce n'est pas possible, ce n'est pas possible!*"

I separated the combatants, knocked heads together, and hauled them over to their protesting nanny. "You'll have to establish a little more discipline before they get back with Nathaniel," I warned her jovially. "These two are angels compared to him."

Janine didn't seem to be paying much attention. She just kept repeating mechanically, "*Zat Marie Francoise, zat Marie Francoise.*"

The lovely restful bullfights

Privately I had to admit that she had a point there. Bing's only daughter was born to shoot J.R. and anyone else who got in her way. With her as an ally, I could really press my advantage. I was now considering some sweet revenge, like recapitulating *The Ransom of Red Chief* and demanding a reverse reward of everything she owned if I were to take the monsters back.

I finally relented, reflecting that nothing in Janine's wardrobe would fit me anyway, and permitted her to tender her resignation to Bing and race home to mother. All in all, there was only one real drawback. My brief reign as the *femme fatale* of the Cote d'Azur had come to a sudden end. There I was back with Harry and Mary Frances.

And that was enough for any three mothers. The next couple of weeks brought me to a point where I would cheerfully have surrendered Bing to Janine, with the sole proviso that she assume full and permanent charge of all his children too.

"Take me anywhere," I demanded despairingly, so Bing opted for Barcelona and the lovely, restful bullfights. Some concept of the level to which I had fallen may be gleaned from the fact that I handed my charges over to my very own mother, and waved a cheerful good-bye, wondering vaguely whether I'd ever see her alive again.

I've never been into torturing animals, but after two weeks with Harry and Mary Frances an arena full of slaughter was a piece of cake. Once again I had time to savor my triumph over Janine, but as events proved I had scotched the snake not killed it. The next morning Bing returned to our room from a quest for cigars, with the self-congratulatory expression on his face that I had learned to dread.

"I have found the perfect nursemaid for the children," he announced loftily. "She's right downstairs in the beauty shop."

"My God, he must have stumbled over another French girl," I thought glumly, "and I'll have to put the kibosh on this one myself, since my troops are daily adding years to my mother's life in far-off Nice."

And so it was that we marched down to meet Manolita, an experience which was certainly worth the hike. From her tinted hair to her four-inch spike heels this was a governess to conjure with. Besides her undeniably flashy looks, the only talent that I was able to search out was an ability to pick up any tune immediately and accompany Bing on the guitar, no mean feat for hands encumbered with three-inch lacquered nails. Also, as far as I could tell, she seemed to be trying to convince me that she loved babies, and indeed she seemed ripe and ready to produce a few.

Resolutely I hauled Bing aside and put one of my size 5's down hard. "I thought you said you wanted the children to learn French," I snarled.

"I've been considering the matter, and Spanish will do just as well. Worldwide it's a bigger language than French now you know, and we'll be spending lots of time in Mexico."

"Good thinking, Bonzo," I snapped. "But it just happens that this girl speaks only Catalán."

"Isn't that a kind of Spanish?"

"No, damn it, it's a whole different language, and it's of use only to a person who wants to spend the rest of his life in Cataluña."

Reluctantly, like a dog separated from his bone, Bing abandoned his perfect find. As he walked away muttering, I could see that he was still determined to find a nursemaid for the children, and had not abandoned his unique screening process. I colored my future dark.

The hussy may have engineered a revenge of sorts. During the next couple of days in the hotel I was overwhelmed at having Bing all to myself, and resolved to play the role of temptress to the hilt. Moderation just isn't my forte, so perhaps I once again overdid things just a trifle. It seemed to me that the members of the staff were casting increasingly suspicious glances at us, while we, unable to speak Catalán, were in no position to allay their doubts.

Finally came the night when we had indisputable proof that we weren't simply paranoid. As we were happily and somewhat

Interviewing yet another nanny

noisily enjoying a bottle of champagne in our room, there was a loud knocking at the door.

"Sir," announced a thickly-accented voice in funeral tones, "You'll have to get that woman out of your room."

Unable to explain ourselves to someone who had doubtless found the command in a phrase book, we felt humiliated, tickled, and actually frightened. Courageously we both pretended that we weren't there, until eventually we heard a couple of men shuffle away. For the rest of the evening we had visions of them returning with a skeleton key and discovering us *in flagrante delicto*.

Since there was no help for it, the next morning we left the hotel in disgrace and returned to our babes in Cannes.

Not a moment too soon. The following day we had long been scheduled to have lunch at the farm of the Prince of Monaco, and I characteristically had repressed the whole affair.

Bing habitually forgave such oversights, but this time he was as nervous as a debutante. Of course I egocentrically assumed that this was on my account, and resolved to reassure him by becoming the belle of the ball. Just to be on the safe side, I first phoned the Princess' social secretary, who informed me that a tea gown would be acceptable attire.

This was a category that I was prepared to handle. Among the trunks which Bing had first forbidden me to bring and then fatalistically lugged over half of Europe, I had secreted tea gowns galore. In honor of the occasion I settled upon the most spectacular number, a splendid chiffon besprinkled with beige and burnt-orange flowers, in a wildly impressionistic style worthy of one of Renoir's drunken acolytes. The jacket was deliciously transparent, and the picture hat would have been right at home in Versailles.

Bing was unaccountably anxious that our children not disgrace us. For the first and last time he watched me prepare them for combat, surveying each step with a critical eye.

Harry uttered only token protests as I stuffed him into his new white suit, but as ever Mary Frances was a different matter. She screamed in feigned agony as I French-braided her hair three times, still managing to leave Medusa-like wisps striving for *Lebensraum* all about her face.

The lord of the manor himself was a model of sartorial splendor in a blue blazer with white ascot. We registered another first when I actually caught him manicuring his nails.

Could this be the same man who had always greeted royalty and ragamuffins alike with the same casual amusement?

It was only when the car arrived that I realized that my mother was to accompany us. "We need someone who can manage the children," Bing had told her decisively.

I worried about them all the way to the farm, with predictable results: They had a grand time and I was carsick.

My stomach was still doing flip-flops as I stumbled out behind our little band, who were following a liveried attendant to an outdoor barbecue.

There on the terrace stood Her Serene Highness in regally grease-bespattered slacks and blouse, competently cooking hamburgers. Equally casually dressed, the Prince was also maintaining his royal cool in the blazing heat.

Staggering in on high heels which should have been made of glass, I felt like Cinderella in reverse, mistakenly donning her ball gown for a picnic. Trying to cover my embarrassment I turned to the children, whom my mother was consigning to the tender mercies of a French governess. I noted with dim forebodings that Mary Frances had already placed a Japanese stranglehold on Albert, and that Harry was enacting his "perfect little gentleman" role for Carolyn's benefit. That was always a warning signal. Combustibles, as I understand it, are all the more dangerous for compression.

Before I could rescue Albert, my mother had stepped into the breach. "Don't give it another thought, Mademoiselle. They're all little savages at that age. Just send them out to play, and they'll work it out for themselves."

Since my first ploy had failed, there was

My angels with Prince Albert and Princess Caroline, the latter still in proud possession of her ballet slippers

nothing for it but to focus my charms on the Prince. His attention, however, seemed fully occupied by Bing and Grace, who had broken the initial tension by the simple expedient of wrapping themselves around each other.

"Unseasonably warm," I ventured. "How nice that you thought of a picnic!" (My talent for brilliant conversation thrives on emergencies.)

My target continued to gaze speculatively at his spouse and her erstwhile costar. I was wondering idly whether this particular monarchic setup had retained its dungeons and torture chambers, or whether I was to lose my mate to the guillotine, when mother, whom the children's departure had left momentarily unemployed, wrapped an ample arm about Rainier and asked him what it felt like to be a prince.

Fresh out of alternatives and abandoned to my own devices, I resumed staring glumly at the couple from *The Country Girl*, who were now chattering like magpies about topics of mutual interest, while absent-mindedly neglecting to unhand each other.

An episode narrated by Rosemary Clooney came to mind. For reasons that I suddenly realized were still unexplained, she had dropped in on Bing one evening, latish and quite unannounced. There she had found Grace curled up in a chair by the fire, attired in cardigan sweater, tweed skirt, and heavy brogans, staring at her knitting through horn-rimmed spectacles.

"Ah domesticity!" Rosemary had breathed before retiring discreetly.

Obviously superfluous, I now did a bit of retiring on my own, following the same liveried attendant to a drawing room furnished in expensive antiques. There I busied myself in a search for something small enough to throw, lethal enough to wound, and expensive enough so that its replacement would bankrupt my feckless spouse.

These blithesome musings were interrupted by the advent of my mother, with the Prince in tow, "Rainier honey," she was explaining cheerfully, "you don't have to worry about sibling rivalries. It's just a phase that children go through. Carolyn truly loves Albert, and she'll come to realize it in time. For the present, just keep knives away from her and give her lots of love."

Noble sentiments indeed, but the moral of the story wasn't helped by the sudden appearance of Carolyn herself, who looked rather as if someone had just given her forty days in purgatory in lieu of the recommended portion of love. Disheveled and caked with dirt she stood, and howled out her hatred of Mary Frances, who it seemed had put her in this state in the course of forcibly removing her ballet slippers. "She wanted 'em and she took 'em off me," the distraught child wailed.

When the Prince looked inquiringly at me, I nodded in wholehearted agreement. That would be Mary Frances all right.

Rainier's stern glance seemed to require something more of me. Could it just be possible that some action was indicated? Could he be unaware of the futility of thwarting Mary Frances? I was about to explain the matter when Albert's arrival interrupted me.

The heir to the throne was not yet barefoot, but this was his one advantage over his sister. "First he butted me in the stomach and knocked me down. Then he kicked me and took all my candy. Then he...."

Yes, that would be my Harry. I smiled benignly and lost all interest in the future sovereign's monologue. I am a relatively quick study, and I'd heard the same lines often enough from the neighbors' children to get them by heart long since.

For the Prince, however, Albert's words still had an air of novelty. He assumed a forbiddingly patriarchal expression quite out of keeping with the role of jovial host. Feeling rather like a little girl about to be disciplined by her father, I was delighted at the interruption when, attracted by the general din, Bing and Grace strolled in, still with their arms about one another's waists.

Absorbed in each other they continued to

With the best quick-order chef in all Monaco

chat amiably for a moment. Then, as if from an immense height, the Princess deigned to take notice of the uproar. Smiling majestically she murmured a few words in French, the burden of which seemed to be, "Cease and desist, my chickadees, or mommy will break your little necks."

The hubbub stopped instantly. Ye gods and little fishhooks, this was sorcery! I resolved to perfect my French.

Her Highness turned back to her admiring escort and favored him with a long, soulful Gallic look, the English translation of which seemed to be, "See, if you'd only married me instead of the over-dressed frump who is now leaving claw marks in the arms of my Louis XVI sofa, you might have had disciplined children, in addition to countless other benefits."

I was about to reply in border Texan, the only language I speak when aroused, but my husband shot me a warning glance and announced that the hamburgers were ready. Whereupon he swept Grace off to sample them, followed by my mother and the Prince, and at a considerable distance by an apparition in an orange tea gown.

Grace and Bing continued their tête-à-tête at lunch, while the French governess appeared at random intervals to lodge savage and doubtless justified complaints against my invisible descendants, and then disappear into the underbrush in pursuit of them. I did my best to follow the conversation, but it seemed to consist largely of code words.

Rebuffed I tuned back in on my mother's voice, and was horrified to hear it slowly, and with immense authority, reciting the entire elementary curriculum for American students. In my acute embarrassment I considered hiding under the table, or joining the children in the bushes. No, there really was no escape. I plucked up my courage and finally stole a glance at Rainier. Methodically and with obvious satisfaction he was taking notes. He looked like a good student who anticipated a test at the end of the lecture, and mother was just the sort of teacher who might administer one.

Fortunately the hamburgers were excellent. Since no one cared to monitor my behavior, or even acknowledge my presence, I favored them with my full attention. Red in tooth and claw, I must have devoured at least a dozen before Rainier regretfully put aside his pencil and announced that Bing and he were overdue at the club for their round of golf.

Robbed of her prey, my mother sadly postponed the test and set off to rescue the governess. Grace and I were momentarily alone and rather at a loss for conversation, even though we would seem to have something, or at least someone, in common.

"Children are rather a problem, aren't they?" Her Highness finally remarked.

"Rather," I agreed. "I'm looking for a cross between a marine sergeant major and a prison warden to take charge of mine."

Surprisingly Grace took me quite seriously. "I'll give the matter some thought and let you know if I come up with a solution," she promised. Perhaps she considered it her Christian duty, or royal responsibility, to save the world from my wombats. I told her I'd be grateful for any relief, and wandered off in the direction of my mother, who was desperately tugging the subjects of our conversation carward.

Rainier beat Bing soundly at golf that afternoon, but my mate could find no excuse other than "a state of distraction." I ground my teeth sympathetically.

Oddly enough I was sent home. The trip afforded me an opportunity to contrast the problems of traveling with Bing with the agonies of traveling without him.

A general with a military band saluted our departure from the Nice airport. An admiral presented two cases of Château Margaux wine, and we were off on the shuttle flight to Paris.

We arrived at Orly in the midst of a strike, so mother and I transported the bags, the wine, and the protesting children from one end of the airport to the other. As it transpired, it was just

Modeling Jean Louis' spring collection

as well there were no porters since I had forgotten to bring money. Without Bing's cushioning presence, my status was simply that of lone, disorganized, civilian female.

In New York our little band raced the whole last mile of an endless concourse only to miss the plane for Los Angeles. To the astonishment of all concerned, after only two-and-seventy further catastrophes we finally did arrive home, somewhat the worse for life.

I had hardly stopped panting, and my children had yet to cease their disapproval of "the mess that mommy always makes," when the following missive arrived from Bing:

"Without the Crosby clan Château Louis XIII seemed strangely quiet last night. The sound track from *Son et Lumière* lulled me to sleep while I gazed upon the Bay of Cannes beneath a full moon.

"It is time for you to stay on top of things until they are fully organized. We have spoken of this many times before, but this time I beg you to devote yourself to it."

For our whole twenty years of married life Bing alternately implored and enjoined me to get organized. It was very much like ordering a government to reduce inflation. A government *is* inflation, and I *am* disorder incarnate. Which way I walk is chaos, myself am chaos. It's my most engaging trait.

It was amply illustrated on the occasion of Bing's return on October 1. In the interest of fairness, it must be stated on my behalf that I didn't know that he was going to appear in the midst of a huge party, which I was throwing in honor of Jean Louis' spring collection. I realized however that his arrival was a possibility, and had resolved that if it did occur I would surpass even barbecued hamburgers served by a royal dish in slacks.

In the event I outdid myself. Bing turned up to find the enormous Scandia buffet scattered throughout house and yard, with inebriated buyers from all over the world dancing to the strains of several orchestras. Resolutely he marched upstairs, only to find his bedroom and most of the second story full of half-naked models, busily changing from one outfit to another under the misapprehension that if they did so resolutely every ten minutes they would eventually show off the entire spring line.

"Just a quiet little homecoming celebration," I remarked airily, but once again Bing was not amused.

"Home is the weary world traveler, hoping against hope for a moment's peace to lick his wounds, and what does he find when he seeks his familial hearth? A *Walpurgisnacht*, a veritable witches sabbath! Well, much as I hate to reinforce this sort of behavior. . ." With which he tossed me a small tobacco pouch with the air of Cyrano dispensing a purse of gold.

I caught it and then held it at arm's length. "You know how allergic I am to tobacco. Is this some sort of vengeance for the time I washed your pipes in Ajax?"

"If you'd stop talking and start opening it up, you might find out."

No one can accuse me of not taking a hint, however subtly phrased. I loosened the string and turned the pouch bottom up, whereupon fifty-two, apple-green, jade beads hit the floor, and rolled into every hidden corner and crevice of the room. I spent the next hour picking them up, and most of the following day playing marbles with them. Then I ran off to the local jeweler, and had them strung into what was my favorite necklace until it was stolen in 1977.

Her Serene Highness made good her promise to find us a governess in a way that almost made me forgive her for her cool blonde loveliness. Marielle, niece of a French count, arrived to assume sole charge of my little varmints, and praise the Lord she was a beautiful six feet tall.

For a full three weeks she ran, cajoled, threatened, and despaired, while I looked on approvingly from a discreet distance.

Of course it couldn't last. My illustrious Amazon just faded away before my eyes, becoming paler, and thinner, and rising later, until she finally locked her door, took to her bed, and swore a mighty Gallic oath not to emerge until I had shipped those terrors off to a well-merited exile.

Marielle with Mary Frances

The Crosby children on their Welsh ponies

Back she went to France, doubtless to spin many a tall tale of the savages in the New World, but the respite had sufficed to prepare me to face up once more to the perils of a hostile universe.

On October 14 we learned that bottled water in France is not the equivalent of distilled water at home. Laboring under the misapprehension that it was good for him, Bing had dedicated himself to it religiously. The mineral content had coalesced into a whole sack of kidney stones, which doubled him up with pain. We raced to St. John's Hospital to see if there was some way to move them into the ureters, through the bladder, and out through the urethra.

Unfortunately the manipulation designed to accomplish this was unsuccessful. Bing decided to postpone surgery, with the hope that a combination of antibiotics and low-mineral diet might improve his condition.

On October 17 he announced that, having had quite enough of my anarchic housekeeping, he was heading for the peace and quiet of the ranch. This was manifestly unjust since I had been working all day every day at the hospital, and had had no time for housekeeping of any description. I did, however, take advantage of his departure to double up my schedule, spending the hours from 7 to 12 and 1 to 4 in the operating room, and then getting down to serious study. When some snake acquainted Bing with the details of my new project, he demanded that I send the children to the ranch, where they would have some sort of supervision from my sister.

As I might have warned him, it did little good. All three felt that they were now old enough to have a whack at their Welsh ponies, which they were indeed able to ride for some seconds before tumbling off. Fortunately their mounts, which looked like stumpy-legged sausages, were so tiny that the damages consequent upon a fall onto the soft turf of the corral were minimal. The children broke nothing, but they finished each day bruised from head to toe.

When I reluctantly exchanged nursing for ranching, Bing made a valiant effort to teach me to handle the feather-light 20-gauge Beretta which I had substituted for those frightening larger weapons. He patiently taught me to creep along the river bank after geese, until he finally made the mistake of turning around and finding me with my eyes closed against the allergen-laden autumn air and the Beretta held straight out in front of me, i.e. with the muzzle practically in the small of his back.

"Why do you carry the gun like that?" he asked cautiously.

"I'm afraid it might go bang at any minute, and I want it as far away from me as possible when it does."

"Very interesting. Tell you what, I think you've practiced enough skulking so that you're about ready to lead. Suppose you walk ahead of me from now on?"

Thereafter I made such splendid progress that on October 27 Bing decided that I was ready to graduate into the big time. We flew off to Weiser, Idaho, the place where he had been scheduled to shoot with Gary Cooper and Clark Gable the week that he married a Texan instead. The subsequent events led me to wonder whether he might not be trying to reverse the process.

It was my first experience with a large, presumably properly-organized shoot. Some thirty massive, determined males and one small equally-determined female circled a field of tall corn, then started slowly moving toward the center. I marched doggedly forward, resolved to do or die in the discharge of my duly-appointed task, until I heard several volleys and experienced a sudden illumination: "There are a number of men with guns directly across from me," said I to myself, "and some of them are firing straight at me."

Dropping my gun and my Spartan pose, I immediately fell flat on my face and clung desperately to the good earth. When I had recovered sufficiently to start worming my way to the rear, I discovered that my intrepid companions had all followed my example. We were shown the way by a goodly number of cock

With Helen and Trader Vic Bergeron

pheasants, who were also leaving this no man's land, but at much better speed and with far more assurance of safety. I was never again to leave on a hunt without first ascertaining whether or not my colleagues were planning to imitate a Polish firing squad.

Fortunately Bing had been equally terrified by the self-appointed presidents of suicide clubs whom we had met in Weiser. He explained that the hunting would be quite different on Kona farm in the Sacramento Valley, whither Trader Vic and Helen Bergeron had invited us for their version of a pheasant shoot.

I accompanied Helen, who looked as if she'd just stepped out of Abercrombie and Fitch's front window, her ascot perfectly tied, her hunting cap at precisely the right jaunty angle, and her posture that of a princess. She appeared to be posing for a portrait, but any bird that came within range would appear on the table that night.

Fortunately the cook was not dependent upon my bag, which remained empty in spite of a great deal of cussing and banging away with the Beretta. So the meals all lived up to Trader Vic's standards, which is the highest praise I can give.

After dinner Bing and I took a last walk through the lovely autumn fields. The ground crunched beneath our feet, and our breath made frost plumes in the frozen air. On such nights it seemed a rotten shame that we weren't immortal. Suddenly I wondered just how much of our scrap of eternity Bing and I had left.

On the beach at Las Cruces

1963

Bing too had been considering the deteriorating state of his health. With increased frequency and for longer intervals he was incapacitated with excruciating abdominal pain. Hoping desperately that it would go away, he avoided all thought or mention of it, and escaped into ceaseless activity.

He played golf all day at Palm Springs, did a special with Mary Martin, flew to the ranch, to Las Cruces, to the Crosby at Pebble Beach, and finally to the Hawaiian Open. But his kidney stones rode with him, and finally brought him to bay on January 29.

A stone moved sufficiently to block a ureter, and Bing went into emergency surgery at 6:30 in the evening at St. John's in Santa Monica. While the operation was in progress, friends took me to Trader Vic's. There I watched in disbelief as all about me happy revelers were devouring Polynesian lamb with peanut-butter sauce, and drinking planter's punch, while for all I knew Bing lay dying on the operating table. It was my first clear look at the ironic contrasts and incongruities of life, which at any moment allow half a world to celebrate while the other half writhes in agony.

For a time I simply sat in a state of shock. Then, urged to eat, I did so with a vengeance, forcing myself to think only of the food, and ingesting everything within arm's reach.

Unable to endure the suspense, I then raced back to the hospital. The news was amazingly good. The operation had gone rapidly with no complications. Bing would soon awaken from the anesthesia. He had had a superstitious dread of this third kidney operation, and for once he would be delighted to have been wrong. Sick with relief, I raced off to disemburden myself of the enormous dinner.

I was holding Bing's hand as he returned to consciousness. His first words were, "Mrs. Crosby, I presume."

"No, this is St. Peter, but our Irish quota is full for the moment, so I guess we'll have to send you back."

"Reserve me a soft cushion," Bing insisted, before relapsing into unconsciousness.

Throughout the night I sat holding his hand and staring at the cheeks sunken in drugged sleep, the clay color of the post-operative patient, the suction apparatus, and the needles administering intravenous fluids. This was where a

My home-made Christmas tree decorations

teenager's romantic infatuation had led her, and now at the end of her twenties she knew what real love meant. I heard my voice repeating, "He's alive, he's alive, he's still alive."

Our absurd Christmas tree decorations were born during this convalescence. I brought to the hospital the cards that we had displayed in the silver bowl on our piano. From them I cut out pictures of children, friends, and madonnas, and pinned them onto styrofoam, adding sequins, ribbons, and rows of decorative pins.

These ornaments have lent a special flavor to each subsequent Crosby Christmas, but I have an idiosyncratic reaction to them. As I unpack them each December, I smell the hospital anesthetic and hear the knee gatch elevated on Bing's bed, while I watch the fluids running into his arms and out of his sides. Silently I give thanks for that convalescence, and for the many that followed it.

With all our experience, we now had the drill down pat. Bing was on his feet almost immediately. He walked around the room and down the corridors, looking like a pin cushion with all the tubes sticking out of him. He forced himself to swallow untold quarts of the distilled water which he was to drink for the rest of his life. From home I brought thick soups, chicken pot pies, and rice and tapioca puddings.

Now that he had been separated from his stones, Bing began to ponder another sort of removal. As we well know, he had always been ready to contemplate buying a house just about anywhere, but for the first time he was actually suggesting selling our Los Angeles home and leaving the area for good, a proposal which posed various familial problems.

First and foremost there was his mother. When he had previously mentioned the possibility of moving to another house in Los Angeles, within the hour he had found his mother's bags in the front hall. "If you're leaving this home, you don't need or want me any more, so I'm going to find my own place. I'm too old to be of use anyway. There's been nothing in this world for me since your father died."

At a loss to counter such arguments, Bing had explained the situation to his prospective buyers, and then helped his mother to unpack. Now, for reasons best known to herself, she suddenly turned adventurous, and actually allowed as how she might enjoy life in a new location.

It was his wife who posed the real problem. In the depths of her little black soul she had never really given up her secret plan to become the queen of the silver screen. She had hid it from a husband who wanted a homebody, from a world which would simply have laughed, and even from herself in a mad confusion of nursing, babies, and travel, but now she had to face the fact that she was leaving the tinsel of Movietown forever. It was time to come to terms with reality, and she had no vocation for that sort of work.

Her dark broodings were interrupted by a problem of manageable proportions. In spite of the surgeon's confident predictions on the occasion of his first operation, the gravel had yet to work its way out of Harry's eye. His mother, who had always had a blind faith that a knife can fix just about anything, demanded that the problem be resolved. Using her pull as an aspiring RN, she decided to make a game of the whole thing. She would take Harry through his tests herself, letting him examine his own blood under the microscope and monitor the entire process.

A little dandy, who would already go to any lengths to improve his appearance, Harry was remarkably amenable to persuasion. Mary Frances, however, was a perennial fly in any and all ointments. She demanded the right to accompany her brother and run her own tests.

In spite of all my preparation, Harry wowled indignantly when I took blood from his finger. But his performance paled into insignificance beside that of Mary Frances, whose screams of rage brought help from all the adjacent labs when I refused to cut her finger off too.

"Harry's no good; he ouched. Cut my finger off; I won't ouch. Cut me, cut me! Waugh!"

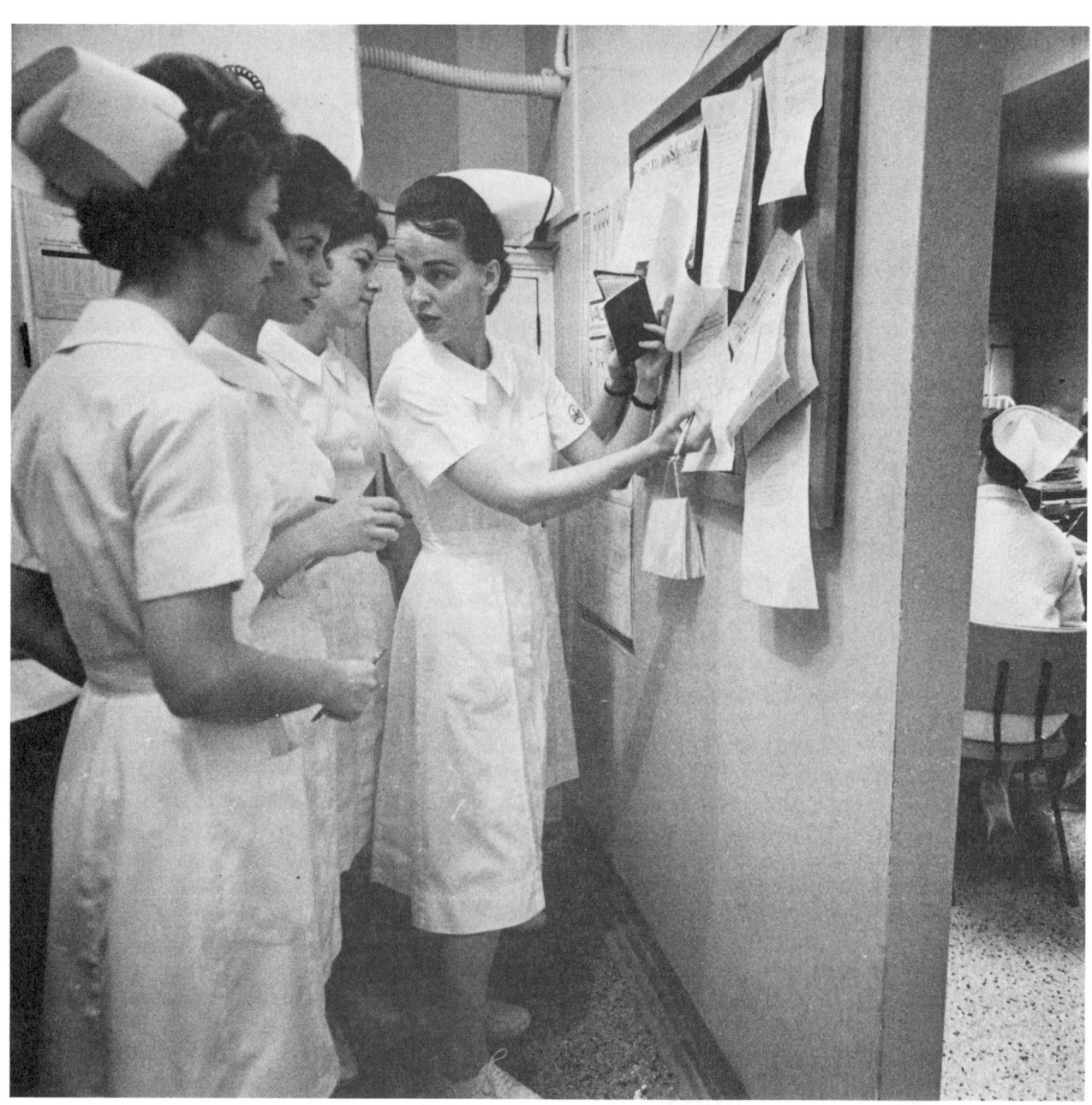
The student nurse and classmates

The child would never be comfortable if she weren't center stage with all cameras running. There was nothing else for it, so I had to prick her finger too, and let her examine her blood under the microscope. True to her word, our resident *enfant terrible* didn't ouch, but inspected her slide with great satisfaction: "See mommy, lots of bugs," she announced proudly.

Once again, with the aid of my trusty pediatrics text, I had prepared Harry for a decapitation rather than a trifling repair. When faced with the actual operation, his only feeling was one of vast relief. Compared to his mother, surgeons presented only minor difficulties.

Their feelings, on the other hand, smacked of ambivalence. "He certainly is a good patient," one of them remarked of the child, who was laughingly fondling a pair of forceps, "but don't you think he's just a trifle odd?"

"It's in the blood," I admitted glumly, and marched off with Mary Frances, who was bitterly disappointed at the triviality of the whole procedure and loudly demanding that they, "Cut my brother some more and make him ouch."

Meanwhile the first generation of Crosby children had not been idle. Phillip, who had always had an eye for the ladies and a way with them, had seen no reason to let matrimony interfere with his dating schedule.

I had had no intimation of this until I was apprised of it rather rudely, when working the swing shift at St. Joseph's as part of my emergency-room experience. While comforting the parents of a child who had accidently shot his brother, I heard a familiar voice from an adjoining cubicle: "Jeeze, doc, there we were makin' love, and just as it was gettin' good something like this had to happen."

Although continuing to show sympathy for the bereaved parents, I kept a wary ear cocked toward the adjacent drama:

"She seems to be having a spontaneous abortion," said Dr. Roger's voice. "Mr. Crosby, would you mind waiting in the reception room while I examine your, er, friend."

That registered. Holy moly, I was presently occupying the reception room! Without a word of excuse, I bolted for the nearest refuge, which just happened to be the laundry room. (When I told Phillip about it years later, his response was characteristic: "Cripes, why didn't you stay and help?")

When Sandra expressed understandable resentment of Phillip's extracurricular activities, he philosophically abandoned her and her two small children, and moved in with Lindsay. Out of the frying pan into the fire. He found that his brother was in an advanced state of avitaminosis, occasioned by a drinking bout of extraordinary length. After observing his condition for several days, Phillip wisely committed him to the psychiatric ward in Santa Monica Hospital, where he would have an opportunity to recover his physical and mental health. Then he less prudently descended upon his convalescing father for spiritual aid and counseling.

When Bing simply looked perplexed, I suggested that Phillip might first consider a return to his wife and babes. If that prospect didn't please, how about life as a roustabout in Afghanistan?

Faced with the dilemma of whether or not to commit Lindsay more or less permanently, Bing so far transcended his own health problem as to grab the next flight for Las Cruces, where he remained incommunicado, sans mail, sans telephone, sans news of any kind, most of which had been bad of late. The utter isolation of Baja California did have its advantages.

In the interim his helpmate remained resolutely at her post, and was rewarded with a visit from the FBI, who wondered idly just what Sandra was doing in Las Vegas with certain figures prominent in underworld affairs. "Probably just trying to stay alive," I suggested. "As I understand it, she hasn't had an income in years."

Foolishly I promised to aid in whatever investigation was going on, and finally located Sandra in her desert playground. "My friends are such perfect gentlemen," she assured me. "They take me to the nicest restaurants and the best clubs, and they leave the biggest tips I've ever seen. It's so nice to have someone opening

Our little church at Las Cruces

With the officiating priest and members of his choir

With the blushing bride and reluctant groom

doors for me and taking care of me again. And they're so interested in everything, particularly somebody named Ray Ryan, who must be a big politician or something. Do you know him?"

As it transpired, Sandra's hoods were out to collect an enormous gambling debt, or to erase the debtor from the book of life. They were simply using her as a cover while they tracked down their prey. In all honesty I couldn't help feeling sympathetic. It certainly must have been reassuring to be associated once more with men who collected and paid their bills.

Meanwhile Bing was trying to reach me on ship-to-shore radio from Las Cruces, and never quite managing it, since if I was awake I was at Queen of Angels Hospital, and if I was asleep I was unattainable. He had to content himself with letters which revealed that, weak as he still was, he couldn't resist the joys of dove hunting. His enthusiasm might have cost him his life, or at the very least returned him to the hospital. Witness the following communication, dated March 16:

"I had a fair shoot at a tiny rancho near Los Frailes yesterday afternoon, but while thus engaged I also had what was very nearly the last thrill of my life. I was standing on a hillside waiting for some doves to come over, when I heard a rustling noise at my feet.

"Looking down, I beheld a five-foot rattler winding along about six inches from my right shoe. Leaping back with an agility I had never dreamed I possessed, I cleanly removed its head with one blast from my puny 28-gauge."

Deciding that my husband was in need of professional supervision, I packed up the children and flew to Las Cruces on March 22. Our lovely new home had been completed at last, and this was our first chance to enjoy it.

While the little ones played on the beach, I sat and fished with Bing. Without noteworthy success I must admit, since I had a strong tendency to doze. Bing, on the other hand, stared silently at the waves. I wonder what he saw there. He was still quite weak, and depressed by the news from his four grown sons.

This was our first Easter at Las Cruces, and we rashly decided that our support for the tiny Mexican church there should not be solely financial. With the children and the entire household staff paddling around in their bare feet, we removed everything, including the kneelers, and to the indignation of a flock of resident swallows, gave the walls and floor their first thorough scrubbing in recorded history, thus initiating a spring rite which unfortunately became traditional.

We flew a priest over from La Paz, and trucked in a load of children, who sang *Adios, Reina del Cielo* with a wild Indian quality in their voices.

Unable to pass up such a prestigious opportunity, our mechanic's friend Paula at last determined to marry him. Since she was expecting her eighth child, I too felt it was high time that they legitimize their relationship. I therefore supplied a bridal costume and saw that all their progeny were shined up to witness the sacrament.

Afraid that his colleagues would make sport of him for marrying a woman who wasn't a virgin, Tavo had refused to shave, but Paula grinned happily through her missing front teeth as the bemused priest gave the blessing which returned the whole motley band to the fold.

Then it was time for a joyous celebration, which combined somehow with the Easter egg hunt that I had been preparing for the preceding four days. Our marineros had hoisted a gigantic piñata with the anchor rope: Tavo's eldest felled it with the initial blow of his baseball bat; his parents became lordly drunk on their first champagne; and a glorious time was had by all, except possibly my errant husband, who had pusillanimously put out to sea, vowing never to return.

Determined to put his new boat, the *True Love*, to some practical use, Bing had become obsessed with the idea that flying fish in great numbers could be netted at night off Espiritu Santo Island, some thirty miles north of Las Cruces. If this were indeed true, it would have been of great importance to the fishermen, who used them as bait to catch marlin. As it was, said

Aboard Bing's new boat, with charter members of The Clams

bait had to be flown down from San Diego at great difficulty and expense.

Bing had obtained a gill net 100 yards long, and persuaded two other boats to rendezvous with him in the lee of the island, where they patiently awaited the dark of the moon and the onrush of the teeming hordes. Thence he would return occasionally to report his failures and restock the boat with provisions.

All to no avail, for he was always in the wrong place at the right time or the right place at the wrong time, or it wasn't light or dark enough, or the net was too high or low, or the ungrateful curs in the other boats had lost faith in the project and gone home to their wives and sweethearts.

For an impatient man, Bing demonstrated enormous motivation and perseverance when the task was right. He was magnificent in defeat, but we never did see any flying fish.

The children remained in Las Cruces with Bing while I returned to California with a curious commission. Since he didn't feel up to it yet, I would search out a new principal residence for the family.

Quite apart from being a total reversal of roles, this was a bit like putting the fox in charge of the hen coop. With my mythical movie career still in mind, I secretly determined to fail so dismally that we'd remain in Los Angeles forever. Thus firmly resolved to preserve the old homestead for Harry's children and their children's children, I proceeded to set impossibly high standards on my pilgrimage from Santa Barbara up through Carmel to San Francisco.

Bing had inadvertently assisted me by setting some standards of his own. "No traffic noise. No possibility of future highways or freeways. Adequate rooms. Suitable architecture for our furniture. Good basement and storage. Solid construction throughout. Concrete, stone, or steel. Excellent heating. Ample kitchen and laundry. About four acres for the children to play in. Church nearby. Also primary schools of high quality."

Up and down the San Francisco peninsula and the northern California coast I trekked, but try as I would I couldn't find a single residence which lived up to those standards. The best of the lot was a magnificient edifice which had just been occupied by the Immaculate Heart novices, but of course neither Bing nor I would have dreamed of evicting them.

From Las Cruces Bing applauded my efforts, and commiserated with me on my inability to find anything habitable. Meanwhile he was having interesting living problems of his own:

"While I was reading in bed the other night a scorpion crawled up beside me. When I flipped him out of there, he made for the headboard.

"Using my book as a club, I valiantly destroyed both bug and board. Thus alerted, I turned both beds inside out, shook out all pillows and blankets, and thoroughly inundated the entire room with Black Flag.

"Since it was then well after midnight, I repaired to the guest room to await daybreak. In the first light of dawn we closed all the windows and sprayed the entire house.

"Charlie Jones assures me that our local scorpions aren't lethal, and Rod supports him in this regard, but I'd prefer not to put the matter to a test."

Bing brought the children back to Los Angeles in late May for, of all things, a family portrait which he had insisted on commissioning. The well-known artist was pompous, slow, and almost incredibly bad. We posed painfully for interminable hours, and the resentful children became simply intolerable.

One noon, toward the end of our ordeal, I failed to notice that Mary Frances was being much too polite for an imp who had been immobile all morning. In the middle of lunch she excused herself and slipped away.

A few minutes later we heard a scream of anguish from the living room. The artist had returned to find that the faces of Harry and Nathaniel had simply been wiped out. In spite of my mother's consoling words to Rainier, sibling rivalry was real enough in our family.

I forsook the joys of domesticity for a

My sister, Frances Ruth Meyer

modeling tour, during which my sister and I showed Jean Louis' new line of spring fashions in Palm Beach, in New York, and prior to the Swan Ball in Nashville. Frances Ruth has never forgotten Teensie Bradford, our hostess there, who upon introduction stated flatly that she never rose before noon. It was the only place we ever stayed in which even the bathrooms sported silver buckets of iced champagne.

I abandoned this luxurious setting to race back to Los Angeles, and tried once more to convince my instructors that they should let me take part in a graduation ceremony. Since I had now been working for five years on a three-year program, and had watched two of my classes graduate, I couldn't help feeling that simple justice was on my side. I had more seniority than most of the teachers, several of whom had been asking me for years now why I was still around.

Finally the faculty determined in solemn conclave that I really did constitute a source of embarrassment and that, even though I owed them another semester, the simplest solution would be to hand me a blank diploma, and trust me to complete the credits in the not-too-distant future. So that is how I finally managed to invite my father to watch me walk across the stage and receive my still-unearned sheepskin.

Since I knew that my five years of early rising and night duties were a very sore subject with Bing, I omitted mentioning the graduation to him. But he had his own sources of information, so as the ceremony got under way I was amazed to see him sitting in the front row of the choir loft between my father and Frances Ruth.

When Cardinal McIntire said, "You have all spent three long years in the pursuit of learning," Bing solemnly held up five fingers and winked. To his dying day His Eminence must have wondered why a simple statement of fact was greeted with a roar of laughter from the balcony, where every eye had been on Bing.

When the English Royal Ballet came to town on June 28, Frances Ruth and I rushed off to the first performance of *Sleeping Beauty*. We had both loved the dance from our earliest years, but it was I who had had the good fortune to be born a bit later into a post-depression family that could finally scrape together enough money for lessons.

Thus from the age of six I had studied ballet with an enthusiastic, if far-from-professional teacher at the West Columbia Community Center. My mother had literally sewn me into my first recital dress because, with typical Grandstaff disorganization, she had neglected to procure a zipper.

Later she drove me the sixty miles to Houston so that I could study with a master teacher. My principal reason for transferring to Robstown High School was the proximity of Corpus Christi, whither my aunt drove me for weekly 8 a.m. ballet lessons.

I read *Dancing Star*, the story of Anna Pavlova, twelve times before completing as many summers, and spent long dreamy hours imagining myself dancing *Swan Lake* in her place. Since I had never actually seen either the ballet or the bird in question, my version of the dying swan closely resembled the more familiar death throes of a chicken.

Throughout college, my acting career, and marriage, I had continued to take ballet lessons at every opportunity. My friends were uncomfortably reminded of Zelda Fitzgerald's dancing madness. Like me she'd been dedicated, inept, and finally just too old.

After listening to some hundreds of hours of my practice tapes, and finding me prancing desperately through my exercises whenever he needed a collar stud, Bing was understandably less than sympathetic. He lived in constant fear that his mother might chance upon me in my leotard, and indignantly abandon his house of iniquity forever. He did enjoy listening to the orchestra at a good ballet but, great ballroom dancer though he was, he remained unimpressed by "all the leaping and twirling around."

Furthermore he had his macho friends to consider. Those devotees of the chase through fen and grot had their own opinion of men who liked to watch boys in tights. On the occasion of the Royal Ballet's visit, the matter was com-

Phil Harris in Western garb

plicated by a scheduled hunting trip with Phil Harris, who proved unreceptive when Bing explained that he would have to cancel it to take Kathryn to the ballet.

"Just how many queers do you have to watch tripping around in tights in one lifetime? When you've seen one fag on tippytoes, you've seen them all," was the Indian's disgruntled comment.

But for one fortunate circumstance, I would doubtless have lost Bing to the pheasants and grouse. Minnesota Mining and Manufacturing had been wooing him to do a series of ads for them. When it became apparent that he wasn't interested, they sent their top brass to town with orders to convince him. This they did successfully in a tour of the local bistros, from which he returned home so thoroughly swacked that he was unmindful of any and all previous obligations.

Seeing my chance, I pounced, and the poor innocent cheerfully accompanied me to see Margot Fonteyn and Nureyev dance *Giselle*, laboring under the misapprehension that we were just dropping by for a few minutes on the way to dinner.

Bing fell immediately into a deep sleep, but unfortunately awoke right at the end of the second act and demanded that I take him home. When I explained that Dame Margot and Nureyev were expecting us backstage after the performance, he decided that presented no impediment. We could simply go right then.

So on we traipsed, past a startled doorman and groups of equally-astonished, naked dancers, with my husband oblivious of everything but his private euphoria. When we finally cornered the speechless stars, Bing suddenly realized that he had no particular message for them and, unprepared to discuss the performance that he had just missed, expansively invited them all to lunch. Back we swept through the cast and out the stage door, trailing clouds of glory and bewilderment in our wake.

The great moment was only a week away. I spent the time planning the luncheon and attending every performance of the ballet. Now that Bing had yielded and accompanied me for once, I was wrapped in dreams of traveling about the world with a captivated spouse, no longer visiting golf courses and grouse shoots, but attending all the performances of the great ballets. Copenhagen, London, Vienna, Paris, and Moscow, we would know and love them all. For the present I was haunting the Royal Ballet in preparation for my subsequent career.

Meanwhile Bing noticed that, even in the absence of his wife, there was an ominous bustle in his household. Finally he inquired suspiciously just what Alan Fisher was doing to the tables on the terrace. When acquainted with details of the plot, he ran me down just as I whipped in the door from one performance and prepared to change for the next.

"Now what's all this about a luncheon?"

"We're having the entire cast of the Royal Ballet."

"Ye gods, who invited them?"

"*You* did."

"Fine, *you* can call it off."

It cost me my attendance at that evening's performance, but I finally obtained Bing's grudging consent to let the luncheon take place, with the proviso that no one demand his presence. The old bear was going hunting.

The luncheon was scheduled for July 6. On the evening of July 5 John Scott Trotter supped with us before escorting me to the ballet. *Swan Lake* was playing at the Hollywood Bowl. It would be my first opportunity to watch the company dancing under the stars.

Jean Louis' wife Maggie was throwing a party for Nureyev at La Scala after the performance, a fact which I realized retrospectively I might have mentioned to my husband, but I fully intended, or I thought I intended, just to drop in for a moment and explain why I couldn't stay.

For those too young to remember, perhaps I'd best mention that John Scott Trotter weighed 320 pounds, wore coke-bottle-style eyeglasses to compensate for his near blindness, and stuttered in stress situations. When we had finally wormed our way through the traffic jam to arrive at the VIP lot, John, who was a director

With John Scott Trotter at a picnic

of the Hollywood Bowl and had conducted numerous concerts there, began to stutter hopelessly when asked to show his credentials.

The guard at the gate favored us with only a brief contemptuous glance before waving us on. Crimson with embarrassment, John was unable to utter anything coherent for some minutes afterward, so he simply drove a mile or so down the road, whence we had to hike back, suffering from the burdens of our respective handicaps, he his weight and I my high heels.

Nonetheless we arrived just as the overture began, and from my point of view it was certainly worth the trip. Margot Fonteyn was exquisite, the dancing was glorious, and I was humming every note of the melody as we stumped wearily but happily all the way back to the car.

When we stopped by La Scala in Beverly Hills to present our excuses to Maggie Louis, Nureyev complimented John, who had just been criticizing the accompaniment, on his knowledge of music and dance, kissed my hand in the gallant continental fashion, and swept me off to the dance floor.

Frankly I don't remember what happened for the next few hours, so overwhelmed was I by the mere fact of dancing with Nureyev, who couldn't lead worth a lick but had an inexhaustible repertoire of steps. Some time in the wee hours of the morning John tapped me on the shoulder, pointed out that we were all that was left of the party, and suggested that I might consider driving home.

Not wishing to disturb my husband at whatever ungodly hour it was, I silently slipped into my nightgown in the dressing room, and then cautiously opened the bedroom door. All the lights were on and Bing, his hair awry, was sitting on the edge of the bed. At first I thought he must have had a nightmare, but he shrugged off my anxious queries and asked in a low tone, "Where have you been?"

"To the ballet," I answered weakly.

Slowly and deliberately Bing slid back under the covers and turned his face to the wall. I put out the lights, got into my bed, and lay there with mouth dry and eyes staring into the blackness, wondering what sort of explanation I should attempt. Just as I was coming up with a good one I must have dozed off, because suddenly it was daylight and Bing seemed to have disappeared.

I had to think for a moment before I remembered my inspiration of the previous night. I then decided that I would write it all down. This would give me a chance to phrase it exactly and stick to it. I've always lied better on paper.

It took me about an hour to compose my masterpiece. Sneaking into Bing's office to leave it on his desk, I found him sitting there, and felt like a burglar surprised in the act of breaking and entering.

"What do you want?" Bing asked in steely tones.

"To talk, I guess. What do you want?"

This seemed a normal-enough question to me, but in the event it proved to be a grave tactical blunder. Bing's voice rose to a pitch of hysteria. "I want a divorce."

"Well, you can't have one. In the first place, you're a Catholic. In the second place, you made me one. In the third place, I wouldn't give you one anyway."

"Why oh why did I ever marry you?"

Idiot that I am, I couldn't resist this opening, "You were pregnant," I shrilled. "You had to marry somebody."

Bing was definitely not amused. "You deceived me," he howled. "You acted like a fragile little southern flower, and actually you're a goddam tank on the loose without a driver. You're supposed to be a wife and a mother, but all you think about is dancing, and acting, and nursing, and modeling, day and night, without ever stopping to ask why. You're crazy as a loon, and stubborn as a mule, and I've tried, and I've tried, and there's nothing I can do about it. Well, I'm exhausted, and I quit!"

"I don't see what has led to such an expression of hostility. All I did was go to the ballet."

"Which lasted until 5 a.m."

"No, John took me to a party at La Scala afterwards. I guess I should have told you that we were going, but I didn't want you to worry."

Trying to imitate

Dame Margot Fonteyn

"It wouldn't have made any difference. I can't do anything with you anyway. You're out of control."

"Are you accusing me of something immoral?"

"No, no, damn it all. Nobody was ever immoral with John Scott Trotter. It's worse than that. If you just had a hankering to run off with a guitar player, I could handle it. I've dealt with guitar players in my time. But that would be too normal for you. You want to spend your time playing Florence Nightingale, or Loretta Young, or Pavlova, or just shilling for a lady's tailor. What in hell do I tell the children when they ask why they don't have a mother? For that matter, what do I tell my friends when they ask if I'm married? I'd hate to have to prove the matter in court."

The trial was not going well, and I wasn't eager to hear any more of the evidence from the prosecution, because I had a dim premonition that its presentation could last for days. The facts just didn't seem to be all on my side.

Well, since the tank wasn't doing so well, perhaps we would have to revive that fragile southern flower. Resolutely I began to think sad, sad thoughts of an unworthy wife and mother, expelled from her hearth to wander the cruel world with no place to lay her weary head. Just why hadn't she practiced her turnouts more diligently during all these years so that she could now run off with the Royal Ballet, or at least have a second string to her bow?

The blessed tears came in waves which engulfed first me, then Bing, and finally the whole office. As usual I was carried away by my own performance, and soon found myself wailing and gasping out magnificently incoherent pleas for forgiveness and promises of reformation.

For all his brave talk Bing was a mere male, who succumbed to helpless femininity almost immediately. The melting magnolia blossom succeeded where the Mack truck would have failed dismally. With a helpless sigh, he picked me up and carried me off to bed. I could just see him telling himself guiltily that the fierce battle was finally over, and that we would never quarrel again. How could he have treated a poor weak female so cruelly?

Meanwhile I was reflecting that I really had pushed him a bit far this time, and had best tread warily in the immediate future.

Bing let me sleep like a log until twenty minutes before our guests were scheduled to arrive. Then he gently roused me, and informed me that he'd seen to the preparations.

I didn't quite wake up during the first hour or so of the luncheon, but it didn't really matter because my husband was gay, debonair, scintillating, and apparently passionately interested in the ballet. Watching him win every heart, I think I could have considered divorce Italian style if the whole function hadn't turned out to be so enjoyable for all concerned.

Realizing that I was skating on thin ice, I became overwhelmingly domestic for the next few weeks. Like any other ham I always overact, and I now devoted myself to my family so exclusively, and with such tenacity of purpose, that I succeeded shortly in suffocating them. Years later I learned that it was Bing who phoned Max Arnow, formerly head of talent at Columbia Pictures and subsequently my agent, and demanded that the poor man get his wife out of town.

"I've got something called *Sunday in New York*. It calls for a week's rehearsal and a week's performance in Indianapolis. Is that far enough? It pays four thousand a week."

"I'd cheerfully *pay them* the four thousand for some peace and quiet and a few rounds of golf."

So off I flew to Indianapolis, laboring under the misapprehension that talent will out. There I stayed with friends, was served breakfast in bed, and started studying my lines.

As Bing well knew, my small head could encompass only one role at a time. Engrossed in the new one, I completely forgot that of model wife and mother. For the time being, at least, he and the children were safe from my cooking and decorating.

Meanwhile, as one professional to another,

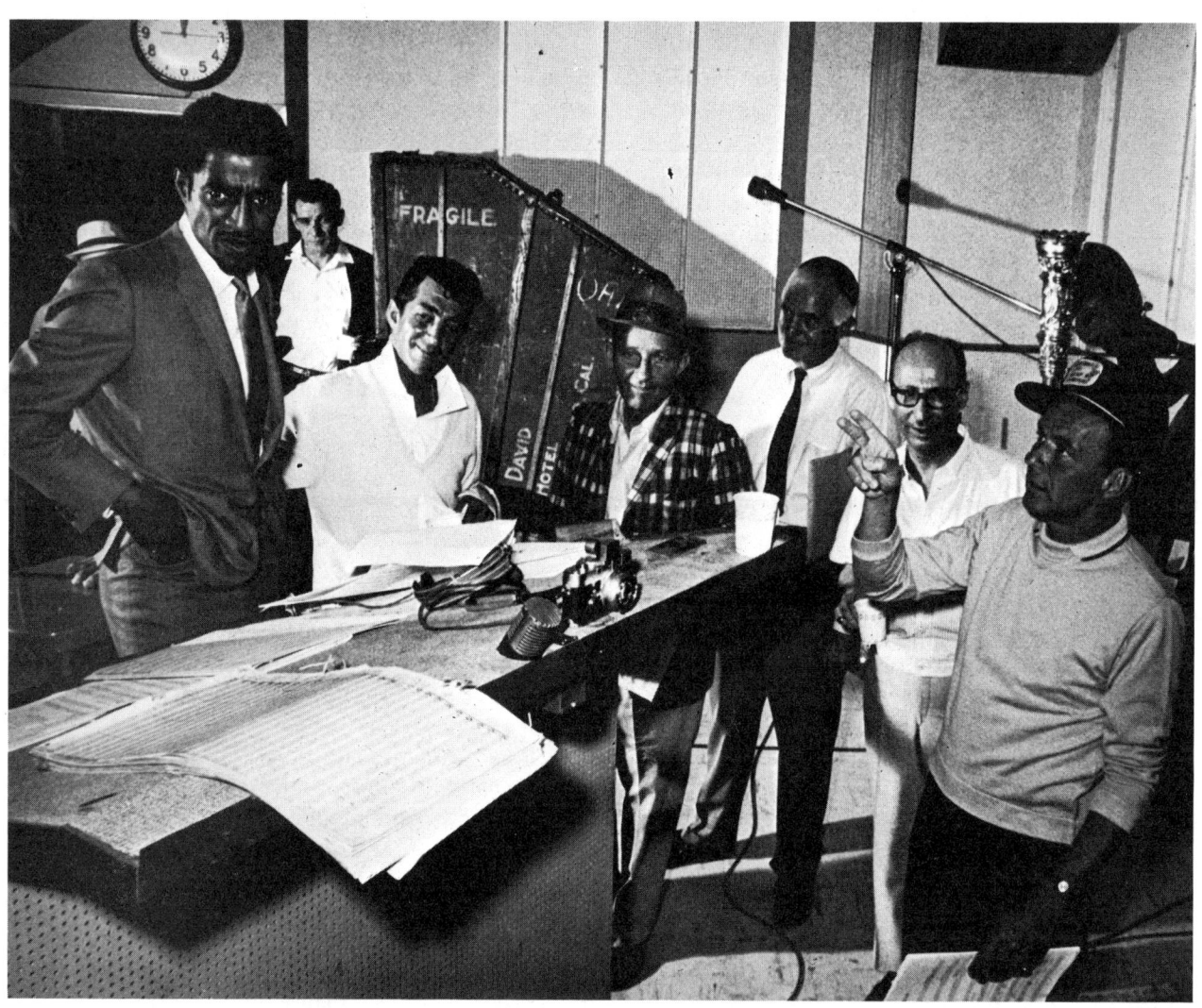

Sammy, Dean, and Bing simply look bemused while Frank tries to conduct a recording session.

Bing wrote about a recording session with Frank Sinatra and Dean Martin:

"The great one had hired a forty-five piece orchestra, a vast cadre of vocalists, and four arrangers and conductors for our songs from the Broadway musicals *Guys and Dolls*, *South Pacific*, and *Kiss Me Kate*. Dean and I watched in bemused bewilderment while Sinatra organized, conducted, arranged, and criticized everything.

"After finishing two sides, Frank, who had spent the night on the town, averred that his reed was tired and dismissed the vast assembly. We had been there less than an hour and a half, a far cry from the old days when I used to record five or six hours with a four-piece band in a warehouse in downtown Los Angeles."

Back in Indianapolis we opened inauspiciously, with a full tent but in a record breaking downpour. To those of us who had never heard a midwest summer rain on a canvas roof, it seemed something like being trapped in a corn popper. We had to halt the performance for half an hour, and when we began again, repeating an interrupted scene, I found that I had lost my jacket, which was a key to the entire action.

Nothing daunted, I simply fixed a woman in the first row with a snake charmer's stare and demanded hers. She complied without batting an eye, and I went on with the scene. Since this was my first appearance on stage since my student days, the director had had certain misgivings. Henceforth, however, he was convinced that whatever might be lacking in talent and experience would be made up in sheer gall.

In point of fact the run was a huge success, both critically and financially, so I returned to Los Angeles with renewed confidence in myself and lovely new dreams of a stage career. Even my stint of domesticity had borne some fruit, because for the first time both my children and Bing's mother seemed to recognize the prodigal daughter on her return.

In other respects, however, Mrs. Senior was having her problems. During the past month she had had lapses during which she walked about the house in the night, disoriented as to time and place. On several occasions she had wandered into our bedroom, singing cheerfully but unable to recognize us. At other times we had found her simply sitting on the floor in the upstairs hallway, leading Bing to fear for her life, since a fall down the staircase would undoubtedly have finished her.

Now she was having hallucinations, claiming that three men had recently invaded her bedroom. We reasoned together on this score, and I finally satisfied her that it couldn't have happened. As soon as she quieted down, Bing decided that we were leaving for Santa Barbara, ostensibly to hunt for a house, but actually to give my baby-sitting husband a spot of rest and recreation on the links.

Our first prospect was certainly large enough and was touted as something of a bargain, including as it did, for a mere million dollars, an artist's studio with a glass wall that provided perfect northern light, just in case I wanted to set up my easel, and a music room where I could play to my heart's content *Clair de Lune* and *Rustles of Spring*, the only two pieces that I'd ever mastered. Almost completed, the house lacked only slate tiles for the roof, which had been delayed by a strike in a Kentucky quarry. Otherwise it was a perfect Tudor monstrosity, created by an architect who had undoubtedly studied under Charles Adams during his early period.

"Heathcliff," I murmured, "if the children survive in this mausoleum, it should do interesting things for their creative imaginations."

Bing seemed undecided, but the real estate agent grasped my meaning, and led us to a Spanish number with adobe walls three feet thick. It was almost windowless, and so surrounded by a forest of oaks that it dwelt in a perpetual damp twilight.

"Fascinating," I admitted. "It wants only a name. We shall dub it the Dark Tarn of Ober, and in it we shall keep our three little ghouls."

As you may have guessed from the preceding, I was still reluctant to leave Los Angeles, but Bing had a suspicious nature, so I was trying not

The older brother of a future U.S. Amateur champion shows his class.

to overplay my hand, difficult though that feat has always been for me. I sought to appear cheerful and optimistic when we repaired to the Valley Club for discussions of real estate, lunch, and golf.

The next day at Pebble Beach, where we inspected an octagonal, grey, stone pile athwart a cliff, I commented only on its practicality. "We'll never have to paint it. It's already the color of the rocks, the sea, and the fog. And we'll certainly have no trouble getting rid of unwelcome guests. An encouraging slap on the back will send them two-thousand feet straight down into eternity."

Bethinking himself of the children's safety, Bing once more abandoned Pebble Beach for the security of the San Francisco Peninsula. I saw his eyes light up when we examined a home whose sole redeeming feature was a gate leading straight out to the 12th fairway of the Burlingame Country Club, and I knew I was in deep trouble. To distract him, I asked if there wasn't something else in the area.

Indeed there was. A little treasure that purported to be an exact copy of Le Petit Trianon, boasting some thirty rooms, none of them large enough for two people to sleep in. Of course in extremity there was always the front hall, where an army might safely have bivouacked, but which had no other conceivable use.

The realtor was, moreover, disposed to throw in a curse and a ghost at no extra cost. It seemed that the structure's five previous occupants had come to bad ends, and at least one of them was to be heard bewailing his fate on windy evenings.

I pointed out that the third floor contained eighteen servants' rooms, doubtless all necessary, and asked if Bing could really imagine our family, or any other for that matter, actually inhabiting the place.

Unfortunately I made these remarks within the hearing of the butler, who promptly carried them to his employer. As ill luck would have it, she attended a party for Barbara Hutton that same evening, greeted Bing icily, snubbed me, and left in a huff, while I tried to explain the problem to a bewildered Barbara.

And perhaps there was a curse after all, because I am sorry to relate that the lady in question, like her ill-starred predecessors, came to a very bad end. Whereas I, whatever my eventual fate, learned to keep my trap shut in the presence of hostile butlers.

The following day, after we had examined a gloomy Gothic tower in the woods of Hillsborough, I was horrified to find that Bing was standing in the dark recesses of what passed for a library, and actually discussing price with the agent.

Keeping a weather eye out for lurking butlers, I hastily observed that the windows would be very practical for our archers to fire their bolts down upon the attacking legions, but were unfortunately too narrow to pour the boiling oil through. As we departed I had to endure the black looks of the agent, and Bing later chastised me for my rudeness, but I thought the price was right if we just escaped with our lives.

Heading south toward Woodside, we finally saw a lovely home with all the accouterments of gracious country living. Between its Elizabethan front and Queen Anne behind, it had gorgeous wood paneling, a huge beautifully-lit library, a living room with a perfect spot for our piano, an enormous master bedroom, and a kitchen where even I might have felt at home.

Outside there were stables for the children's horses, and acres of sunny fields for them to play in. In fact the only defect that I could discover was the lack of neighbors and schools. Bing left, vowing to give serious consideration to its purchase, and even I was tempted. Perhaps after all, despite my ambitious plans, I was destined to end my days far from the madding crowd.

For the time being it was back to Beverly Hills baroque and Roxbury rococo. But as I wearily followed the coast southward along Route 1, my mate still kept scenting the wind like an old hound on a hot trail. Finally there

House-hunting with Mary Frances and Harry

was no help for it. We just had to stop in Santa Barbara and see one last house, which our agent had represented as the most glorious bargain of them all.

It seemed that a little band of Oklahoma Indians had arrived in these parts in the dear dead days beyond recall, and had lavished vast sums of oil money on a magnificent edifice. The sole survivors were a pair of ancient sisters, who had kept to themselves for lo these many years, but were rumored to be ready to return to the land of their ancestors, just prior to a final ascent to the happy hunting grounds.

Charitably, as it seemed to me, the agent classified the style of their present dwelling as eclectic. In translation, this seemed to mean that one architect had set out to do something Moorish, loosely based on the Alhambra, before being succeeded by the director of *It Happened One Halloween*, who had completed the edifice in early Metro-Goldwyn-Mayer.

But if the externals were disquieting, the interior was truly appalling. To the agent's credit, it must be said that he was seeing it for the first time. What little was visible, that is, for without exception the halls and chambers were filled to the ceilings with periodicals of every description, leaving only the narrowest of passageways for the ancient recluses to slide along.

Fortunately the two squaws were so emaciated that their treasures offered small impediment to their progress, but our would-be vendor, who wouldn't have given away many kilos to a sumo wrestler, experienced considerable difficulty in keeping within hailing distance of Bing and one of the crones, while I followed the other off to reconnoiter Manitou knew what.

We wandered for what seemed like hours, and saw only endless stacks of magazines and newspapers, which effectively concealed all structural details. I had just about despaired of ever being reunited with my spouse or civilization, when we rounded a stack and came face to face with an equally astonished opposing war party.

"How," I enunciated solemnly, raising my right hand, palm outward, in token of peace and friendship.

Somehow Bing managed to extricate us all from the maze and resume the journey southward, not without apologies to the agent for his wife's dubious sense of humor, and a subsequent lecture to said culprit on the observance of the bare minimum of social proprieties.

I'd have felt bad if I hadn't been punished for that one, but I needn't have worried. Bing deposited me in Los Angeles, and departed alone for his meeting with Minnesota Mining and Manufacturing in Minneapolis, muttering something about thus sparing the local Red Men gratuitous insults.

While he was there, a reporter unearthed the marriage record of Catherine Harrigan and Harry L. Crosby, who had been married on January 4, 1894 at the respective ages of 21 and 23 years. Bing insisted that I show the resultant articles to his mother, and I did so with some trepidation, since she had always manifested great sensitivity to the subject of age, going so far as to rip the vital statistics page from the family bible, and to admit only that she was over 21 when registering to vote, or when applying for a passport or for admission to a hospital.

My fears were unfounded. For some days the senior Mrs. Crosby had been too busy hallucinating to lend any credence to external reality. When I finally captured her in a semi-lucid moment, she considered the problem gravely and finally allowed as how that mother of hers (whom she evidently considered to be the Catherine of the clipping) "never had had any taste in men."

From Minneapolis Bing flew directly to the ranch, leaving me to the tender mercies of mother and monsters, until my mounting cabin fever prompted a phone call to Max Arnow who, still acting under Bing's previous instructions, immediately shipped me off to do *Sunday in New York* in Warren, Ohio. As a parting gesture of love and trust, I took the preliminary precaution of flying the children off to Bing,

A rancher has to eat hearty to keep up his strength.

who in his initial shock accepted the boys, but recovered sufficiently to return Mary Frances on the next plane.

I took her to Ohio with me, and commiserated with her father in a series of epistles. Bing was perturbed at having twice apprehended Harry in the act of drowning Nathaniel in the bathtub. He evidently awaited some deep psychological explanation from me, and was rather disappointed at my practical suggestion that henceforth the boys bathe separately.

Harry had also discovered the joys of motoring. He not only wanted to drive a car, but also understood every detail of how it worked, and was ready, willing, and able to take off on his first cross-country tour. Bing complained that repeated spankings hurt daddy's hands, but had no appreciable effect on Harry.

Once again I went straight to the heart of the dilemma with my recommendation that he hide the car keys. (Since I had no knowledge of hot-wiring, I mistakenly assumed that the same was true of our firstborn. Live and learn.)

Meanwhile, in far-off Ohio, Mary Frances had captivated John Kenley, the producer of my show. From the far corner of his attic he had dragged out an antique tricycle with an enormous front wheel. It was the answer to a maiden's prayer. Our daughter had always been a devotee of speed, who gazed wistfully after each passing motorcyclist. Now that she had wheels of her own, she used them to maximum effect. Up and down the theater lobby she raced, while bewildered playgoers dodged for their lives, and finally concluded that she must constitute part of the show. Kenley was no help. In his free moments he simply played tag with her.

A story in himself, John was adored by all the little old ladies of Warren as "the sweetest man," which indeed he was. A licensed, card-carrying, full-blown hermaphrodite, he had been faced from his earliest years with the problem of making an arbitrary sexual decision. The situation might have destroyed a lesser personality, but he had carried it off with great courage and considerable élan vital.

To begin with, he had resolved the dilemma of which accomodation to visit in an emergency by adopting a seasonal approach. Since he was known throughout the theatrical world as a male whose business was summer theater, he cut his hair short in the spring and wore men's clothes from that time through the fall, at which point he could ease back into the dresses in which he spent the winter incognito.

Edie Adams was one of the chosen few from the entertainment world who were privileged to visit him during the cold months in his New York apartment. She finally became overcome by curiosity as to how such a hyperactive producer managed to hibernate for those lengthy periods.

"Just what do you do during the long winter months?" she asked indiscreetly.

"Roll sailors," was the cheery reply.

When I arrived in Warren, John had shown a normal producer's interest in my wardrobe. Toward the end of my stay, as his hair lengthened and the witching hour approached, he kept wanting to try my dresses on.

When Bing finally arrived to check out my performance, he was distracted by Mary Frances, seated possessively on his knee and glibly beating mother to the punch on every line, and a very attentive producer, who sat beside him and endeavored to hold his hand. "Just what the hell. . . ." he began, when he finally reached my dressing room.

"Tut, tut," I admonished. "Politeness above all else, you know. We wouldn't want to offend the chief of the local Indians, whatever native costume he may wish to assume."

The performance itself had been a monument to what Bing termed the "shout and duck school." The enormously long, absurdly narrow theater left no room for subtlety. Each actor had his moment in the spotlight as he leaped to center stage, delivered his lines directly to the audience, and leaped away to provide room for his successor. All that I added to my repertoire was a series of nostrums for dealing with laryngitis. If I'd ever contemplated a political

A confrontation between brother and beau in *Sunday in New York*

career, I suppose it would have been a preparation of sorts.

After the last performance, we flew in a private plane to Piqua, Ohio, where friends occupied a house so lovely that I would have seriously considered abandoning Los Angeles and the rest of the world for it, had it or its equivalent become available on the coast. Its early American furniture, black-and-white marble floors, and superbly-paneled walls gave an impression of formal elegance, which was belied only by the legend embroidered in Gothic script across a panel of our Victorian bedroom: "To the best of our knowledge and belief, intercourse is the principal cause of pregnancy. Having disclosed this fact, the management refuses to accept any further responsibility."

Our room was provided with hot coffee, bowls of fruit, dishes of biscuits, vases of flowers, and current issues of every conceivable magazine. We found our suitcases unpacked, and their contents pressed and hung. Bing accepted this treatment as a matter of course, and I was prepared to become accustomed to it. Indeed the stage would have been set for a second honeymoon if Mary Frances had not decided to occupy one of the room's two canopied beds. Even so, it remained an oasis of calm to which we both recurred frequently during the hectic days that followed.

Indeed Bing was so charming that I should have suspected that something was in the wind, but I remained in a fool's paradise throughout our stay in Piqua and the subsequent return to Los Angeles. We had been home a full week before he finally admitted that he had sold our present home out from under me, and acquired a new one in far-off Hillsborough. Ordinarily this would have led to a pyrotechnic display of temperament, but his mother had neatly upstaged me by throwing a series of what we of the medical profession technically denominate *conniption fits.*

For some months she had nightly disturbed Bing's sleep by wandering about the house conversing with ghosts from her past. Bing was terrified that she might fall down the staircase, so his sleep, which was poor enough at best, was now practically nonexistent. I therefore decided that, in the interest of his sanity, I would hire a night nurse to sleep in his mother's room. To my astonishment, she agreed that this would be a fine arrangement: "That way I'll have someone to talk to when I wake up at night."

The *someone* turned out to be pleasant and competent. I installed her in a day bed in a corner of the senior Mrs. Crosby's large room. All went well until late evening when Bing's mother threw her out.

My talent for negotiating is proverbial in the better circles. I speedily called a truce, and reinstalled the nurse. An hour later Catherine Harrigan Crosby threw her out again.

Well, if you want a thing done right. . . . I let the nurse go and decided to occupy the day bed myself. My superiority was clearly evidenced by the fact that I lasted a full two hours before getting the old heave-ho.

At this point Bing suddenly decided that it was time for the man of the family to assert himself, and raced in to remonstrate with his mother. Ten minutes later he joined me in the hall. "I'm calling my doctor," he decided.

When the physician learned that Bing's mother had failed to recognize him, and had sent him from the room, he told us to bring her to the hospital for some tests. That was easy for him to say. Knowing that she wouldn't go without a struggle, and that he could never face up to the ordeal, Bing suddenly recalled a business appointment at the crack of dawn. After he left, Alan Fisher and I tried to cajole his mother into accompanying us to St. John's Hospital.

To our relief we found her fully dressed and purse in hand, but determined to visit Bob or Larry, in whose dwellings she anticipated better treatment. Pretending to follow her wishes, Alan and I managed to lure her as far as the servants' dining room, at which point she voiced her suspicions of our motives, sat on the floor behind the door, resolutely grasped its knob, and refused to budge.

A Bing Crosby Special with Dean Martin, Frank Sinatra, and Rosemary Clooney

While the cook hid in terror behind the refrigerator, Alan and I pried Mrs. Crosby loose, and carried her, kicking and screaming, to the waiting car. It seemed that she knew in her bones that she would never come back.

Bing had always been a dutiful son. Now in his 60th year, he still catered to his mother's wishes when at home. He was permitted neither to take a drink in her presence himself, nor to entertain any of his Hollywood friends, who without exception failed to measure up to the moral standards of Spokane.

I stayed with her throughout a day of tests, leaving only to grab a bite in the hospital cafeteria. When I returned to her room, I found that she had become violent, and had had to be strapped into bed. Her old arms were black and blue from struggling against her bonds.

I forced Bing to come and see her, and tried to convince him that she should be permitted to die at home. He asked her what she wanted, but she furiously refused to speak to him, and finally pretended to be asleep. Sick with guilt, we slunk home and simply sat staring into space. I knew that Bing couldn't face any action that might in some way contribute to her death, and would therefore be forced to leave her in the hospital.

The next day Mrs. Crosby had a stroke and, after three days in the intensive-care unit, was removed to a convalarium. There I stopped to visit her each day, on my way to or from the Veterans Hospital, where I was fulfilling my psychiatric nursing requirement. She was no longer able to walk, but seemed more lucid than she had been in years.

She was very eager to leave the hospital, and we spent hours discussing the decoration of her rooms in the new house in Hillsborough. For the most part she seemed delighted with the prospect, but she had occasional moods when she spoke darkly of the better living conditions which she might enjoy with her other children, all of whom I knew to be skulking in the hinterlands, terrified at the very prospect.

Since Bing was unable to look at his mother's empty room, I am sure that he would have left home if his Christmas special had not come along at just this time. On the ragged edge myself, I finally blurted out something that I had been wanting to ask for the past six years: "Why don't I have a part in it?"

Bing agreed to discuss the matter with the producers, and finally got them to agree that I should be allowed to read a commercial. This was too much. Had I not recently starred in *Sunday in New York*? Why couldn't I sing and dance like the other guests?

The hand that rules the cradle rocks the world. To the astonishment of all concerned, Bing finally agreed to read the commercial himself, while I sang a glamorous solo and danced a number with Peter Genero.

This was more than I had hoped for, and it seemed that I might have overreached myself. I promptly caught cold dancing in the air-conditioned studio, and what little voice I had was reduced to a croak. There I was, standing before a symphony orchestra and backed by a full chorus, but feeling like a princess recently turned into a frog.

At this juncture Bob Hope, who as ever was guest-starring on the show, came in to inform us that he had a detached retina in his left eye: "Would you mind if I do my song early so that I can fly north for a shot of laser?"

Watching the way this courageous man ran through his jokes and his song with Bing, without exhibiting a trace of his fear of blindness, I felt my little problems pale into insignificance. Resolutely I entered the isolation booth, started to sing, and promptly dissolved into tears.

Evidently disgusted at my lack of professionalism, the man who had vouchsafed me the opportunity left the rehearsal and didn't return that day. Rosie Clooney, always my friend, told me that a lyric often got to her, and assured me that I would be fine when the big day came. Sure enough, the next day at the studio when John Scott Trotter and I took a cold run at the ballad, it sounded much better. When even Bing stayed to listen, I thought we might have a hit on our hands.

Just a perfect friendship

As if his mother's plight weren't enough, Bing was once again experiencing the lower back pains that he recognized all too well as a prelude to kidney surgery. The house had the festive air of a morgue, and the members of the staff were tiptoeing around him like funeral attendants.

In a desperate effort to cheer us all up, I decided on a Halloween party. True to the adage that misery loves company, I invited Rosemary Clooney, who had been experiencing marital problems, to bring her entire brood, and the widowed Edie Adams Kovacs to come with her daughter Mia. Bing supervised, sang, did a juggling act, and even played the spoons. In his efforts to keep small heads from staying under too long as they bobbed for apples, he briefly forgot his fears for his mother and the sharp pains in his back.

After the little ones had toddled off to their trundle beds, Bing raised a convivial glass or two with Rosie's Uncle George, whose horses had vied with his host's for last place on the "leaky roof circuit" in the merry days of yore.

Suddenly the look of pain returned to Bing's face and he abruptly left the group. Having experienced an unbroken chain of disasters of late, I expected the very worst, and nearly collapsed in relief when our minstrel returned caroling, "Rock of ages passed for me, so tonight I'm finally free."

Bing went through an entire soft shoe routine on his way to handing me a jagged kidney stone the size of a Texas pecan. I forgave him the totally out-of-character hint of blasphemy, when I realized that the elimination of the ugly object had saved him from surgery.

"What did it feel like?" I asked in awe.

"Like delivering a set of broken dishes, but I'm now enjoying the full fruits of maternity."

On November 29, Bing invited us to watch *Robin and the Seven Hoods*. The children and I spent the morning at a pre-Columbian art exhibit at the Los Angeles County Museum, then stayed for a frightful lunch from the cafeteria in the basement of the building. Famished from their exposure to culture and trained in the harsh school of their mother's cooking, they took it all in their stride, wolfing down vast quantities of unidentifiable but possibly Mayan dishes.

In the course of their orgy they became thoroughly bespattered, and I congratulated myself on my foresight in bringing along a change of clothing. In the ladies room I dressed them in their very best, so that they would be radiant for their father at Warner Brothers.

Before our admiring eyes Bing completed his big production number of Jimmy Van Heusen's *Don't be a Do-Badder*, backed by a full orchestra and a chorus of some thirty kids. To my amazement and relief our whole brood behaved beautifully, laughing at just the right times and destroying nothing of consequence. Bing was so enthralled by the vision of these model children that he picked up all forty pounds of his youngest butter-ball and asked "Well, bubbles, what did you think of that?"

Nathaniel smiled weakly, and then deposited the contents of a very large pre-Columbian lunch all over his beaming father. I reflected that I had at last found a specific that transformed my bobcats into models of deportment, and resolved to keep the cafeteria at the County Museum in mind as a court of last resort. As for Bing, I'm not sure just how he reacted to the implied criticism, but in retrospect I can say that it was the last musical he ever made.

In the first weeks of December I finished my practical work in the maternity ward with flying colors. Modesty forbade that I take my triumph too seriously, since with my practical exposure to the subject I had an unfair advantage over my teenage colleagues.

The children were permitted to leave their classes at the Buckley School in order to share this, my finest hour. They stood beside me in the cafeteria of the Queen of Angels School of Nursing, as its director finally handed me a real diploma with my name on it.

At long last I was a graduate RN, a circumstance which seemed to occasion some concern in the ranks of the faculty members

"Don't be a Do-Badder" from *Robin and the Seven Hoods*

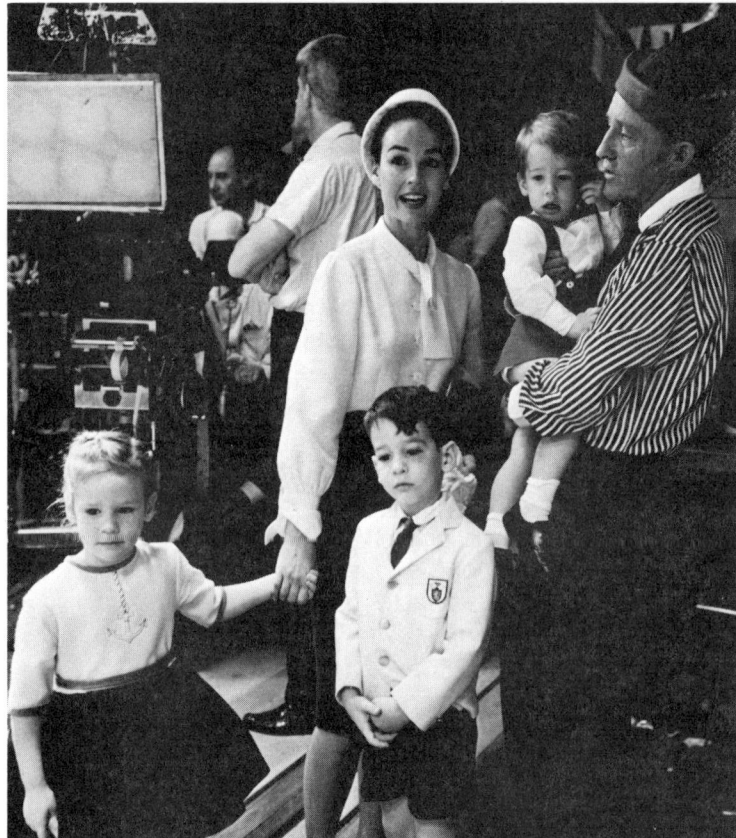

Nathaniel prepares to be very sick.

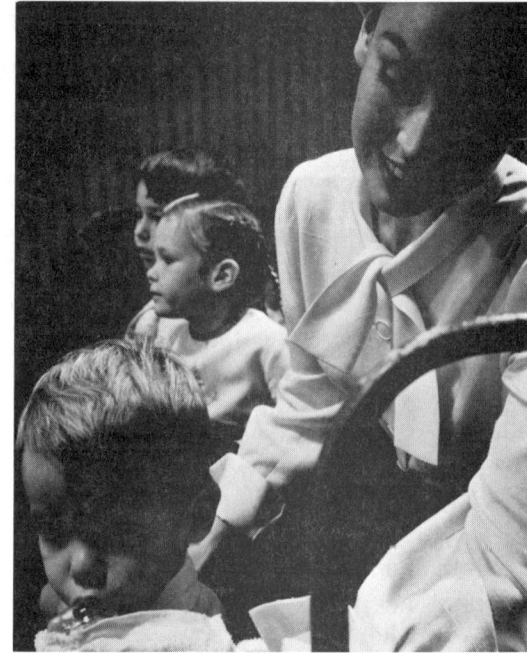

Afterwards nurse applies ice to her patient.

present. One asked apprehensively if I were really planning to exercise my talents in a nursing career, while another admitted that they would have to give the matter some thought before admitting other "mature students." And here I'd thought I had been preparing for an ingenue's role!

Before I left, several of my teachers did apologize for their frequent efforts to expel me for such crimes as absenteeism and pregnancy, in the course of my long and checkered scholastic career. It had been their first look at my brood, and perhaps they had concluded that I was more to be pitied than censured after all.

Louis Armstrong once remarked without rancor that, although he had worked with Bing for thirty years, he had never been invited to the Crosby home. Somehow the remark was circulated with the implication of racial prejudice. What Louis was actually saying was that neither he nor any other entertainer had ever been invited to visit Bing. The fact of the matter was that Bing was a very private person, who neither entertained nor accepted invitations within the Hollywood world.

His natural penchant in this regard had been reinforced by Dixie's lingering illness and his mother's absolute refusal to have actors in her house. Nonetheless Bing had so enjoyed costarring with Sammy Davis Jr. in *Robin and the Seven Hoods* that he accepted an invitation to dine at the Davis' home on the evening of December 23. Rat-pack leaders Frank Sinatra and Dean Martin had also been invited.

Frank had to cancel early, but dinner was delayed for an hour while we waited for the Martins to appear. I could see that his wife Mai was suffering for Sammy, who obviously wanted to impress Bing. Finally she phoned the Martins, and heard from a bewildered Jean that she knew nothing of the engagement, and had long since served dinner.

In the meantime Sammy had regaled us with his incredible repertoire of songs, jokes, and dramatic recitals. He knew Cyrano by heart, obviously identified with the position of outsider, and was the only person I've ever heard who could match Jose Ferrer's performance on the great monologues.

When we finally settled down to dinner, Bing related anecdotes from the running "race war" between Sammy and the other members of the rat pack. They had painted the name Smokey on his golf cart, had placed a sign over his star's dressing room that read *Downstairs at the Back*, and had dismissed his hard-won proficiency in the complicated dance routines as "natural rhythm."

Sammy himself had brought the joke home, with constant reminders of the topsy-turvy world in which his minuscule black self was wedded to a statuesque Swedish beauty, and their brown offspring had a white nursemaid. When newsmen had asked him what sort of children he hoped to have, Sammy had replied, "Black, brown, grey, white, or pinstriped, we'll love them just the same."

On and on the stories went until I finally ventured to ask, "Don't you ever get tired of so many variations of the same old joke?"

"Yes," said Sammy Davis Jr.

I knew that his mother's absence from our Christmas festivities would make them a sad occasion for Bing. In need of advice, I finally solicited my own mother's help in livening up the household. As soon as she arrived from Texas, she suggested a dinner on the 24th for our entire staff and their chosen guests.

Fortunately for all concerned my culinary aptitudes are not inherited. Pressures of time had done terrible things to my mother's housekeeping schedule, but her moments in the kitchen were nearly always productive. She was, however, inexperienced in preparing meals for more than three people, and the prospect of forty-five guests proved a bit much. In desperation she reverted to the grab-and-throw method, filled the kitchen with flying ingredients, and inevitably omitted the key one from each recipe.

The want of baking soda transformed mother's delicious southern biscuits into hardtack. Potatoes whipped without cream tasted

At long last, a graduate RN

like Elmer's Glue. Her banana cake, a specialty of the house, died a horrible death from lack of cream of tartar in the mix, or sugar in the divinity icing. Meanwhile the legs had fallen off the turkey, which had been abandoned in the oven for too many hours at much too high a temperature.

"I've long suspected that you wanted to get rid of us," Alan Fisher remarked, "but couldn't you have picked a more civilized way to communicate your message?"

Catastrophe or no, we had established a tradition which would endure throughout the remainder of my mother's lifetime. Years later I learned that our annual rite had become known in sacrilegious downstairs circles as *The Crosby Christmas Crucifixion*.

The great day itself was a sequence of minor catastrophes. Desperate to get rid of the game birds in the freezer, I had decided to serve pheasant. I instructed the cook to exhibit one bird under a blanket of plumes, while the others were burning in the kitchen.

"Cripes," remarked Dennis' wife Pat when the tail feathers passed beneath her nose, "it's a good job you're not serving buffalo."

Meanwhile Bing, who was inexperienced in such matters, had made a rare trip to the wine cellar to bring back a sample of our rarest old vintage, then worth some 500 dollars a bottle. The corks first refused to budge, and finally slivered into dozens of fragments which had to be fished out of the wine. By the time the guests were ready, the delicious bouquet had turned suspiciously sour. Sure enough, a half-hour's exposure to the general atmosphere had sufficed to transform the lot into the world's most expensive vinegar. I tried to console myself with the fact that for once no blood had been shed among the children.

Immediately after Christmas we were off to Kona Farms to join Alice Faye, Phil Harris, June Haver, and Fred MacMurray in Trader Vic Bergeron's California retreat.

As Bing had planned it the girls were simply to watch, but by purest accident Trader Vic's opening monologue went approximately as follows: "Hell, I wouldn't go on a hunting trip without Helen. What's the fun of a bunch of dirty old men seeing who can drink the most booze or tell the filthiest stories? When my Helen steps out with that little silk scarf at her throat, and nails the first pheasant that pops up out of the kaffir corn, that's my idea of class. Right, Bing?"

Bing had devoted much of his life to seeing which hunter could drink the most booze or tell the dirtiest stories, but he was neatly trapped in a situation where he could only nod and acknowledge Vic's authority. Regretfully he broke out a gun for me, and summoned my new dog Patrick J. O'Toole, an Irish Setter that Trader Vic had been keeping for us in his kennels while the trainer worked with him. Bing was agreeably surprised when Patrick actually found us several pheasant during a brief trial run.

Unfortunately, once we reached the field the following morning, all traces of training seemed to have fled from Patrick's dim doggy brain. Obeying some faint premonition, Bing had insisted that a chain be placed on his collar, and had warned me that I must hang onto it for dear life.

Off we marched into the sunrise. At the first hint of birds my canine companion took off like a rocket, chain waving behind him and tail high in the air. Through the dewy kaffir corn he bounced, presenting alternate visions of flying auburn ears and plumed tail. My screams mingled with his barks, and then with Bing's desperate whistling. Soon all the dogs were racing through the fields, and the pheasant were up and off for parts unknown, bright feathered meteors against the morning sun.

Vic howled and swore first at my dog, then at his dog, then at all the dogs, and finally at poor little open-mouthed me. Bing became astonished, tickled, outraged, and finally sullen. Of course it was all my fault, so I was in tears as we retired to the main house for lunch. It was only 9:30 a.m. when we arrived, but now that I had ruined the hunt, no one had any idea of what to do with the rest of the morning.

To fill up the empty hours Phil Harris began

Our first formal family portrait

mimicking my screaming at Patrick, first with a strong, high-pitched female shriek, then with a hopelessly cracked voice, and finally with a tense, hoarse whisper. Eventually I developed an appreciation for his gallows humor, and joined the others in their roars of laughter.

"It would serve those dogs right if none of them ever came home," the Indian decided. "They disturbed my sleep with their damn barking last night, and they ruined my hunt this morning. The Chinese may have something at that. What would you say to roast hound as the *pièce de resistance* for dinner tonight? It's only poetic justice after all. They cost us our meal of pheasant."

We settled for roast beef with Chinese pea pods and water chestnuts, after which we had songs from Bing, Alice Faye, June Haver, and Fred MacMurray, all of whom joined Trader Vic and me in a final rendering of *Sweet Adeline* that served as the curtain closer for 1963.

I said good-bye to my spiral staircase at 594 South Mapleton Drive

1964

For the new year I had resolved to admit that I had lost my underhanded battle to remain in Los Angeles. Just between us I had no alternative, since Bing was about to move with or without me, but my resolution made it official.

My worst fears were realized when I flew to Hillsborough to view the new house. Bing had outdone himself this time. It combined the most deplorable characteristics of the last ten we had seen. To begin with it was dark, dank, absurdly proportioned, and totally ill-suited to our needs. As I approached it the acacias, which lined the driveway, occasioned an immediate allergic attack that made me beat a hasty retreat.

Plucking up my courage, I covered my face with a handkerchief and finally made it through the front entrance. When I opened the door to the first closet, I was greeted by a swarm of termites. The second closet had been designated as the office that I had always wanted but never had. I was replacing the silverware, which it had previously contained within dimensions so tight that I wondered how poor Sterling could have managed there.

Bridget Brennan, who had accompanied me, took one look at the stairs leading down into her quarters and burst into tears. Apparently there was some medieval Irish tradition which placed the lesser servants in the lowest dungeons, and she felt that she had suddenly regressed to the nightmare images of her youth. Somehow she managed to conjure up a cup of tea in the gloomy, antiquated kitchen, wherein we sat staring at each other through rheumy eyes, wiping our runny noses, and repeating sadly, "It's all wrong. It's just all wrong."

We decided that, if we were to deal with the house at all, we would have to classify it as a challenge. We returned to present Bing with our plans for remodeling it completely.

"Oh I don't know," Bing murmured dreamily. "After all this is just temporary. I'm thinking of buying another house or two, or perhaps building some new ones. I've been talking to an architect who likes to do Japanese moderns."

Out of the frying pan into the fire. I decided that we would make do with what we had. The

Discussing the new winter fashions with Jean Louis

prospect of moving once was bad enough. I didn't want to repeat the process every six months for the rest of my life.

Meanwhile I continued to visit Bing's mother, who had had another stroke. After his first view of her in the convalarium, Bing had never been able to force himself to go back, but he worried about her all the time, and asked me for news of her every morning and evening. He was still trying to convince himself that she could make the move to Hillsborough, and insisting that I prepare her quarters there just as she would want them.

On January 5th we loaded the last of our furniture onto the mover's vans that would take it to Hillsborough. I bade a fond farewell to the home where our three children had played as infants, and where I had hoped to hold their wedding receptions. Bing's own memories antedated mine. The scars on the Waterford chandeliers bore mute witness to the games of football that his other boys had played in those halls.

We had removed much of the paneling for our new home. I ran my fingers lingeringly over that which remained, wondering if the glass from the powder-room wall would survive the trip north. (It did, and *faute de mieux* was placed in my new dressing room before the windows, which focused the brilliant rays of the morning sun upon it, and blew it into confetti-sized pieces.)

On Monday morning I paid my daily visit to Mrs. Crosby at the hospital, and then flew to Hillsborough to supervise the installation of cabinets, paintings, draperies, and curtains. With no place in Los Angeles to lay their heads, Bing and the children repaired to Palm Springs, where I joined them late that night.

On the following afternoon we received word that Catherine Harrigan Crosby had passed away quietly in her sleep at 3:30 p.m. I awaited some agonized reaction from Bing, but he just looked stunned and bewildered. After some hours of staring blankly at the walls, he finally took Remus out for a walk, which lasted the entire night and much of the following morning.

The funeral arrangements were complicated by the fact that we now had no home in Los Angeles. The family gathered at Larry Crosby's before and after the rosary, funeral mass, and burial in a grave beside Bing's father. At 4 p.m. on January 9, with no place else to go, we finally returned to Palm Springs. Each time that I awoke that night I heard Bing sobbing.

On January 13 we flew to Hillsborough, determined to overcome our grief by burying ourselves in activities related to furnishing the new house. I had been particularly spurred on by Bing's conversations with a series of architects about constructing still another residence on the four acres surrounding our present one. Terrified by the thought of more dwellings looming on my immediate horizon, I frantically supervised the installation of all the rugs and furniture that had arrived from Los Angeles.

My feelings of inadequacy and my frequent mistakes brought me to such a fine pitch of hysteria that I finally came down with an acute case of the shingles. As my sort of therapy, I fled with my sister to Pittsburgh to do a fashion show for Jean Louis. Thence I proceeded to New York, to carry out my cherished project of purchasing wood paneling from the William Randolph Hearst warehouses.

With John Scott Trotter's help, I scanned a book of pictures and selected two superb rooms. We then ascended eight floors in a freight elevator, picked our way through a series of musty corridors to an ill-lighted corner of one of the bins, and were shown piles of pine boxes marked X-4027 and X-5694.

"There they are," the caretaker said.

"May I look at the wood?" I asked.

"No, Ma'm, but it's there all right, and in good condition too. I see to that."

John Scott Trotter then guided me through the Frick Museum, so that I might learn more about period furniture and the other accouterments of gracious living. It had taken me

"Kathryn, will you kindly shape up or ship out."

a while, but I had come to realize that Bing wanted to lounge around a very formal house. He delighted in dusting his pipe tobacco all over the rug of a perfectly-furnished library. The chairs over which he draped his raincoats and hunting jackets had to be delicate antiques, and the bedspreads on which the Labradors lolled must be museum pieces. The books which he dogeared, during the endless reading sessions to which his insomnia condemned him, were necessarily first editions.

Firm in my belief that I had accomplished much and learned more during my two weeks away, I flew home free of shingles and full of righteousness. I was met at the airport by a driver, who informed me that Bing was out to dinner. He failed to return, and was unavailable for the next few days, which I spent teaching the children to read in the schoolroom that I had improvised in the attic.

When I finally cornered my husband, I presented him with his valentine, a Fabergé letter opener that I had purchased in New York. He grunted, refused to look at it, and disappeared with Harry on a hunting trip.

When they returned, I foolishly demanded an explanation and got it. "I've told you a dozen times that I don't like your modeling. Furthermore I don't like the idea of your traveling to Pittsburgh or puttering around New York alone. We have just moved to a new home. I should think that you would try to furnish it, make it run, and hopefully enjoy it."

As luck would have it my agent chose this moment to phone, with a part in a new TV series called *Breaking Point*, a Bing Crosby production. All I needed was the approval of the entrepreneur himself.

I had really played my cards wrong this time, and no amount of wifely devotion or false eyelashes seemed to have any effect. Bing turned me down cold, and left for the golf course while I moved lamps, selected stationery, supervised children, scattered rugs, and mourned my vanishing youth and lost career.

My husband finally demonstrated his approval of my new routine by presenting me with a German short-hair named Lady, a replacement for Patrick J. O'Toole, who had been returned in disgrace to his previous owner. Bing remarked uncharitably that he regretted that he didn't enjoy the same privilege with me, but I informed him that he was out of luck there since my father knew enough not to take me back.

Grimly I resolved to become the children's friend. On the first sunny day in mid-February I packed an enormous picnic basket, and shepherded them first to the DeYoung Museum, where they were bored by the pictures but loved to play in the water fountain. Next we visited the aquarium, where they preferred the crocodiles to the fish, and did their level best to pet the vicious reptiles.

I decided that we'd have our picnic in a tree-shaded area in front of the band shell. It proved so cold there that we were forced to take refuge in the Japanese Tea Garden. After some negotiations, the proprietors agreed to sell us hot tea, but flatly refused to permit us to eat our picnic lunch.

I must have carried that cursed basket for five miles, in the course of which we all caught colds and never did get to eat. As might be expected, the children spent the evening telling their father the sad tale of how their mother had mistreated them.

In point of fact said mother didn't know quite what to do with them. If there was one subject on which Bing and I were in total agreement, it was the children's education. We were prepared to spend any amount of time and money to give them the best that the modern world could offer, but we had been unable to determine just what that might be.

In Los Angeles they had simply terrorized a highly-recommended private school. The parochial school in Hillsborough was hopelessly understaffed, and all too ready to spoil Father O'Malley's "angelic children." In the local public schools we sensed the same want of discipline that they had known at home.

When at my wits' end I always phoned Dr. Barkley. As usual she had a ready suggestion.

With Beverly Garland, Bing's TV wife

"Try to contact Dr. M. W. Sullivan. He is the only one who has applied modern learning theory to the education of children. His research facility is hidden in the Santa Clara mountains somewhere in your area, but I'm told that he's almost impossible to reach. Perhaps Bing can think of something."

Oddly enough the name rang a bell. I must have heard it in the courses that I had taken for my teaching credentials. I also had a vague association with Spanish plays in the drama department at the University of Texas, but that must have been some other Sullivan. I leafed through the peninsula phone books, and persecuted the information operators, but could find no listing.

At least I had a temporary solution. I would rescue our home and the neighborhood from imminent destruction by flying the children off to Las Cruces. We had already had a nasty fire in the bathroom, when Harry discovered that he could burn toilet paper in the electric heater.

Now his mother almost duplicated the feat on the occasion of our first formal dinner in the new house. At the close of a sumptuous repast, in which I'd had the good sense not to involve myself, Alan Fisher ceremoniously flung open the doors to the dining room and announced, "Coffee is served in the drawing room, madam."

The animals marched in two by two, and nearly died of asphyxiation. I hadn't known that I was supposed to engage a chimney sweep before igniting the enormous pile of logs that I had prepared so carefully in the fireplace. The room was black with smoke, which the now-open doors were permitting free access to the rest of the house. The men raced outside, pulled open doors and windows, and retired gasping and coughing to the library. The only permanent damage was to my ego.

Then it was off to hunt and fish in Mexico. After my failure to control my dog at Kona farms, I was assigned a seat on the hillside, while the men hiked through the cactus after birds. This I minded not at all, because the time for my state boards was drawing near, and after some months away from school I was feeling very rusty. Furthermore Bing and I had a bet on the outcome. If I passed he would buy me a Fabergé flower, while if I failed he would buy himself a trip to Tierra Del Fuego.

Fishing trips were another matter, because I became seasick almost immediately when I tried to read on a boat. I was wrestling with nausea in the cabin when a marlin took it into his silly pointed head to strike my line. "I can allow you only five minutes," I announced grimly in my most authoritative tones.

By some trick of fate I had hooked a perfectly splendid fish that chose to charge the boat. All I had to do was reel in like crazy. When the boatmen announced a phenomenal total elapsed time from strike to release of only seven minutes I smirked, "I'd like to give you some more pointers, fellows, but that's all the time I can spare for now," and daintily passed the rod to my bewildered spouse, preparatory to returning to my book-filled bunk.

After a moment's hesitation Bing biffed me on the shoulder and growled huskily, "You old son of a gun," which accolade so puffed me up with pride that I almost remained on deck.

Back we sailed to Las Cruces, to arrange for the Immaculate Heart nuns to establish a marine biology summer school at our house. Producer Steve Gethers arrived from Los Angeles, and as usual I got things backwards. I thought he was offering my husband a part, whereas in point of fact said spouse was producing the Bing Crosby show, and currently appraising Steve to see if they could work well together.

When I finally got the notion, I put out a few feelers about the availability of a certain potential costar or, failing that, the possibility of a Kathryn Crosby show. Oddly enough there were no immediate takers.

As you may recall, we had worked not wisely but well the previous year in establishing an Easter tradition. It was now a Crosby duty to mop the floors of the church, fill it with bougainvillea from our house, supply it with new candles, import Padre Luis and a choir

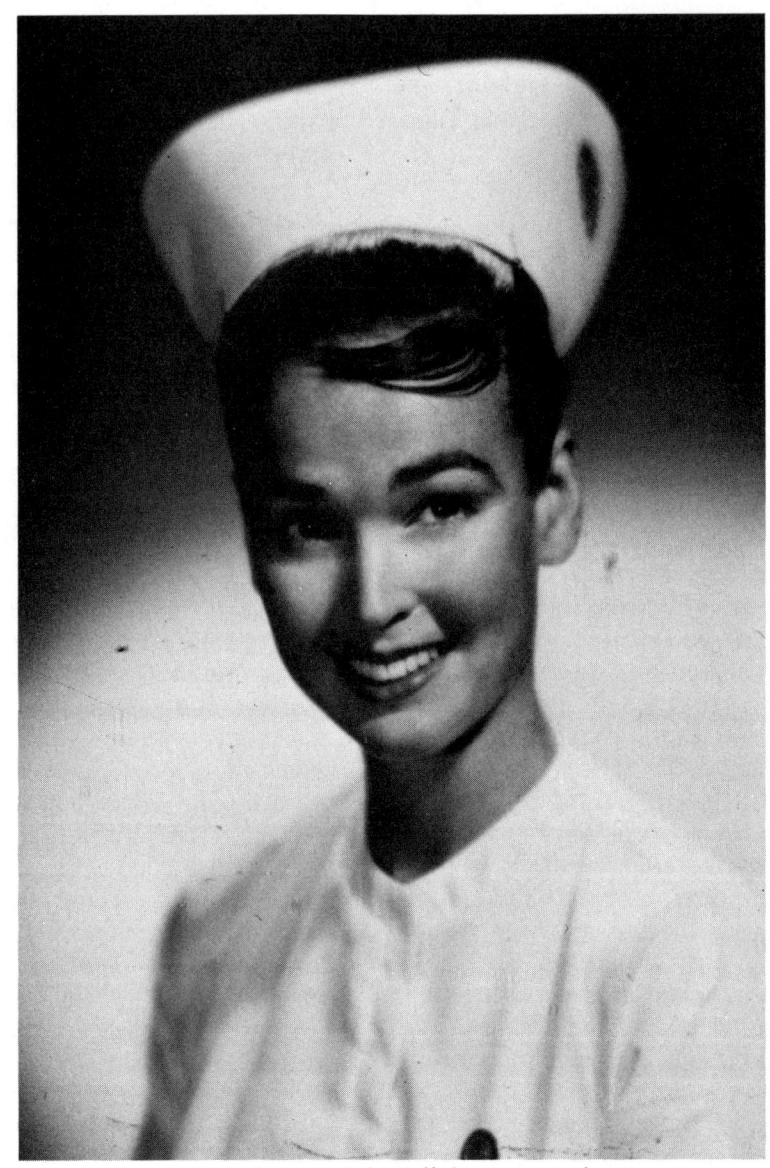
"But darling, I did it all for your sake."

from La Paz, and purchase and distribute the ice cream, cake, and piñata for the ensuing party.

Then it was off to Santiago with all three children. While the men hunted, I herded my babes through the fields, trying to share my scanty store of knowledge: "Don't try to pick the flowers off the cactus, because those spines sting like bees. Don't touch the milk that oozes out of the paper tree, because it will take your hide clean off. Don't eat those pretty but poisonous oleander blossoms, and don't wander off into the underbrush where the rattlesnakes play." How I longed to be back in the thick of the shoot where a girl was safe.

Upon our return Bing was felled by a sudden fever. He dropped into bed, and I started playing diagnostician. "There is always the threat of kidney stones," I suggested. "If one of those little devils starts to move, how in the world can I get you back to Los Angeles fast enough to do any good? What if it was a centeroides, the little straw-colored scorpion with the lethal sting? Right now it could be causing the nerve damage which leads to convulsions and death due to respiratory failure. Have you noticed any symptoms of salmonella dysentery? We've been very lucky so far, but it's always a threat here in Baja California."

On and on I went while Bing listened solemnly. At length he favored me with his solution: "Go play doctor with the children while I get some sleep."

I left the ungrateful old curmudgeon to his own devices while I chased the burros out of the plumaria under his bedroom window. After allowing him an hour to recover his spirits, I woke him to see how he had been resting. He was furious.

"If by some crazy accident you ever get your license, I'm going to see that it's revoked. Do you know that you threatened me with some fifty forms of grisly and immediate death, without even bothering to take my temperature? What were all those ridiculous years of nursing for anyway?"

He did have a point there. I had been so busy diagnosing that I had somehow overlooked the first step, which seemed to be attention to the patient's symptoms. But I couldn't stand to be castigated in front of the children, who had just poured in the door.

"Obviously you're feeling much better or you couldn't possibly be so angry," I announced authoritatively. "I don't need to take your temperature. You have just let off all the steam that you had bottled up. But you might be a little more appreciative of my nurse's training. After all, I did it for your sake."

"You did what?" Bing was first incredulous, and then livid, "Do you mean that you're trying to use me as an excuse for the agony that you've put us through over the past five years? How many thousands of times have I begged you to drop that nutty nursing? And now you try to blame it all on me! I'm as healthy as a horse and you know it. Or at least I was, until you got your hands on me and started playing Doctor Know-it-all."

My treatment, though unconventional, had certainly been efficacious. Bing bounced up out of bed and went stamping off to his fishing boat. Stung by his ingratitude, I was left to console myself with the reflection that all was not in vain. In spite of the macho image that forced him to deny his problems and present himself as the dauntless outdoorsman, his health really was in a precarious state. My nursing background had made me very useful to his mother, who had labored under the misapprehension that I was a physician to her dying day, and it would benefit him throughout our future life, whether he liked it or not. Mutter, mutter, mutter. A girl's best friend is her mutter.

Off we went to Mexico City where, after a visit to the zoo, Bing took the boys for haircuts. When I saw the state in which they returned, I required an explanation.

"I tried to tell the barber in Spanish to cut it short, but I didn't know the right words," Bing replied. "I'm glad the boys didn't know the words either, because they were yelling to leave it as long as possible."

My menfolk seemed to think that their contradictory messages had lost something in

Dilettante scholars in my class at Las Cruces

translation, but it was apparent to me that the barber had understood all too well. Harangued at from both sides, he had effected the sort of compromise that we were later to denominate a Mexican standoff. With true peasant cunning, and in alternate strips, he had simply left half of the hair long, while cutting the other half short. The result was something that only a mother should have been able to love, but once again I failed the test. We do have our limits you know.

The Crosbys took a side trip to Pueblo, where we purchased a set of Talaveras pottery, actually the rejects of those that had been made for the Dutch Queen Wilhelmina. We thus earned the potter's scorn, but found that our treasures resembled Zen art in their intriguing imperfections. I was reminded of a remark by a connoisseur in San Francisco: "Don't you love my Talaveras? All the right things are wrong with it."

Right or wrong, I had come to welcome bargains in our more fragile purchases, since I knew that their days were numbered in our household. As we jumped back onto the plane that we used as a sort of Mexican taxi, I appreciated more thoroughly Mary Frances' five-year-old estimate of the world. Her first question upon meeting a new friend was, "Where's your airplane?" It was the only form of transportation with which she had any real familiarity.

Back to Mexico City and a visit with Merle Oberon, who described in detail how she had decorated her exquisite home. Bing listened entranced, while she discussed the importing of antique columns, the design of rugs, and the planting of pine trees and wisteria.

I reflected on my own inability to make Bing concentrate for a moment on household matters between rounds of golf, and wanted to kick them both. But then I reminded myself of how Merle had helped me with subtleties of hairdos and make-up right after my marriage. I would never forget the way she had reclined against tiny lace-covered pillows in her Louis XVI bed and explained that, though she had pneumonia at the moment, she always did try to look presentable.

She had succeeded then and was certainly managing now. I jabbed an elbow into the ribs of my mesmerized husband, and introduced the subject of Merle's pre-Columbian art collection. She rose to the bait and suggested a trip to Oaxaca, to see the excavations and museum there. "I'm all tied up at the moment," she explained, "but if you'll wait till Tuesday, I'll have our chef fix a lunch and we can all go."

As Bing's head started to bob up and down, I announced sweetly that we would have to be getting back home, but that we would certainly drop by Oaxaca on the way. Merle's husband Bruno nodded his solemn assent. I was glad to see that someone was on my side.

My prime recollection of Oaxaca is of the attempt that I made to down enchiladas at the tiny restaurant beside the museum. No one else would touch them, but my Texas pride was up, so my mouth and throat burned for a week.

We had been remarkably short on catastrophes during our little idyll in Mexico City. To be sure the children had interchanged the guests' shoes in the hallway of the hotel, while Bing and I were at dinner, but this was hardly on a par with their customary crimes. I was feeling much more confident about life in general as I entered the kitchen of our Las Cruces home and asked Brunhilde, the resident Nazi cook, "What's for supper?"

Brunhilde was an elemental force of nature, who had come as housekeeper with our new home. Alan Fisher, with his penchant for playing god, had decided to convert her into a cook. In this capacity she had shown a certain flair, and a propensity for banging pots about and concocting heavy pastries decorated with the legend, "Velcome, Katryn und Bing."

In Las Cruces she had filled the pantry shelves with cans of supposedly-frozen Minute Maid, while placing the tomato juice, which ordinary mortals thought required no refrigeration, deep in the freezer. Not that this simple exchange had mattered much, because she had elected to "defrost" the freezer with an ice

(Above) Mary Frances and Harry admire Brunhilde breasting the waves.
(Below) Bing with hotel kitchen staff

pick, punctured its aluminum innards, and rendered it *hors de combat* forever.

To Bing's amazement and delight, in Las Cruces she had determined to go native. Punctually at two each day, when she had finished breaking the crockery, and the burning desert sun was at its worst, she stretched her Gertrude Ederle swimsuit precariously over her mighty frame, pulled an enormous bathing cap down into her eyes, and marched straight as an arrow through flowering cactus and neighboring driveways to the beckoning beach, upon which she dropped her blanket-like, terry-cloth robe, before swimming unhesitatingly precisely one-half mile straight out to sea, wheeling with military precision, and retracing her strokes.

Now Brunhilde was kneeling resolutely before the stove. "Ach, Gnädige Frau, you vill luf mein. . ."

Fortunately she had turned toward me as she spoke, for at that very moment the oven door flew past her head, followed by an enormous explosion, and a casserole containing the dinner which she had been about to describe.

As usual she had had the luck of the just, her linguistic difficulties having preserved her from instant decapitation. In the event she had suffered only singed hair and eyebrows, and a mild case of shell shock, which seemed to have transported her back to the good old days of WW2, for she was muttering something about the filthy British with their night raids, interspersed with comments to the effect that, "I vas only following orders, but I did not know how to put the little pipe back into the big pipe after I haf cleaned the gas ovens."

I gave Leutnant Judenhasser a brief but well-merited furlough, and burned the family's evening hamburgers with my own little hands on the patio grill.

I have perhaps neglected to mention that, thanks to some chicanery on the part of Lillian Barkley, and leniency bordering on criminal negligence from the Immaculate Heart nuns, I had been allowed to take a series of exams, without being forced to participate in the dreary education courses designed to prepare me for them, and was now a fully-credentialed teacher in California.

Feeling that my activities in Las Cruces lacked scope, I added the sons of our laundress to my own brood and sent out a call for more volunteers. Class hours were from nine until noon, and my neighbors soon learned to stay away lest they be commandeered into listening to pupils read, or calling out multiplication tables. From noon on, teacher and class repaired to the beach for swimming and snorkeling.

One day, while helping to prepare the lunch which separated my academic from my maritime pursuits, I noticed that a slight girl who assisted Brunhilde in the kitchen was coughing frequently. Motivated by simple curiosity, I asked her *desde cuando* she had had her nasty summer cold.

"Toda mi vida," was the disquieting response.

"No cause for alarm," I reassured myself. "She doesn't seem to be overly burdened with brains, and she probably just didn't understand." Nonetheless I sent a culture by the next plane to the clinic in La Paz. Before evening they had returned the verdict of tuberculosis.

I hastened to make further inquiry, and learned to my horror that for the past six months my new-found patient had functioned as tortilla-maker in the local hotel. My next step was a consultation with their cook, which led nowhere. My Nazi was a babe in arms compared to this model. A stiff-necked Castilian, she was inordinately proud of the fact that she had never had a case of *turistas* among the hotel guests. The waiters reported to her, and she separated and boiled the tableware of anyone whom she considered to be sick. She stated imperiously that she maintained the highest standards of cleanliness among all the helpers in her kitchen.

And indeed she did constitute an enormous improvement over her predecessor, whose first and perhaps last step in the dishwashing process had been to consign the plates to the

(Above) Bridget, the children, and our laundress, potential shills for my anti-TB campaign
(Below) More potential victims for my Tine tests

local hounds until they had been properly licked clean. "My kitchen is spotless," my paragon insisted.

Desperately I tried to pierce the barrier of mutual linguistic incomprehension, but words like *bacteria* and *microbios* failed to elicit a positive response. Finally I made the mistake of screaming, "Bugs, bugs, your kitchen is full of terrible bugs. *Está muy sucia.* We have to scrub it down with Ajax and Clorox immediately.

Right after I was forcibly ejected from the kitchen, I nailed Bing, who was just leaving for Los Angeles, and told him what serum to bring back. When he returned, he found that my class had added seven more Mexicans, and that his bed was occupied by our laundress' two-year-old, who had an unusually severe case of the measles. The mother and Bing looked on resentfully while I removed the child's wool cap and heavy clothes, washed him in the sink with tepid water to bring down his fever, cut his long fingernails, and scrubbed away two years of dirt.

Then I lovingly unwrapped the parcel that Bing had brought me. It was the wrong move at the wrong time. He knew these people much better than I did, and realized that it was time to make a stand.

"What are those four-pronged objects that you're hauling out?"

"These are Tine tests for turberculosis. See, I just jab one into your forearm. If a large red circle appears three days later, you've had a positive reaction, and I ship you off to Dr. Von Borstel in La Paz."

Bing leaped back as if I'd just been transformed into a rattlesnake. "Oh no you don't," he said. "You've violated enough local taboos already. We have to live with these people, you know, and if they don't want to wash, or be jabbed in the arm every day or two, that's their business."

"All you have to do is come down to the hotel, where the workers can watch, and lend me your good right arm. When they see that you haven't been harmed, I'm sure they'll let me test them too."

"Listen, Miss Busybody, I'm not going anywhere with you. Why can't you leave these poor folk alone? And now that I'm on the subject, what is this mob of kids doing in my bedroom?"

"They're learning how to read and write. That is to say, they will be as soon as I figure out how to teach them. Isn't it wonderful? They won't be illiterate like their poor parents."

Bing regarded me balefully. "You really should have been a missionary in China," he decided, "or a nurse in the Boer War, or anything, anything but my wife!" He stalked regally out of the room.

And would you believe it, he stuck to his guns. So it was poor Bridget whom I dragged off to set a sterling example of Anglo-Saxon *sang-froid* for the lowering locals. Unfortunately I had chosen not a lineal descendant of Richard the Lionhearted, but a hysterical Celt, who fainted at the mere sight of the needle, thus falling somewhat short of the desired impression.

"You didn't even stick her yet," Mary Frances announced disapprovingly. "I want to see you stick her good, and then get Harry and Nathaniel."

"No," I reflected, "I think it's your turn."

To my utter surprise the reply was, "Oh yes, stick me, stick me. Everybody watch while mommy sticks me!"

There is, after all, something to be said for having a psychopath in the family. Her daddy's darling was ready to play any role, providing only that it be the lead. Basking in the attention of a large and obviously impressed adult audience, she cheerfully submitted to the needle herself, and then grabbed for it to attack her brothers. When I made to restrain her, she insisted that I jab first them, and then her friend Rod.

Señor Rodríguez had a superstitious terror of doctors, nurses, hospitals, and sharp objects in general. But his Mexican machismo wouldn't let him escape a fate to which three children

Pygmalion at the University of Texas

had now submitted. Grimly he formed his workers into a line, and placed himself at the head of it. I held my breath, but fortunately he didn't faint, so my antitubercular campaign was at last safely launched.

Indeed once my initial "volunteers" realized that they had survived the ordeal, they developed a splendid *esprit de corps*, and turned in their friends and neighbors with an enthusiasm that was truly touching. As Bing remarked, I seemed to have unleashed the latent sadism which lies just below the surface of every modern-day Aztec.

Now that the battle was won, mopping up operations were in order. One of my patrols discovered our boat captain, cowering in the engine room, and dragged him forth into daylight and retribution. The bartender at the hotel finally yielded to social pressure, where force had proved vain. "Nobody will speak to me," he confessed, regretfully baring his mighty forearm.

I scoured the hillsides in a jeep, busily innoculating bewildered cowhands. Aware of the existence of bovine tuberculosis, I also cast a lascivious eye upon their charges, but the skins looked dreadfully tough and I was unsure of precisely what would constitute a positive reaction. At the end of three days, if there was an unstuck native within five square miles, I was unaware of him, though I am certain that he must have been aware of me, and a pretty sneaky customer to boot.

I wish I could state categorically that my precautions saved Las Cruces and its surroundings from a terrible fate, but as luck would have it I identified only one positive reaction, that of a stalwart neighbor from Keokuk, Iowa, who certainly didn't look tubercular but, as I insisted to all and sundry, one never can tell.

While Bing, the only unvaccinated featherless biped within miles, looked on in disbelief, said neighbor jumped into his private plane and raced to San Diego for chest X-rays, which unfortunately showed that he was solid as a rock, though prone to allergic reactions to dirty needles.

"Best stay away from those unsanitary Mexican clinics," his doctor warned.

All in all, I can't say that the results of my campaign made me an Evita Perón in the eyes of my constituents. The net effect of my efforts had been the removal of one resentful, tubercular teenager to La Paz for treatment. There was a general feeling that a mountain had been in labor, and a mouse had been born. Unflinching in the face of adversity, I consoled myself with the reflection that virtue, after all, is its own reward.

Bing was less certain of the truth of the old adage. He suggested that we might be able to nip a revolution in the bud by shipping me back to save the United States of America.

Let it never be said that I can't take a hint. Back I flew to the Lone Star State, where true talent is always appreciated, to begin rehearsing the role of Eliza Doolittle for a university production of *Pygmalion*.

Shortly thereafter Bing himself had to return to begin work on *The Bing Crosby Show*. He had every reason to skulk in Hollywood, after selecting Beverly Garland for his screen wife, when a much more natural choice was ready, willing, able, and waiting in the wings.

I wasn't the only one who complained. Rosemary Clooney refused to watch the show, insisting that Bing was betraying her before the whole nation with "that other woman."

In Rosemary's favor it must be said that she tried to help me with my little contribution. Determined not to be left out entirely, I had written *Love Overlooks Those Little Things* as a theme for the show. John Scott Trotter had furnished the music for my lyrics, and Rosie had done everything for them that a great voice could. Imagine my disappointment when such an array of talent was rejected for a mere Jimmy Van Heusen number.

God tempers the wind to the shorn lamb. The three children were with me in Austin, and it was a delight to watch them become Texanized by their grandparents, who were staying with me at the Chi Omega House, which I had rented for the duration. While I mastered a

Governor John Connally

cockney accent, they went crabbing along the gulf and bass fishing in Lake Jackson, picking up the dreadful local dialect along the way.

Meanwhile Bing was scribbling off a note every time that there was a pause in his crowded schedule:

"We finished shooting the first episode this morning. The work isn't too difficult but it's constant, and all other activities and interests must be excluded. We work straight through from 8 a.m. to 7 p.m. every day. By the time I bathe and dress for dinner it's 9 o'clock, and I collapse into bed by 10. I have to rest a minimum of nine hours because, as you well know, only about five of them are spent sleeping."

Three days later he complained that, "Overwork has aggravated the bursitis in my shoulders and I have another terrible schedule today. To make matters perfect, I have just slammed my fingers in the car door."

I could generate some sympathy for his aching fingers and shoulders, but none for the perils of overwork. I would cheerfully have slaved twenty hours a day for the rest of my life if Hollywood had called. Yet here I was dividing my time between nature walks with the children and a college production destined for a total run of four days, with a Professor Higgins whose true vocation was selling grills for backyard barbecues.

Thus Bing: "I made a Christmas album with Sinatra and Fred Waring over the weekend. Also taped a panel show called *Los Expertos Contestan* for Latin American release. I tried to do it in Spanish, but got all tangled up. We'll have to find time to learn that language one of these days."

Thus Kathryn: "I took the children to see the governor's lady at the mansion. You may think that fans trouble you, but tours are run through her home every day. Can you imagine a daily influx of nine busloads of sixth graders?"

Bing, June 28th: "Gary has been invited to Calgary to be Grand Marshal of the Stampede. He may have trouble making it because he's in a film, and we're planning to use him in one of our episodes. Lindsay drops in on the set prac-

tically every day, and Denny works right next door. So we'll probably write in some parts for them too."

Indeed there seemed to be parts for every member of the family but one. I wondered idly what the cameramen might do with an avenging fury who crashed through the door and pursued the lot of them offstage with a buggy whip. Ironically I was engaged at this time in interviewing summer students in the drama department, who desired to make their way to Hollywood and wanted tips from an ever-so-successful actress.

Bing, June 30: "There's been such a marked improvement in my shoulders that I'm back to playing golf again. The doctors are unable to account for it, but they hope it's more than just temporary relief."

I could have accounted for it if anyone had asked me. In a sudden fit of remorse, I had removed two pins from my Bing doll just yesterday. I decided to read on before replacing them.

Bing, July 2: "Nini sent me a clipping with the picture of you as Shaw's Eliza. It's perfect typecasting. You look like a girl who has spent her life hawking fish heads."

Silently I replaced the pins.

Kathryn, July 3: "Governor Connally still lives dangerously. He offered the children cokes in his office today, and then showed fabulous reflexes in catching the drinks before they hit his gorgeous new carpet. Not a fast learner, he then let Harry play with his beautiful gold pocket watch. My heart stood still, and I'm sure the watch will too, through all eternity."

Bing: "For two weeks now I've been searching attic to basement for the velvet, gold-initialed, lounging slippers by Maxwells, that you gave me for Christmas. I wanted to show them off by wearing them to dinner with Beverly Garland and her husband. In desperation I finally appealed to Fisher, who insists that you spirited them off to Texas. Explanations are in order. Are you an Indian giver? Are you keeping a man? Signed, Perplexed."

Kathryn: "Dear Perplexed: Right on both

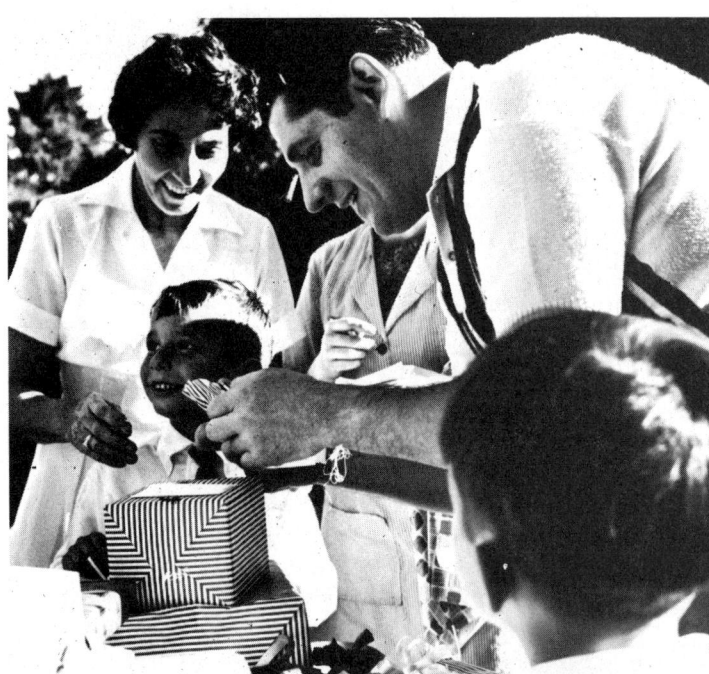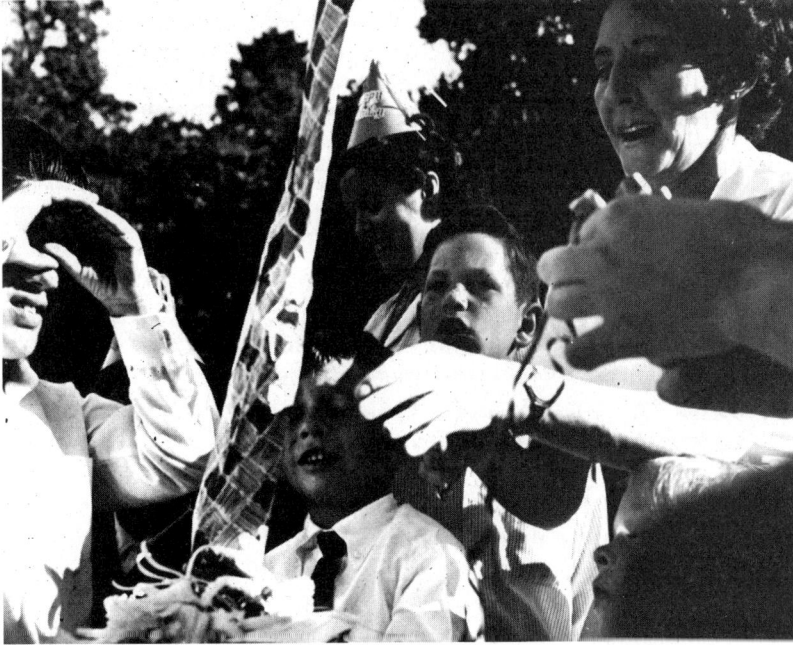

Bridget helps Alan and Norma Fisher with Harry's birthday party.

counts. Eliza threw them at Professor Higgins every night, and to judge from the ensuing applause they were perfect in the role. Incidentally, so was I. Your slippers and I may never make it in the big time, but Texans are loyal to their own, and we were a smash in Austin."

After *Pygmallion*, I did *Sabrina Fair* in Indianapolis. Bing wrote on August 2, to say that he was now finding time to spend weekends with the children in Hillsborough. He was trying very hard to get his obstreperous daughter to speak softly and act like a lady, and also applauding Harry, who was undefeated in the swimming races at the club. Bing admitted that he was on a paternal kick only because the pain in his shoulders prevented him from playing golf.

Bing, August 8: "As I write, Harry's birthday party is in full sway. The entire yard is decorated with balloons, streamers, and Donald Duck placards. Only one serious conflict has developed. Nathaniel is quietly and seriously insisting that it is his birthday too. He's not given to impassioned outbursts, but he's steadily, relentlessly obdurate. At this point it looks as if we'll just have to yield and find another cake.

"I now share your opinion of the inadequacies of this house, but I have grave doubts about building again. I just don't know whether I have the energy to deal with the inevitable worries, decisions, and frustrations."

Hallelujah! I breathed easier after that paragraph, but as the sequel proved the snake had lured me into a false sense of security.

It was standing room only in Indianapolis throughout the entire week. Flushed with success we moved on to Detroit, only to find that a total of 19 tickets had been sold for our first performance. The producer ordered the cast into the streets in a vain effort to drum up sales. Since there was a newspaper strike, our only publicity contacts were underground periodicals.

On we went to department stores, supermarkets, senior citizens groups, and ladies teas. It was something between a sorority project and a PR tour for a movie. Social creature that I am, I loved every minute if it. But I had overlooked the fact that when touring for Columbia I had a picture that was already in the can. Now I was in the position of dragging my weary limbs onto a stage each evening, to confront the small but hostile audience which we had bullied into attending.

I mistakenly described my activities to Bing, who had his own views of what behavior might be considered appropriate for his wife. "You are doing just what I asked you to avoid—agreeing to every request, no matter how silly or futile. Why do you think you need to get up at 7:30 a.m., rush about furiously all day promoting the play, give a performance in the evening, and then entertain the backers and promoters until 1:30 a.m.? Are you afflicted with a pathological inability to say *no*?"

The answer of course was *yes*, but I was tactful enough to treat the question as rhetorical. Even I, however, had to admit that he might have a point there, when I found myself somehow scheduled for a fashion show in Holyoke, Massachusetts, our next tour stop.

My delight in such events had always been a bone of contention between Bing and me. I enjoyed the lovely new dresses, the society of the other models, the social flavor of the event, and the conversations with experts on apparel from all over the world. But in this case I hadn't had sense enough to ask how closely the show fit my image, before leaping in with both feet and agreeing to do it.

I was driven to a country club full of reporters and photographers. When I asked to meet the other models, I was told that there weren't any. When I asked what wardrobe I was to exhibit, I learned that it was to be my own. Who then would be the narrator? By this time you can guess the response. Finally, in desperation, I asked a character player from the cast to fill in for me, while I changed clothes behind a screen.

"Sorry," she answered. "I have to do my laundry."

Solemnly I went through my paces, presenting a complete fashion show for a room totally

Finally Nathaniel had his own birthday party.

innocent of buyers or audience. The representatives of the press, who were as taken as I was, gleefully photographed my every move, and presented me in the local media as an enormous success.

So it goes.

Bing, August 16: "Shoulders sufficiently improved to permit cancellation of hospitalization, and rescheduling of the recording session with Rosemary Clooney. I'm delighted because there was a great deal of pressure from Capitol to get it done before she left on tour.

"Gary doing very well in this episode. Quite a revelation to me. He's punctual, knows his lines, and is cooperative and receptive to directions and suggestions."

I would be too, damn it, if someone would only give me a chance.

Bing made a dramatic arrival for my last performance in Holyoke. The tiny local airstrip was fogged in, and the pilot had to make three passes before he could land. The state police then drove Bing to the theater with sirens wailing, arriving just before the beginning of my last show.

Word of his coming had leaked out, and the place was mobbed. The manager had to hide him in his office until curtain time, a procedure ill-calculated to add to Bing's enjoyment of the performance. Once the lights had dimmed, he sneaked into a seat at the rear, where he was safe until intermission, at which time a squad of state troopers had to rush him into a phone booth and guard him with their lives.

The show had completed its run, and we escaped to visit Bing's brother Everett on his farm near Canaan, Connecticut. Then it was home to Hillsborough, after a few days of shopping and theatergoing in New York.

Now came a respite from frantic activity. New inflammation in Bing's shoulders kept him off the golf course, so I found that I had a househusband to entertain for the first time in my life. I responded characteristically by sleeping for the first week or so, as I gradually recovered from the eighteen-hour days of my summer tour. Thus it was Bing who first noticed that we had a problem on our hands.

"Your kids," he remarked severely, "are spoiled rotten. Alan and Norma treat them like young royalty, and they've made a slave of Bridget, the woman who's supposed to be in charge of them."

"Better her than us," I suggested hopefully.

"This is no time for levity; we have to do something."

"Short of the thumbscrew, the rack, and the iron maiden, just what would you suggest? I know when I'm licked, and I'm seriously considering surrender."

"Didn't Dr. Barkley suggest somebody the last time you talked to her?"

"Yes, but she didn't know where to find him, and I've forgotten the name anyway."

"Well, it can't go on like this. I'll give her a call and see what I can do."

For the next few days I made a serious attempt to work with the children in our hopelessly inadequate attic "school room." As a credentialed teacher, I felt that I should be able to make some sort of progress, but I didn't. I could feel the critical eyes of my mother and all the other schoolmarms in my immediate family condemning my obvious ineptitude, and I would have suffered more if it hadn't been right at this moment that I received the news of having passed my state boards in nursing. If I couldn't be a John Dewey, I might still settle for Florence Nightingale.

It was somewhere along here that I noticed that Bing was conspicuous for his absence. If he wasn't at home, hunting, filming, or playing golf, where on earth was he? One evening after dinner, I finally collared him in his study for a showdown.

"Let me have it straight," I began with my usual subtlety. "What's her name?"

The wide blue eyes were innocence itself, and now I was really suspicious. "What are you talking about this time?" he inquired mildly.

"You know perfectly well," I insisted, feeling like a comic-strip version of Maggie with a

Dr. Sullivan programming in his mountain retreat

rolling pin in her hand. "Where have you been the past week?"

Unaccountably Bing looked pleased as punch. I tried to maintain a severe expression, but felt that I was losing my grip on the situation. My husband's air was more that of a cat who has just polished off a bowl of cream, than of Willy Sutton and his ilk.

"All right, all right," I said. "Spill the beans."

"Well, I called Lillian Barkley and she'd finally got a line on that fellow she told you about. I tracked him way up into the Santa Cruz mountains, and I think I know what to do about the kids."

"Are you planning to ship them off to the mountain each day?" I inquired hopefully.

"No, that won't be necessary," Bing smiled infuriatingly, "but it's going to be all right."

Somehow I doubted that, and I wasn't at all sure that I liked Bing in his new role as an educational consultant. This had been my province, and I was prepared to relinquish it only if he would yield the role of film star to me. Meanwhile the children were getting a bit lost in the shuffle.

I had always been jealous of people who took up Bing's time, and it seemed cruel that he should disappear for such long periods each day, just when there were no other activities to separate us. If I had known what was happening, I like to think that I would have been delighted. Bing had devoted a lifetime of largely sleepless nights to devouring the best available books. He had read more widely in the English classics than anyone I have ever known. As a consequence, he had a superb verbal sense and an easy polysyllabic virtuosity that stupefied the best of his writers. His brightest friends had often remarked that the lines which he delivered spontaneously in the course of his daily activities were far better than anything that he was given to say in his films. Now he had discovered a world which recognized this ability alone, and he was reveling in it.

A week later Bing brought Dr. Sullivan home to dinner, and I was thoroughly disappointed. I had the children dressed to the nines and on their very best behavior, but the sage seemed uninterested. Where I had awaited some magic words that would solve my problems with pre-reading and math, he and Bing spent the entire dinner reliving scenes from their favorite books.

"I don't see how he's going to help," I told Bing. "He doesn't seem to be quite human."

"Ah, but that's the secret," Bing smirked. "He isn't trying to be."

"Well, when does he start helping the children?"

"He's going to send us some programs."

"And just what are those?"

"All in good time." Bing's smile was so smugly superior that I'd cheerfully have strangled him.

"Just thank your lucky stars that you're bigger and stronger than I am," I warned.

"I do that every day," he informed me, and went happily on about whatever secret mission engaged his attention at that moment.

On the afternoon of October 1, after a lunch in the backyard, I discovered just what it was. "We're going to see a house," he announced without preamble.

"Oh dear God no! I still haven't unpacked the lamp shades from the last move, and I won't know where to put them when I do."

You can't say that I didn't leave him an opening, but Bing said no more. With the conspiratorial air that I had come to recognize and dread, he chauffeured me past the club to the other side of Hillsborough. We drove through massive stone gates toward an edifice that I was prepared to condemn on sight.

I opened my mouth to give vent to the diatribe that I'd been preparing during the drive, and then uncharacteristically closed it again. The house looked like something out of my private childhood fantasies. Suddenly my only thought was that someone might take it away from me.

"Is it for sale?" I breathed.
"Yes."
"Whose is it?"

Trying to break Buzz in on quail

"It belongs to the Cochrans, who are living in it now, but Joe's been commuting to Pebble Beach in his own plane for ten years, and he's getting a little tired of taking her in through all that morning fog."

"Did he build this house?"

"No, it originally belonged to Lynn Howard, my partner in horse racing. Lynn's dad owned Seabiscuit, and trained him right here."

I wouldn't have let on for the world, but I had lost all interest in Seabiscuit. The white bricks of the outer walls had a bit of rose peering through the paint. Enormous French doors were shaded by cypress, pine, oak, and eucalyptus trees, which still admitted oceans of brilliant light. Queen Elizabeth tree roses nestled against columns on the terrace, and acres of lawn swept away into park-like forest.

The inside of a round tower was a dining room on the first floor, and a spacious airy room upstairs, that I immediately assigned to Harry and Nathaniel. There were huge fireplaces in the living room, the library, and the master bedroom. The ceilings were fourteen feet high, and what the present occupants had mistaken for a third-floor playroom was obviously my school.

Once again we had a complete role reversal. Suddenly I was demanding that we buy a new house immediately, and Bing was cautioning me that we had yet to settle the price, examine the neighborhood, or for that matter decide how we could best ease out of my megalomaniac remodeling schemes for the now-hated edifice that we presently occupied.

"None of your nonsense," I commanded. "Get me this house."

Bing's eyes twinkled. "Actually I'm pleased that you feel that way," he conceded. "It would be cause for divorce if you didn't."

"How did you find the place? Had you ever been here before?"

"I once watched George Pope ride a horse in the front door and up and down the hall. One of us must have been quite drunk; I've never been able to figure out which."

"Let it be the horse for all I care, so long as we don't lose this home."

It seemed impossible that Bing could have still more surprises up his sleeve, but he retained his air of secrecy. When I found that I'd passed the state boards, I had tactfully refrained from mentioning our little wager, though I certainly wasn't ready to finance his trip to Tierra Del Fuego. As we left for the opera on the eve of our seventh wedding anniversary, Bing summoned me to the bedroom to look at the vitrines.

I couldn't help thinking that domestic trivia were out of place at such a moment, but in I swept to find myself staring at three jeweled Fabergé flowers. The only thing I could think of was that I'd been overpaid. "But, but, but we bet only one," I stammered.

"And you get only one," Bing announced triumphantly, retrieving a fourth flower from behind his back. "This is for taking me on that cursed bet. The other three are for the children."

Bing also gave me Buzz, a beautiful, temperamental German short-hair. I trained him with a professional dog handler, and took him to the ranch on November 4 to demonstrate our mutual skills to the family. Mindful of my difficulties with Patrick J. O'Toole, I decided to take him out for an initial solitary hunt before our debut in front of an audience.

And so Damon and Pythias went trotting down the lane which was richest in covies of quail. I was delighted to see Buzz come on point almost immediately. Then I watched him hesitate, take another deep sniff, shudder, race back to me, and dive between my legs. Whistling would obviously do no good since he was already as close to me as he could get. I essayed the firm voice of command, shouting "Hie on," and "Move out," all to no effect.

Stoically I hauled Buzz along by the scruff of his neck until I finally succeeded in scaring up a covey of quail myself. At this point he made an earnest effort to wrap his paws around my legs. The only direction that I could move him was

Hope and Crosby

homeward, so we repaired thither to request advice and counsel from Bing.

He laughed in the superior fashion that had become characteristic of late, and declared that I was obviously doing something wrong.

"Doubtless," I agreed, "but perhaps you'd best demonstrate the correct technique. Nothing like this happened with the trainer."

"What sort of birds did you work with him?"

"Pigeons and pheasants."

"Well, we'll just have to break him in on quail."

Back down the lane we marched. Buzz, who seemed to have the drill by heart now, came to a staunch, picture-book point, inhaled a great whiff of quail, whirled, and leaped into Bing's arms.

In grim defense of his ego picture, Bing forced the dog further down the lane. The result was an identical sequence of events, with the exception of the climax. In his eagerness to get back home, this time Buzz knocked Bing down. My sister and her husband, who had appeared behind us, were holding their sides. On the way back to the house, they pointed out that while their Labradors might be a trifle sloppy on point, they seldom fled from the scene of action.

This was an emergency. Grimly Bing phoned the trainer and demanded an explanation. The poor man was incredulous. If it hadn't been Bing talking, he wouldn't have listened at all. As it was, he said he'd never heard of such a thing, and wouldn't believe it until he saw it.

"Fine," Bing agreed. "We've just had two demonstrations, and we'll stage a third as soon as you arrive."

So the professional filled his truck with game birds of known and dependable qualities, and drove the whole ensemble for six hours to give the amateurs a lesson.

We repaired to a field near the river, where the trainer planted some of his pheasants. As we all watched, Buzz trotted bravely into the long grass, snapped to a magnificent point, and held his bird until we arrived.

After Buzz had repeated the process with a partridge, the trainer was looking askance at Bing. "He does seem to be working out," Bing admitted. "Let's try him on a field of quail."

I'm sure that Bing felt as stupid as I did, as we watched Buzz lope confidently into the field, and snap to one of those perfect points of his. We were, however, vindicated at long last when the dog's cool collapsed at the first sniff of poisonous quail scent and he ran right over his trainer, who just happened to be standing on a bee-line between him and the kennel.

Silently the trainer dusted himself off. After a few minutes of sober reflection, he ventured an explanation:

"Buzz came from back East, where he might have been trained on quail. Some German short-hairs have hard mouths, which permit them to swallow a few birds before they realize that they're supposed to retrieve, not eat. If Buzz was too badly punished for eating a quail, he'll never touch another."

He never did. We sent him right back with the trainer, destined for a future which might include many a pheasant and partridge, but nary a trace of quail. Meanwhile I was developing a reputation of my own, as the curse of Allah where hunting dogs were concerned.

November was a long, lazy dream of relaxing, hunting, and fishing in the golden fall weather. We felt like pilgrims as we prepared our own venison, duck, and goose for Thanksgiving. It was all much too good to be true, as we learned when we returned to work in December.

This time we both went down to Los Angeles. During our idyllic past months, I had availed myself of every opportunity and all my wiles, to wangle bits on Bing's television show and Bob Hope's Christmas special.

Back on two such sets again, I was in my element, reveling in the constant interplay between cast and technicians, and playing a social role disproportionate to the brevity of my scripted one. I felt as if I had come home.

Bob loved to work late into the night. After doing a takeoff on a current television commer-

"And just what, pray, do you consider to be your profession?"

cial, in which a lady lay on a tigerskin rug in a filmy gown and advertised men's cosmetics with lines like "Sic 'em, tiger, grrrrrrrr," I returned very late on Saturday night, or rather early Sunday morning, to The Townhouse where Bing was waiting for me. Bubbling over with gossip about the cast and the changes in scenes and scripts, I announced proudly that there would be work for me on Monday too.

"You are going home tomorrow." Bing announced flatly.

"I can't do that. I haven't finished my work on your show or Bob's."

"And you're not going to."

Belatedly I raised my antennae. Could it be that I had an unhappy husband on my hands? Yes indeedy. There were deep creases around the corners of his mouth, and the crows feet at the edges of distant and withdrawn eyes might have graced a bird of prey.

"What's the matter?" I inquired with brilliant originality. "Have I done something wrong?"

"You will return in the morning to your home and children, and this time you will stay there."

I stared at Bing solemnly, and waited for his better nature to assert itself. No luck. He glared back at me until I finally dropped my gaze. By the seven gods of Mongo, it was the night of the ballet all over again.

I had been told to start packing, so I stalked into the next room and did just that, meantime commiserating with myself on my unhappy fate. I was condemned to be a frump, and to live in a hole in the wall in Hillsborough, and I didn't even know why. Somehow I found time between slamming suitcases to call the airport and reserve a seat on the 7 a.m. flight north.

Then for about an hour Bing kicked the walls in one room, while I stamped the floor in the other. Since this sort of Mexican standoff didn't seem to advance my cause, I finally bearded the lion in his den.

"Just for the record, I'd like to know what the hell is going on."

"If you don't know by now, there's no point in repeating it for the thousandth time."

"Is it just because I got in late? You know how Bob works, and surely you know what goes on in a TV studio."

"I certainly do."

Evidently I had struck the wrong chord there. I would try another tack. "I never once complained when you arrived home from work in the wee hours, or when you stayed in Los Angeles all week for that matter. It seems to me that you might accord me the same consideration."

"I'm a professional," Bing stated curtly.

"And so am I!"

"And just what, pray, do you consider to be your profession?"

"What is that supposed to mean? What are you accusing me of anyway?"

Bing shrugged his shoulders in defeat. "I don't know really. Of not wanting to be my wife, I guess."

"I've never wanted to be anything but your wife. Does that mean that I have to stop breathing?"

"It means that your place is at home with your children."

"How about you? Is *your* place at home with your children? Why can't I be right here with you, doing the same work?"

"Because I'm a man, and I won't have my wife off flirting with every gaffer on the set."

"That's nonsense and you know it. But speaking of flirting, you've never been regarded as an icicle among your costars. Why should I behave any other way?"

"Because you're supposed to be a woman and a wife."

"And a man and a husband can conduct himself differently, is that it?"

"Yes."

That did seem to settle the matter, at least so long as Bing's word was accepted as the final criterion. Which it evidently was, at least by him. I stamped out, sat on the bed by my suitcases to brood, and was awakened by my morning call at 6 a.m. Grimly I marched off to the elevator, a suitcase in either hand.

Trying to upstage Beverly Garland on the Bing Crosby Show

An apparition rose from a chair in the lobby and blocked my path. Bing had already been down for breakfast, but he looked and must have felt like the wrath of God. It was evident that he hadn't had his usual two hours of sleep.

"Where the hell do you think you're going?" was his opening ploy.

"Home, in due obedience to the orders of my lord and master."

"Get back into that elevator."

Here I hesitated. I really had had some vague notion of sweeping up the children and taking them home to mother in West Columbia. On the other hand the lobby was small, intimate, and rather well-peopled for such an early hour. We were attracting inquisitive stares, as Bing would certainly have noticed if he weren't beside himself, because above all else he hated a scene.

Since I just stood there, Bing grabbed the bags from my hands, and simply marched me before him into the elevator. I must admit that I didn't put up too much of a fight, a) because that was the best direction anyway, b) because I hated the thought of losing those two parts, and c) because, as I believe I've mentioned before, I just adore masterful men.

A half hour later we entered the elevator arm-in-arm, descended into workaday reality, and wended our respective ways off to the sets. For the time being the tempest was over, but it was obvious that the basic issue remained unresolved.

Still I had had a triumph of sorts, and only in retrospect did I realize that it had been my last. My one tiny scene on that show was the only time that I was ever to work as an actress on a Bing Crosby production.

"We don't photograph well together," Bing decided, and thus limited my future performances to his Christmas specials, from which he could eliminate me only by finding another wife, an expedient which he must have seriously considered from time to time.

1965

This was the year that I determined to dedicate myself to good works of every description. Not that I hadn't always had a tendency to interpret God's will to my fellow man, but my devotion to the theater had complicated the issue. Since Bing disapproved of my acting, so be it. I would now reveal myself as a full-fledged, card-carrying Goody Two-shoes.

This I say was my New Year's resolution, and I was determined that it should last, at least until someone offered me a role.

While biding my time, I helped Bing fulfill certain social obligations. On January 2 Merle Oberon gave a dinner dance. Bing had admired the easy grace of this serene beauty when she was his costar, and he was even more impressed by the perfection of her household.

Trying to avoid tripping over my own feet, I made my way to her side, stuck like glue all evening, and busily took notes. To her credit she was as helpful as possible, but some of her precepts and examples just didn't work for me. The admonition to "put all signed pieces together" had no immediate application, since my only one had been an ancient piano with the name *Phillip* on it, and I had long since disposed of that.

Bing was obviously intrigued by Merle's splendid expanse of bosom, and I considered attempting something along those lines, but was immediately halted by his stern injunction to "keep your coat on for God's sake, or you'll have the waiters spilling hot soup down your throat."

Still I kept Merle's image in mind, and tried to play the mature, gracious charmer when we entertained General Eisenhower. In preparation I had boned up on matters of state and prepared a series of provocative questions for the great man, but he and Bing spent the entire meal either reminiscing about silly incidents in which both had been involved in Paris toward the end of World War II, or discussing the theory and practice of chip shots.

On the several occasions when I tried to force a comment in edgewise, I provoked only startled glances, a momentary hiatus, and then a hasty resumption of the previous conversation. This was definitely not the *femme fatale's* way. I had an uneasy feeling that Merle would have managed it better somehow.

So much for the social graces. It was now time for Good Deed Dotty to strike. Bing had espoused the cause of the Immaculate Heart

Plotting to put nuns into Jean Louis dresses

nuns, and we had already lent them our house in Las Cruces for their marine biology lab. Now I decided to contribute my invaluable assistance to whatever was going on. For a start, I would follow Pope John's advice to modernize church institutions, by bribing Jean Louis to design some devastating habits for the sisters. A similar effort had already done wonders for the recruitment of United Airlines stewardesses.

And then there was the subject of hair, a problem which hadn't afflicted nuns for the past thousand years or so, but had suddenly come to the fore. If they were to abandon their shaved pates, what sort of coiffure should they substitute? Resolutely I faced the challenge of designing the first provocative-but-ever-so-discreet nun's hairdo.

"The bubble," a sort of modified beehive, was very big in those days, but to my mind it didn't strike quite the proper religious note. After examining all the other alternatives, I finally settled, oddly enough, upon my own style. This consisted of a ponytail, screwed up into a figure 8 and covered by a hair net. It seemed to be ideal for the nuns' purposes, since it had a preparation time of about a minute, and a durability factor of weeks if need be. Furthermore it had been sufficiently unsuccessful in the world to demonstrate its obvious spiritual advantages. Bing had once suggested that I had earned several centuries of indulgences just by wearing the thing.

When I solemnly discussed my new project with him, his first reaction was consternation. "You're doing what? Designing dresses and hairdos for nuns?"

"Well someone has to do it, and no one else who is properly qualified seems even to have considered the matter."

"That I can readily believe. Couldn't you just preoccupy yourself with the mounting illiteracy of your own brood?"

"You always said we should do as much as we can for the church. And besides, Pope John says. . . ."

"I hope they'll let me off with less than a million years in purgatory for whatever hand I had in bringing you into the fold. I am unhappily reminded of the private audience that Claire Booth Luce, another convert, had with his Holiness. It ended with the Pope insisting in resonant, albeit guilt-ridden tones, "But Mrs. Luce, you see, I already *am* a Catholic.""

"I hope you're not putting in doubt the Pope's infallibility. You Irish seem to think that you invented Catholicism, and are therefore exempt from its rules and obligations."

"Well at least we're not *más papista que el Papa*, and I hope you don't drag this poor Irishman into a religious controversy, when you start designing lifestyles for nuns. Are you so sure that you've totally mastered those of a wife and a mother?"

Ignoring that last sally as beneath me, I took wing for the Immaculate Heart Novitiate in Santa Barbara. There I counseled each of the novices individually on the wonders of makeup and *haute couture*, forgetting for the nonce that they had yet to leave the world, and were in most cases closer to present trends than I.

Some however proved gratifyingly otherworldly. When I inquired of a recent doctorate in physics what hairdo she contemplated adopting, she explained in some embarrassment that it just hadn't been a subject of her meditations. Resourcefully I suggested a ponytail, screwed up into a figure 8. . . .

Then I was off to relate my success to the Mother Superior, and to acquaint her with my plan for a religious fashion show, in which her postulants would display Jean Louis' latest town-and-convent attire for the sister who had everything.

The Reverend Mother seemed a bit bewildered by all this, but when I explained that I was sure that we would be carrying out the wishes of the Pope, she bounced back with the suggestion that perhaps I might serve on the board of the order's college. After all, she must have reasoned, anyone this close to Father O'Malley couldn't be all bad.

Never having sat on a board before, I was in some doubt as to the precise nature of my duties, but I did have a vague notion of making

Vainly contending for primacy with Molly MacNeal, whom even Remus preferred

earth-shaking decisions that would determine the future policies of the college and perhaps the world. Our first meeting disabused me of that misconception. Lest any other innocents share my delusions, let me state clearly for posterity that the function of a member of the board of trustees of a Catholic institution is to beg money, if necessary from oneself and one's loved ones. As my chairman put it succinctly, "You either give, get, or get off."

For openers, I decided to give till it hurt— Bing, that is. Since I had no personal connection with the family finances, I felt the sting not at all. In addition to contributing our houses in Las Cruces and Palm Springs, I funded the summer school in Mexico, the development and purchase of the new nuns' habits, the style show which demonstrated their suitability, and finally a raid on my home state with the traitorous object of pillage and looting.

Naively supposing that we were all Catholics together, I first suggested that we check in with the local bishop, but was immediately enlightened by our president, who explained that it wouldn't do at all, since we were "poaching on his territory."

In the event, she needn't have worried, because I was new at the game, and my arrangements were so amateurish that I failed at my first leap, and had to go growling back to the jungle, contenting myself with inviting the sisters to my old stamping grounds at the University of Texas, where my puzzled former professors showed them the school of drama, and took them on a guided tour of the rest of the facilities.

All this made perfect sense to me since Sister Marie Fleurette wrote children's drama on occasion, and we would certainly need a drama department for the vast new campus that I planned to construct with all the funds that I brought in. Curiously enough no one else seemed to consider the trip much of a success.

If I had failed as an amateur mendicant, I was now to be favored with a lesson from a professional. I had returned from Texas with the intention of settling into the role of Bing's model wife. Imagine my consternation upon discovering that he already had one. Comfortably ensconced in what I had fatuously considered to be my home, and fully in charge of staff, progeny, and husband was a large, angular, and horse-faced Irish woman, whose legs were adorned with the most flamboyant varicosities it has yet been my privilege to view.

Not much of a mate for Bing, you might remark, but tarry awhile for I at first reached the same conclusion, and then had to revise my estimate of her. Molly MacNeal, as I shall christen her for the good and sufficient reason that it is not her name, was the relict of an ancient Irish family that had fallen upon difficult times. Like any good survivor she had developed a specialty, namely that of handmaiden to the lord of the manor.

In that capacity she had traveled about Europe, disemburdening the aristocracy of problems occasioned by unwanted children, aged relatives, or country homes in need of management, social directors, tour planners, or simply obliging and immediately-available dinner guests. While I was traipsing about Texas, she had met Bing at a neighbor's house where she had outlived her usefulness, seen her opportunity, and moved in through the enormous opening which I customarily left in my defensive line.

My approach to Bing's idiosyncrasies had been as American as apple pie. I simply set out to change them to suit my view of the world. Molly, on the other hand, offered the European plan. She studied Bing's desires, needs, whims, and foibles with total absorption, and with the sole view of gratifying them all. Under her regime Bing's day was perfectly arranged to suit him, from the preparation of his morning cup of espresso, to the cutting of the right cigar after his favorite evening meal. My husband was being spoiled rotten and loving it, and so were the children and staff.

Hard as I had tried to convert Bing to my own way of thinking, I had never dreamed of directing his daily activities. Molly arranged his golf dates, hunting trips, fishing expeditions,

Girl with man and mink

and dinners far better that he could have himself, and without all the effort that his own involvement had entailed. Furthermore she ordered the staff to obtain his favorite delicacies, to prepare them to suit his fancy, and to have his room and his clothing arranged just as he might wish to find them when he returned to the house.

Wonder of wonders, she had even transformed Bing into something of a social lion. He, who never accepted invitations, had dined out with Molly three or four times a week during my absence. How could an artless Texan, nurtured on the "pick up your own clothes and mine too if you have a moment" philosophy of my mother, ever hope to compete with such a paragon of the continental pipe-and-slipper school.

Foolishly I started by trying to beat her at her own game. During Alan Fisher's entire regime, I had never even considered giving him an order. In the first place I wouldn't have known how, and in the second it was obvious to both of us that he understood the workings of the household better than I did. Nonetheless I now lowered my head and plunged in, loudly countermanding Molly's instructions to the staff.

This resulted in startled looks, momentary interruption of activities, and then resumption of Molly's schedule. It was obvious to a child that she knew what she was doing and I didn't.

And indeed the children were full participants in the general euphoria. As in the case of Bing, Molly had simply ordered them to do just as they pleased, and was fulfilling their wishes faster than they could express them. They gazed with sullen hostility upon the traveler who had returned to demand that they show evidence of progress in their studies.

As ever when in dire straits, I telephoned Dr. Barkley. After listening to the full recital of my woes, she asked, "Is there any way that you can compete with this woman?"

"No."

"Then what are you planning to do?"

"Throw her out."

"Will Bing and the children go along with that?"

"They won't like it, but they'll have to."

"Hmmm. It seems to me that, even if you succeed, you'll have to deal with a lot of smoldering resentment, and they'll always compare your future performance unfavorably with hers."

"Then what should I do?"

"Nothing at all."

"Are you sure of that? Nothing? Nothing at all?"

"That's right, nothing at all. In fact I'd encourage her by giving her lots of rope."

So for the next three weeks I watched my household running like clockwork, my children living a fairy tale, and my husband becoming the social sensation of the season. A true altruist would have rejoiced in their happiness, but one small rotten person was in a blue funk.

I perked up only when the chinks began to appear in Molly's armor. The subsequent mutiny came with remarkable speed. All in the same wondrous week, Alan Fisher decided that the house was too small for Molly and him, the children did their level best to assassinate her, and Bing, who now that I thought of it had been wearing a hunted look of late, informed me that, if I didn't get that Irish woman out of his house, he would leave immediately for Las Cruces.

Alas poor Molly! She had suffered the fate of many a benevolent dictator with an ungrateful flock. All my little puritans were revolting against a life of mandated and regulated indulgence, and Bing, in particular, had had enough partying to last him for a decade or so.

In sharp contrast to Miss Efficiency, I was inept, congenitally disorganized, and at last truly appreciated. I escorted her to the airport, and returned in triumph. That afternoon Bing swept me off to the finest furriers in San Francisco, and rewarded my general inability to cope with a full-length, black-diamond mink coat. I wore it the rest of the afternoon and evening, and was dissuaded with some difficulty from sleeping in it.

Harry and Mary Frances with their new teacher

Harry with Bing's captain and a puffer fish

Now Bing would not have to depart for Mexico alone. The whole family decided to celebrate our recent reprieve with a long, disorderly, typically Crosby vacation in Las Cruces.

And for a while it was just that. Then Bing tired of the school in his bedroom, which now embraced some twenty less-than-avid students. "None of their mothers care whether they learn to read or not, you nitwit," he informed me uncharitably. "They just want to get them out of their houses and into mine."

Not only did he have a point there, but life as a schoolmarm on the frontier just wasn't what it was cracked up to be. Once I had given my usual TB tests, and vaccinated all and sundry for polio and rubella, the real fun was over, and I had to face the fact that I didn't know how to teach those stolidly-uncomplaining Indian faces how to read. Also I was in danger of losing a husband, who unreasonably objected to being banished from his house.

Fortunately the problem practically solved itself. Whose fault was it, after all, that these children were growing up without a school? To determine this, we need only examine the recent history of Las Cruces.

It had been a land grant to Abelardo Rodríguez, whose father had been president of Mexico. On it Rod had built first a hotel for vacationers, then a splendid residence for himself, and finally five more homes for special friends.

For the workmen who had built these residences, and then tarried as hotel employees, mechanics, sailors for the boats, gardeners, majordomos, and laborers, Rod had first erected dormitories; and then, in the goodness of his heart and softness of his head, had permitted the construction on his land of cabins to house the womenfolk that they imported from La Paz without benefit of clergy. In the fullness of time, the biological consequences had been the little wave of humanity which was now cast up on the threshold of one crooner, who strenuously insisted that some other disposition be made of them.

With my remarkable facility for going straight to the heart of a matter, I cornered Rodríguez and demanded that he live up to his social responsibilities by constructing a school.

"I don't think so, señora. It would only lead to trouble."

"What could induce you, the son of a progressive president of Mexico, to make such a statement?"

"Sad experience, señora."

"Well, I've had enough of your defeatism and pessimism. If you don't start work immediately on a school for these poor deprived children, I'm going to talk to the mayor of La Paz and the governor of the territory."

I left Rod sitting at his desk with his head in his hands, but was uncertain as to whether this constituted a hopeful sign until I saw construction begin on the school building three days later. Within a month we had a cheerful little one-room schoolhouse and, as a consequence of a further demand on my part, a dapper, amiable, government-trained instructor, in whom I immediately demonstrated my complete confidence by consigning my entire brood to him.

Two days later he returned the favor by inviting me to come to school and help control them, and I was thenceforth enrolled as an honorary Mexican first grader. To those accustomed only to the informality of bedroom instruction, the organization of our new curriculum was impressive indeed. There were government lesson plans, government workbooks, government recesses, and government games.

Harry and Mary Frances roundly rejected the first two elements of a Latin education, but warmly embraced the others. Their favorite games came to be tackle-tag on the school roof, skip-rope in the broken glass, and catch the scorpions by the tail.

After the teacher's first four weeks of exposure to them, recesses became longer and longer as he developed what seemed to be an inordinate interest in tea breaks. As it transpired he had finally discovered his true vocation, which was wooing waitresses in the hotel.

Hunting at Todos Santos

But I had inadvertently sown the seed of far more than an ineffectual literacy campaign. Through me the Mexicans who worked in our houses and in the hotel had learned the false but impressive lesson that they enjoyed the full rights of American citizens. Led by the five gardeners, and fully supported by a silly Texan, they demanded an elected council, a mayor, a minimum wage, twelve months of salaries for eight months of work, and everything else that they or I might think of next.

It saddens me to report that the sequel was undemocratic in the extreme. Without warning one sunny afternoon, Rodriguez ordered his foreman to round up the workers' families, deposit them in trucks, and drive them off to comfortable residences which he owned in La Paz, where they could enjoy the benefits of the city's school system and social programs.

Thus it was that the gardeners were sent back to their gardens, the fishermen to the sea, and I to bed without my supper. I was left with a profound mistrust of politicians, and the grim knowledge that the finest of social programs may lose something in translation.

Noting that my popularity was on the wane with all factions in the immediate area, Bing spirited me away to the wilds one step ahead of a lynch mob. With the pretext of hunting in an unspoiled area, we settled in a thatched-roof cottage at Todos Santos on the Pacific side of the peninsula, where it was regularly some 20 degrees cooler than at our home on the Sea of Cortés. Unfortunately during our stay a cold front rolled in off the ocean, and transformed our unheated shack into an inadequate igloo.

With my abnormally low blood pressure, I tend to shiver on what humans consider to be hot summer days. Under the conditions at Todos Santos, I donned every bit of apparel that I had brought with me and everything that I could steal from Bing. Without removing a stitch, I then wrapped myself like a mummy in the sole bedcover at night. Ironically it was an electric blanket in this spot devoid of electricity, hot water, and all the other concomitants of civilization except rats, and the huge spiders that were evidently attracted by water, and perched on the bathroom ceiling beside the bare pipe which protruded from the wall in lieu of a shower.

In all fairness, I can't say that I troubled them unnecessarily during the course of my stay. After my initial attempt to endure an icy shower by the unique expedient of screaming in agony while performing a war dance under it, I surrendered the facility to the amused Bing, who felt that such penitential rites were part and parcel of his image of great white hunter.

The uninitiated might conclude that I was a less-than-romantic figure, as I shivered through the days and shook through the nights, and this shows just how accurate an uninformed opinion may occasionally be. If, in spite of all my conscientious efforts to reform the world, I am eventually consigned to outer darkness, dear God, let it be hot down there.

Slowly the months passed while my nimrod wreaked havoc among the local wildfowl. Curiously enough the calendar marked these enormous expanses of time as mere days, and I learned what the simple inability to get warm can do to a girl's time sense. At long last our stay in paradise came to an end, as all things must, and we returned to Las Cruces, whose inhabitants had presumably learned to forgive and forget in the interim.

As it turned out they hadn't, so I prudently decided that it was time to remove Harry's ailing tonsils, a problem of which I had been forcibly reminded by the constant sore throat that had plagued me at Todos Santos, and still remained upon my return to civilization. Off I flew to Los Angeles with a very reluctant Harry, who had wanted to remain in Mexico and fish with his father.

When faced with an examination by our ear, nose, and throat specialist, Harry declared that he felt no pain, and flatly refused to open his mouth. Since he had been known to bite viciously upon similar occasions, I decided that further preparation was in order, delayed the operation, and sped off to Santa Barbara to model Jean Louis' new line of nuns' habits.

Bing and Mary Frances

There I presented a full style show to mixed reviews from a heterogeneous audience composed of a hanging jury of old-line nuns, an enthusiastic if somewhat bewildered intermediate group attracted by high fashions and fitted, knee-length gowns, and the disinterested novices, who had been accustomed only to blue jeans, and were not yet into clothes. All in all, I considered that my presentation of spring fashions with the theme *What The Well-Dressed Nun Will Wear* had experienced a modest success, although as the sequel proved, the styles were never to be adopted, so Bing had unwittingly financed their development and the entire show in vain.

It was back to Los Angeles and a tonsilectomy for the still-unconvinced Harry. When a doctor tried to examine him with a speculum he howled, "You're not going to shove that spatula down my throat," and dived behind the examination table. (As he often explained to his admiring peers, his impressive familiarity with medical terminology derived from the fact that his mother was a "registal nurd.")

You can catch more flies with honey than with vinegar. I took Harry's place on the table, opened wide, and demonstrated conclusively that it didn't hurt a bit. The results were ambiguous: Harry did indeed crawl out of his lair to watch wide-eyed as the doctor examined his mother's throat, and he did thereafter submit to a similar examination without causing any irreparable damage to the doctor's fingers. From my point of view, however, the diagnosis left something to be desired. Whereas Harry's tonsils were in a borderline state which left their removal a matter of choice, his mother's were practically terminal. We were scheduled for consecutive tonsilectomies on the morrow.

I spent the intervening hours preparing Harry for his ordeal, and to his credit it must be said that he survived it admirably, demanding boatloads of ice cream within hours after he emerged from the anesthetic. I, on the other hand, was nauseated for days, with a throat so swollen that I was unable to eat, and a horrendous case of *pityriasis rosea* from the hospital sheets.

Harry, who was up and about by evening, spent the next couple of days taking care of his mother and explaining to bemused hospital personnel, "She's just a woman and they hurt worse."

When Bing phoned, Harry discussed with his father at great length just how fortunate it was that he had been there to help his poor mother. I could hear Bing agreeing wholeheartedly from the other end of the line, and silently deplored the lack of voice that prevented me from roundly cursing them and all other self-satisfied males.

To amuse me during my recuperation, Bing sent a long account of his doings in Las Cruces: "The marlin are scarce and satiated these days. They swim up to the bait, scrutinize it carefully, and invariably wander off. It must be because the small fish are so plentiful in the bay this year.

"Mary Frances is fascinated by the little puffer fish with the big 'meet me in the moonlight' eyes. She pulls one up and scratches his belly, until he puffs up like a little balloon and covers himself with spines. She has also discovered the trigger fish, which has a face like a little pig, and a dorsal fin which is absolutely rigid and sticks up about three inches. Try as she will, there is no way Mary Frances can bend it, but when she touches the smaller fin just behind it, the big dorsal fin suddenly slips into a slot on the fish's back and lies completely flat. She is now tending the lobster pots for everyone in the area. Doesn't care in the least about the catch; just enjoys putting the trap down one day and hauling it up the next to see what's in it.

"That enthusiast Bill Brady, the Chairman of the Board of Corn Products, has a new undertaking, the development of a medicine for arthritics. The researchers on the project begged him to bring back the pancreas of a marlin, on the grounds that it's the strongest, toughest, most active thing that swims, walks, or flies. For reasons I still don't understand, this seems to make it perfect for their new product.

A confident Peter before the first dress rehearsal

"So Bill brought down a container for a marlin pancreas, which he intended to freeze and take home with him. It was only then that it occurred to him that he didn't have the faintest idea of what one looked like. I finally found a vacationing doctor, who said he'd never seen one but that he just might be able to identify it.

"Bill and I went off to Cabo San Lucas where catching a marlin is a certainty, hooked one, beached it, and told our boatman to gut it and put the entrails in a pail. Bill then walked off to the hotel with his pail of guts, leaving two astonished Mexicans kneeling over the carcass of the marlin, and asking themselves why a crazy American would catch a beautiful fish, remove the guts, and abandon it on the beach, without even weighing it or taking a picture.

"The doctor finally did pick out a slimy something which he identified as the pancreas, arbitrarily as he later admitted to me, and Bill rushed it up to New York, where it should soon be curing us all of arthritis.

"Trader Vic has flown down a team of zoologists and paleontologists to investigate the fossil field near Santiago. We spent a day climbing the hills and rocks to examine skeletons of whales and millions of shells from the Miocene Period. We also discovered a field of diatomite, composed of countless trillions of minute organisms whose skeletons formed a chalk-like substance on the sea floor. An excellent abrasive or pottery glaze, it is now also used in filters, and we are told that the field is of a size to be commercially exploitable.

"The next day we took the *True Love* to Ceralvo Island, to observe the sea lions and try to determine where they give birth to their young. I showed Dr. Orr our colony of fish-eating bats, which he considers to be a rare find since, to his knowledge, they exist in only one other place in the world.

"The researchers refer to Mary Frances as 'the competition,' since she is an even more avid collector of crustaceans than they are. She never wearies of wading along the shore, and returning with all manner of slimy, repulsive-looking things to frighten Nathaniel before eventually abandoning them on the back porch, where they expire and exude a pestilential stench.

"I've been trying my best to determine what profit these two kids may have derived from your ill-fated educational experiment. All the indications are that you simply succeeded in producing illiterates in two languages. Not one of them has the faintest notion of what reading is about, and Mary's Spanish remains hideously ungrammatical.

"Contrary to expectations, however, Nathaniel has finally succeeded in picking up a couple of random words. The other day I tried to pull them together for him by asking, 'What do you say in the morning?'

He looked at me solemnly and finally admitted that it might be 'Buenos dias.'

'Fine,' I continued encouragingly, 'Now what do you say in the afternoon?'

It was like pulling teeth, but I finally got him to say, 'Buenas tardes.'

'Great,' I persevered. 'What do you say in the evening?'

This took a bit more thought but he finally came up with, 'It's gettin' dark.'

"Oh well, even if they don't speak like Mexicans, Nathaniel and Mary Frances are now so tanned that they look like them, and with that accomplishment I guess we'll have to rest on our laurels."

When Bing realized how slowly I was recovering from the tonsilectomy, he phoned to say, "If I had known that it was going to be so serious, I'd have come up with you."

We both thought this over for a minute before bursting into simultaneous laughter. If he had known that it was going to be serious, he'd have left for Outer Mongolia.

So much I knew at the time. It wasn't until much later that I learned how guilty Bing had felt when Eddie Lang died. Eddie was the great jazz guitar player who always accompanied Bing. He had chronically inflamed tonsils, which Bing finally advised him to have

Help!

removed. Reluctantly Eddie submitted to the tonsilectomy, and died of an overdose of anesthesia.

As we approached the mid-year mark, my convalescence afforded me an opportunity to pause and reflect. In spite of my wholehearted expenditure of enormous energy, my dedication to good works could not be said to have borne much fruit. My family, the nuns, and my neighbors at Las Cruces had all proved ungrateful. Could it be that my talents lay in a different direction after all?

Just as I was brooding on these matters the telephone rang, and a good fairy, in the guise of my Jewish agent, offered me the lead in an Indianapolis production of Peter Pan. I leaped to my feet and emitted several huzzas from my still-aching throat.

So carried away was I that it was a full ten hours before I began to reflect on how my husband might receive this bit of news. He had just announced that he was returning to take us all to Europe for the Irish Sweeps Derby, and could have no inkling that the path now led through Indianapolis.

Bing arrived home on June 13. When I broached my plans to him, he seemed stunned. "Hadn't you promised me not to play in any more of those nonsensical summer productions?"

"Yes, but I didn't have any offers then."

"Was that what made you change your mind?"

"That and the fact that I made such a mess of all my charitable enterprises. The strike in Las Cruces was enough to discourage anyone."

"That line of reasoning sounds specious to me."

The fact was that it did to me too, but it was the only one available, so I had to make do with it. To Bing's credit he voiced no further criticism. He simply wrapped himself in a mantle of silence, and took no subsequent notice of my preparations for departure, or for that matter of my continued existence on this green planet.

I flew to Indianapolis on the evening of June 14. There my mother joined me at the home of my friends, the Ruckelshauses, where we were both to stay. Once there I felt much better. I'd had a surfeit of failures these past months, but hadn't I always wowed them in Indianapolis?

My first meeting with the producer was auspicious. Determined to give me the very best, he had brought back a favorite son, who had actually played roles in Hollywood, to direct our little play. Serving under him would be a stage manager who had recently graduated from a leading school of drama. Enthusiasm was very high among cast and crew, and he felt that he had every reason to anticipate a smash hit.

So did I. Our read-through went swimmingly and so did the first rehearsals. To be sure we had a director who had never directed before, and an equally unblooded stage manager, but all the actors knew their parts, and the whole seemed to be jelling into a perfect interaction of personalities.

The first signs of trouble appeared at the dress rehearsal. It was then that the lights and the myriad stage gimmicks were to have their initial test. After we had missed the first four light cues, the director became hysterical and screamed piercingly at the stage manager, who continued to stare serenely outward at an imaginary audience. This was the first hint we had that he was stone deaf and a lip reader.

Most of the props simply failed to materialize. Missing were such essentials as Nana's doghouse and the alligator who had swallowed the alarm clock, simply because no one had realized that it was his job to procure them. Most ominously of all there was no *Peter Foy Flying Apparatus*, invented for Maude Adams, and the mainstay of all Peter Pan productions since her time. Consisting of an elaborate and time-tested combination of pullies, harnesses, and invisible wires, it permits Peter, Wendy, and the other two children to fly with safety and verisimilitude.

Once this problem had been fully faced, the stage manager resourcefully attached a hawser to a thick belt around my middle, and prepared to haul me into the air. When I objected that the device was absurd, completely visible, and not

Stranded flyers, smiling through their tears